LORE OF FAITH & FOLLY

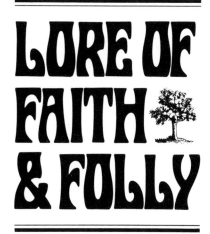

LORE OF FAITH & FOLLY

Compiled by the Folklore Society of Utah

Edited by Thomas E. Cheney ; V I
Assisted by Austin E. Fife
and Juanita Brooks

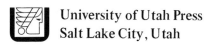

University of Utah Press
Salt Lake City, Utah

Because few states have a more colorful history than Utah, few states possess a richer store of folk traditions. Yet few states have in the past seemed more reluctant to collect and study their traditions. To remedy this circumstance, a number of folklore-minded college professors and interested laymen founded in 1958 the Folklore Society of Utah "to collect, preserve, and interpret the folk literature, music, thought, and crafts of Utah and adjacent areas; and to make these materials available to scholars and the general public by maintaining archives and publishing and encouraging publication." This book, compiled and edited by Thomas E. Cheney, past president of the Society, represents the Society's first effort to meet its commitment to publication, to bring both the lore of the state and interpretations of that lore to the attention of the public. The Folklore Society of Utah sponsors this volume with the hope it will be the first in a series.

William A. Wilson, President
Folklore Society of Utah

To Dean Harold Bentley
without whose interest a Folklore Society of Utah
might not have been organized

contents

foreword

This book might well be viewed as the culmination of and a memorial to the first decade in the life of the Folklore Society of Utah, organized in 1958 through the initiative of Dr. Wayland D. Hand, Director of the Center for the Study of Folklore and Mythology at the University of California in Los Angeles. The unique folk heritage of Utah and the Mormons was in Dr. Hand's awareness both through his own cultural roots and through early publications concerning the folk life of Mormonia by Juanita Brooks, Olive W. Burt, Kate B. Carter, Thomas E. Cheney, Austin and Alta Fife, Hector Lee, Wallace Stegner, and others.

Annual or semiannual meetings of the Society have been held, one of which (at Utah State University in July 1963) was jointly sponsored by the Folklore Society of Utah and the American Folklore Society. Membership in the Folklore Society of Utah has always been and is now open to all who are interested in the lore and legends of Utah and neighboring areas: professors, professional or sometime writers, and laymen with a flare for values that are inherited and transmitted through the centuries in the media of the folk.

It was during Professor Cheney's tenure as president and on his initiative that the idea for this volume was conceived and the first draft thereof completed. Several of the contributions had indeed been prepared for and presented at meetings of the Society. It is important that readers be advised of guidelines which we have followed. Above all, we have felt that the work should represent the whole membership of the Society and not merely its academic wing, or its few professionally trained folklorists. Popular literature is itself a kind of folklore and as worthy of publication as are scholarly adumbrations thereof. We have felt that the book should be, for the main part, by, about, and for persons formed in the mainstream or in the backwaters of Mormonia and sensitive to its distinct cultural set, yet should not exclude lore of minority groups of the intermountain area. We have wished to keep our sights on the lore of the folk and not upon the industrial, political, religious, scientific or artistic development of Utah as a state save insofar as they intrude upon or form a juncture with the materials and processes of folklore which, as great folklorists have affirmed, are older and more universal than civic or religious institutions. Transformed, mutilated, subjected to the onslaughts of church or state, they still survive, giving continuity and hence a kind of intuitively felt security to the minds of men who need more answers to questions than science alone can give.

The notion that folklore and scientific or religious truth are opposites is of course to be dispelled: "lore" itself means both knowledge and belief, and the mental baggage of men, even ignorant men, is not all folly. All men, indeed, behave to a large degree in a folkish manner, and the greatest scientists or humanists are often the first to avow that the known is but an atom in stature compared to the unknown and the unknowable. Hence, men base most of their decisions more on faith than upon knowledge, and such acts of faith are always couched in the traditions and customs of the folk.

Even in decades before the founding of the Folklore Society of Utah, a few investigations into the realm of Mormon folklore had been made and a few public and private manifestations thereof brought into being. Under the W.P.A. Utah Writers Project, directed by Dale Morgan, tales, legends, songs, and other lore had been collected and files established in the folklore section of the Library of Congress and the Utah Historical Society. Thomas E. Cheney had made an early collection of folk songs in the Mormon zones of Idaho, presented a master's thesis thereon at the University of Idaho in 1936, and had subsequently initiated courses in folklore at Brigham Young University. Austin and Alta Fife had recorded folk songs for the Library of Congress and completed other field research which culminated in their *Saints of Sage and Saddle,* published by Indiana University Press in 1956. The Daughters of Utah Pioneers, under the energetic direction of Kate B. Carter, had collected data on Mormon history, pioneer reminiscences, and other oral tradition, and had begun to publish the voluminous collections of *Heart Throbs of the West* (1939-1951) and *Treasures of Pioneer History* (1952-1957), both series immersed in pioneer lore and legend. Hector Lee had established the Utah Humanities Research Foundation, and the *Utah* (later *Western*) *Humanities Review,* which once gave a prominent place to folklore. His doctoral dissertation entitled *The Three Nephites* was published by the University of New Mexico Press in 1949. Lester Hubbard had taught courses on the ballad at the University of Utah and had gathered songs which culminated in his *Ballads and Songs from Utah* (University of Utah Press, 1961). Artifacts of our pioneer culture had been acquired by the Sons of Utah Pioneers and placed in the Pioneer Village Museum, thanks largely to the efforts and affluence of Horace Sorenson. Slim Critchlow and his "Utah Buckaroos" had learned a repertoire of cowboy and western songs, and strummed them back to the folk over KSL Radio.

Wallace Stegner, professional writer, had kept an ear to Utah's soil and produced his *Mormon Country* (Duell, Sloan and Pearce, 1942), a work steeped in the lore of Utah.

But let the past be prelude: The Folklore Society of Utah wishes now to offer a collection of essays covering a wide range of Mormon lore and encompassing several points of view and distinctive techniques of presentation; the essays range all the way from fiction and other narratives in direct participation in or observation of folk life to the well documented and analytical presentations of scholars in the field.

The scope of folklore is much broader than the typical reader is likely to think. In the verbal sphere alone it ranges from simple traditional metaphors ("as swift as greased lightning") through sayings and proverbs ("the squeaky wheel gets the grease"), rhymes ("Red sun at night/Sailors' delight"), riddles, and even tombstone inscriptions (see "The Cycle of Life Among the Folk," p. 223); jingles, songs, ballads, and folk poetry (see "Ditties of Death in Deseret," p. 153); parlor jokes, anecdotes, folk tales, tall tales, fairy tales, family reminiscences, oral history, legends, and myths, and, in some cultures, orally transmitted epic poems. What makes these materials folklore is not that truths are wanting, but that truths have been stereotyped, magnified, intensified, altered, or stylized to give them a formalistic or artistic expression and hence human content which makes them live for decades, even centuries, though any actuality which lies behind them may be lost. Robin Hood's conflict with the English barons dates from the early thirteenth century, yet ballads about him have been recovered in the folk song tradition of the United States in our own century, seven hundred years after his death. Obviously his myth counts for a good deal more than his actual exploits, and its importance lies not in what the myth reveals about Robin Hood, but rather in what it reveals about the people who have nurtured his memory in anecdote and song. Will Jesse James or J. Golden Kimball live as long in American or Mormon oral tradition? And, if they do, what relation will there still be between the historical and biographical facts and their story as preserved in the lore of the folk?

Folklore includes nonverbal behavior wedded to appropriate verbalizations: rituals, taboos, fetishes, beliefs, practices, gestures, ceremonies, hand signals, games, dances, pantomimes, receipts, and remedies are all manifestations of traditional human behavior which is transmitted through the processes of the folk through space and in time in an unbroken chain. They bind groups together (or separate them irretrievably), they give meaning to every human act, they contain, sustain, and project the systems of value which differentiate one culture from another, and all mankind from other species. Van Gennep has wisely observed that more than twenty centuries of economic and political vicissitudes have had but a small impact upon the folkways of the French people.

Folklore also has a material and tangible content in arts, crafts, and popular mechanical devices by which man has supplied some of his immediate physical needs: clothing and costumes; devices for the procurement or production of food; equipment to domesticate animals and to bend them to his will; shelters, sheds, barns; fences, gates, gate hinges and gate latches; hay derricks, horseshoes, ox yokes; quirts, ropes, knots, thongs, thread and fibers; quilts, rugs, drapery, and embroidery—crafts of skin, bone, stone, fiber, wood, hair, metals, fats, and fluids. Industry and mechanization, of course, have come to the aid of man in these areas—but only in the last two centuries and then largely in the technologically advanced nations. A great proportion of mankind still remains untouched thereby. Building fences, for example, is an absolute necessity for civilized societies because it permits the specialized use of land and makes possible the concept of private property. Little wonder then that western pioneers gave hours, years even, of their lives to the construction, maintenance, and repair of fences, using materials which the frontier offered and mechanical devices which men have acquired, used, and transmitted since the dawn of history.

In the second century B.C., Terence, a freed slave and author of Latin comedies written and produced in ancient Carthage, had already expressed the underlying mood which inspires folklorists, including the contributors to this collection: "Homo sum: humani nihil a me alienum puto" ("I am a man: nothing that pertains to man escapes my scrutiny." In "The Man Who Punished Himself," I, 1, 25). It is in this humane and inquisitive spirit that we invite the readers to examine the content of this book. An expression of appreciation is due each contributor, and especially to Professor Cheney whose dedication, initiative, and editorial expertise have brought the work into being.

Austin E. Fife

about the authors

This book is the work of an unsurpassed group of Utah writers. Over half of the nineteen contributors have published full length books. The total bibliography of publications of the group would be startling in its scope. Eight are women, eleven men. Six, Wayland Hand, Austin Fife, Alta Fife, Olive Burt, Juanita Brooks, and Thomas Cheney, can be called professional folklorists. Some of these writers have been recognized beyond the state. Wayland Hand has been president of the American Folklore Society; Austin Fife is past president; Thomas Cheney is serving as board member of the National Folk Festival Association. Juanita Brooks, Olive Burt, Thomas Cheney, Alta Fife, Austin Fife, Wayland Hand, and Claire Noall have all published sizable works which can be classified as folklore.

Writers of articles appearing herein have contributed significantly in other areas than folklore. Frank Robertson, professional writer, now deceased, wrote nearly forty books of fiction, drawn largely from his own folk experience. And the daily newspaper column he wrote for many years preserved folk thought. Jack Adamson, Juanita Brooks, Karl Larson, Gustive Larson, William Mulder, and Karl Young all continue to publish knowledgeable works in history and literature.

Of the group ten are college professors; one, Wayland Hand, a native of Utah, directs the folklore studies at the University of California at Los Angeles; two are at the University of Utah, Jack Adamson and William Mulder; one at Utah State University, Austin Fife; four at Brigham Young University, Thomas Cheney, Dean Farnsworth, Gustive Larson, and Karl Young; two served at Dixie College and now are retired to do research and writing, Juanita Brooks and Karl Larson.

Austin Fife is past president of the Folklore Society of Utah. In 1969 leadership went to William Wilson. At the time this book was compiled Thomas Cheney was president, Juanita Brooks and Austin Fife, vice presidents. Both of the latter assisted in choosing and editing materials for this volume.

introduction

Of Utah and the West we have many fine histories both secular and religious, many writers of historical fiction (Maurine Whipple, Vardis Fisher, Sam Taylor, Paul Bailey, and others), a profusion of biographies, and many doctrinal writings. But we have a limited number of works of folklore, recorded tales and reminiscences—the area to which this work belongs. To the extent that it presents traditional customs, beliefs, tales, and sayings preserved orally among the group, it is folklore. Peripheral to folklore as some items in these articles are, they are still presentations of customs and behavior patterns, the very heart of the culture they represent.

The notion many people entertain that the word *folklore* means something untrue must be dispelled. Folklore is not merely the myths, the superstitions, the fairy tales, the foolish unprincipled traditional customs and beliefs preserved and promulgated by the folk—it includes a good deal more. The folk includes all the people; their lore includes their traditional beliefs, patterns of thought, and behavior. One person's belief or behavior pattern may not constitute folklore. Yet if many people follow a similar action or harbor a similar belief, it becomes a folk pattern, a folkway worthy of attention. If, for example, in the pioneer Mormon Church sacrament service, one man breaks the sacred custom of taking a sip of wine from the large cup in memory of the blood of Christ shed for him and instead drains the full cup, it is a human-interest incident; but if others too drain the cup until the practice becomes a characteristic group action, then a folkway has been established. In any case one's oral account of such an event can become a folk tale. Much of the work herein is not presented with parallels to establish it as folklore—it is folk material. Moreover, this book is not, nor is it meant to be, a definitive work on Utah or Mormon folklore. If it were, it would have to include the spice of J. Golden Kimball stories, the myth-like flavor of Nephite legends, and a multitude of other items. It is not meant to be a basic study of folklore in Utah with all the scholarly comparisons and annotations of a thesis or dissertation.

Few areas are rooted as firmly in unique lore as is Utah. The Mormons who colonized the state went there for refuge. They had withstood the ferocity of men (who expelled them from their former homes) and the cruelties of elemental nature upon whose inhospitable lap they had fallen. The ethnic unity was developed through two unifying forces: first, belief in revelation and in their prophet leader, Brigham Young; and second, a mutual confrontation with malign nature in the intermountain basin—they had suffered and hoped together. Loyalty to authoritarian leadership, theocratic in its operation during the years of orientation, led men to respond when called to settle outlying areas where nature demanded the utmost in strength to survive. This loyalty to religious concepts and spiritual leaders led women to raise families in polygamy with astonishing serenity and men to manage several families with the authority of patriarchs and with sincere belief that their course of action was a priestly calling. This devotion is reflected herein. These things—life in an unconquered desert country, a hostile environment, in a carefully organized, prophet-dominated society with unique social customs—make Utah's early folk experience distinctive.

Unlike other regional cultures which retained foreign customs—the Pennsylvania Germans, the Louisiana French, and the Hispanic Americans of the Southwest—the Mormons emerged as a distinctive group within American society. Although shipload after shipload of Mormons came from England and Scandinavian countries, they were quickly amalgamated. Mormonism was a sizable, orderly community, established on a moral principle and a religious order which had brought trouble in the East and Midwest from which they had fled. But they were soon to learn that no group can remain in isolation; other groups invaded their insularity. This too is reflected in the folk history and folkways presented herein.

The book contains a variety of types of lore as a glance at the table of contents will reveal. It is made up of two distinct types of materials: Part I is folk narratives, local stories, reminiscences and oral history. Articles vary in style and tone, reflecting the individuality of the writer. Although this weakens total unity, it provides variety and novelty, characteristics which make or break writers; for all men, it seems, pay homage to the new and unique. None of the stories in Part I is the pure fabrication of a creative writer. All are stories which the writers accept as folklore. This is the real lifeblood of Utah folklore—the pioneer, Western American folk heritage. Part I begins with the same material as did the first folklore in America, the Indians. Soon after establishment of the American Folklore Society in 1888, anthropologists were concentrating on Indian tales. But in Utah, stories of Indians are not only studies of the habits of Indians, but also stories of white men trying to survive with Indians in peaceful coexistence or at least to live in Indian country without being molested. This is exactly the problem of all pioneer America.

Here also are regional stories of coal miners in Carbon County with its immigrant groups and their economic and social problems; of small communities, oral history, and folkways; of coyotes and men in conflict; of small-time traveling stock companies; of faith healing and family cures and practices; of strange gifts of premonition amounting to clairvoyance, of reminiscences of the old Silver Reef mining town, or pranks and pranksters.

Part II is analytical. It contains not only the lore of the people, but critical studies of it, probings into the reasons for its existence, and the meanings it suggests.

The folklorist and the sociologist as well as the general reader will find in this area subject matter of interest and value. Sufficient recurrences of certain types of behavior are presented in the articles on polygamy and wine-making in Utah to suggest culture patterns. Samuel Brannan and Orrin Porter Rockwell are well defended as emerging culture heroes. In the final section scholarly studies are presented which show depth and perspective in studies of folkways in courtship and marriage, in cures for common colds, in meeting the great world of the unknown, and in creativity and craftsmanship to meet common needs.

T.E.C.

1

Of Indians

Indian folklore of Utah is of two distinct types: one reveals Indian customs and beliefs, and the other deals with race relationships. Two significant articles appear herein which reveal Indian customs. "Our Annual Visitors" gives a vivid picture of the death-ceremony tradition of a tribe as well as their ways of dealing with the intruding settlers. "Red Magic" reveals an Indian's faith in the magic of the medicine man.

To the critical reader this group of four articles may appear heterogeneous and slight in relation to the great mass of Indian lore; yet it is sufficiently germane to Utah folkways to be significant. Because of the individuality of each of the three contributors, the styles of presentation are varied. "Red Magic" is presented in good, creative narrative form and might very well appear in a volume of literary works with subjects or motifs derived from folklore. "Spinning Wheel Hairdo" and "Sing, Tom! Sing!" are subjective and sentimental. They are told purposely, it appears, to play upon the emotions of the reader. Part of their charm lies in the conscious-unconscious folk sentiment so typical of Mormon society. "Our Annual Visitors" is a series of reminiscences reflecting a pattern of folk behavior toward Indians which was indigenous to the Utah pioneer society.

To point out significant folk motifs involved, I will give some background of Mormon experience with Indians. Brigham Young's method of dealing with Indians has been profusely told in oral and written communication from 1847 to the present time: "It is cheaper to feed them than to fight them." He said in a message to the Utah legislature in 1854, "I have uniformly pursued a friendly course toward them, feeling convinced that independent of the question of exercising humanity toward so degraded and ignorant a race of people, it was manifestly more economical and less expensive to feed and clothe them than to fight them."*

Following this policy, bishops all over the church advised their flocks essentially as did the bishop referred to in "Our Annual Visitors"—"Give as generously as you can." People in all the settlements felt that it was bad luck to refuse to give to an Indian beggar.

The result of this philosophy of giving food and clothes to Indians was not all good. The unrequited beggar often became a thief who then frequently resorted to violence. Therefore, many stories survive from pioneer days of experiences with Indian thieves and beggars—the white people trying to save their

*Clarissa Young Spencer, *One Who Was Valiant* (Caldwell, Idaho: Caxton Printers, 1940), p. 107.

meager supplies and the Indians manipulating their every means to steal them. Stories such as "Spinning Wheel Hairdo" abound. For example, Lorenzo Young's wife in Salt Lake City refused an Indian food, whereupon he aimed his arrow at her heart. She moved to the next room pretending to get food only to unleash a huge dog which, ordered to attack the Indian, complied and the Indian was driven away.

My own grandmother left a story to her descendants. At home alone, she was afraid when a huge and frightful Indian came to beg bread. She told him the truth when she said she had neither bread nor flour, but he did not believe her. He was threatening her life when an old man appeared (presumably a Nephite), convinced the Indian that there was no bread, and induced the intruder to leave.

In the April conference of 1854, Brigham Young told the people not to invite Indians into their homes, for their familiarities became oppressive, and if asked to leave they would become angry and quarrels would follow, causing difficulties. The problem with the Indian beggars and thieves is the most widespread motif in tales about Indians in Utah.

Other Indian themes emanated from the church leadership and from such important men in Indian affairs as Dimick Huntington, Jacob Hamblin, John D. Lee, and Porter Rockwell. As well as "Feed-them-rather-than-fight," the people must "Never lie to an Indian," "Never act afraid," and "Never kill or the red man will retaliate."

Retaliation or "eye-for-an-eye" justice is the motif for the story of "Sing, Tom! Sing!" and for that of the boy known to the Indians as Wamptun Tunghi (Grandpa Dudley) in "Our Annual Visitors." In this incident is another aspect of folklore—superstition. The white man takes advantage by playing upon the Indians' fear of magic. Closely related to this is the belief in the power of the medicine man, a belief surviving to the present day as is demonstrated in "Red Magic."

The Indian whose name arises most frequently in pioneer lore of Utah is Chief Walkara, known to the white people as Chief Walker. He died in 1855, so honored by the Utes, whom he led, that two squaws, two children, and fifteen horses were killed to accompany him to the world beyond. Yet to other tribes of Indians Chief Walker was a terror and to the white people an ever-present threat. Pretending friendliness to the Mormons, he continued to steal their cattle and horses and to keep outlying settlements in constant fear. It appears, however, that the greatest travesty of justice was the Indian practice of stealing children and youths from other tribes and selling them as slaves. Both Juanita Brooks and Gustive Larson mention Chief Walker but they tell no story related to the slave trade. Its history and lore is one of many areas not treated here.

T.E.C.

Juanita Brooks

Our Annual Visitors

No Indians lived near our little village of Bunkerville, Nevada, but once each year they came in a band and camped near town across the Big Ditch, where they set up their wickiups and stayed several days. This was usually around Christmas time. The Big Ditch was like a magic line above the town, protecting it from the desert and from all the unknown beyond. A log bridge spanned it near the camp, but no child crossed the bridge, nor did the Indian children come over to our side. Only the squaws came into town. They carried with them baskets of their own weaving—large clothes baskets with woven-in handles made to carry piles of wet clothes to the line, square, loosely-woven lunch baskets with attached handles and lids, and small sewing baskets finely woven and decorated. These they would trade for flour, molasses, bacon, or for such combinations as could be agreed upon, for we had no money and they needed none.

Then on Christmas Day, or on any day from then until New Year's, they visited every home systematically, each squaw carrying a sack, to rattle the screen door and call, "Crees'mas geef, Crees'mas geef!" Always they were given something—it was bad luck to turn them away empty-handed—a quart of flour to add to what they had already collected, a dozen potatoes, a bottle of molasses, or a piece of bacon. (How the squaw beamed to get this bacon!) Ma was always generous, so they left our door smiling, but we heard that some housewives received glowering looks and muttered imprecations.

But no house was ever visited twice. They evidently planned their campaign carefully on their side, and on ours the bishop counseled us to give as generously as we could, but not so much that our neighbors would be at a disadvantage or that the Indians would be encouraged to press this begging too far.

Their real influence did not come from this annual visit, but from the long past. Our grandparents had come with the first missionaries to the Southern Utah and Nevada Indians, had lived among them and learned their language. Thus some Indian words became part of our common talk: "tick-a-boo" was a very good friend and "too-wich-a-weino tick-a-boo" a dear friend who would stand by you in any emergency, even when you were wrong. A person was "tobuck" if he became angry; one was "heap tobuck" when he was fighting mad or filled with blind rage.

We often used "pike-e-way" to say "get out" or "be gone." With the local "P.D.Q." appended for emphasis, it meant to go instantly and with all speed. (P.D.Q. was the abbreviation for "purty-damn-quick." The English equivalent, then, was "get the hell out of here!") A similar word, "yake-e-way," meant to leave permanently or to die. "Him yake-e-way" was to say he is dead or he was killed.

Of course, our parents who dealt with the Indians or talked to them understood and used many words that did not come into our speech patterns. A few mothers still warned their little children that "Old Sanpitch will get you!" if they wandered away. This was a throwback to the earlier times when Chief Walker and his brother Sanpitch would raid the weaker Indian bands of the south and steal their children to sell as slaves in Mexico.

My first experience with an Indian came when I was only six years old. I was playing with the younger children and some neighbor youngsters in our sand village under the pomegranate bushes, where we had little houses outlined in the damp sand and roads between them. A guttural sound behind me brought me instantly to my feet, face-to-face with an Indian—a full-grown man, dressed like a white man, but undeniably an Indian.

"Where's Hen?" he asked. "Hen live here?"

"Yes," I stammered, trying to appear calm. "He lives here, but he is not here now. He is down to the field. He comes home before sundown."

He glanced at the sun, low in the west. "I wait," he said, and walked back to sit on the edge of the porch.

Our play was ruined. No one had any interest now in the little rolled-up-rag ladies or forked-stick men, in the "bony" horses or sardine-can wagons. We whispered together; the neighbor girls gathered up their doll-rags and went home to tell their mothers that an Indian was sitting on Uncle Hen's porch—just sitting as quiet and still as a statue. We watched him a while, and soon one and another of the children began to approach him gingerly to try to attract his attention.

I had gone down into the garden to tell Ma that he was here, and returned just in time to see the game–children creeping up almost near enough to touch him and then squealing and dodging around the corner. I scolded them and sent them packing, but not before one little mischief had thrown a tomato and hit the Indian right on the side of his bare head. Now he came to life! Leaping to his feet, he looked fierce enough until he saw Pa's wagon out in front. Then he turned to walk out to the sidewalk, wiping his head as he went.

"Mi-ek! Mi-ek!" Pa called out from the wagon, echoing the Indian's greeting. "Why Simon, you old scamp, what are you doing here? Long time, no see!"

Pa had pulled the team to a stop, wrapped the lines around the brake and leaped to the ground all in one quick movement, and the two men almost ran toward each other. They met in a strong right-arm embrace, Pa's hand patting the Indian's back.

"Come on out while I take care of the team," Pa said, as they separated, and to me, "Go tell your mother we've got company for supper."

Pa drove the load of melons and squash into the stackyard, and a little while later the two men came toward the house, Pa with a casaba under each arm. Simon stayed outside while Pa brought the melons in. Ma asked in an undertone if he was going to have the Indian eat at the table.

"Sure he's going to eat at the table," Pa said, "Fix a place."

After we were all in and seated, Pa brought in the Indian and said pointing, "My squaw. My papooses," taking us all in in one gesture. To us he said, as they settled themselves, "Simon was my friend when I was a boy at Gunlock. We herded cows together. I give him one of my biscuits and molasses; he give me some of his jerky. Sometimes his mother made little round cakes for us, hot and good. And we set traps for chipmunks and quail and robbed mudhens' nests in the sloughs."

Simon smiled a little at this, but attended to his eating in silence, as though conscious of our curious stares. They finished quickly and went outside again to the corral fence where they could talk, away from any listening ears. By the time Pa came in again it was dark. He sat with a half-smile on his face and then said, "It took him quite a while to get around to letting me know what he wanted. He said they were going to gather pine nuts on the south mountains, and he thought there were mountain sheep near the top of Noon Peak. If he had a gun, he might get one."

"You didn't let him take your new .30-.30 sure?" Ma guessed, surprised.

"I sure did. The gun and a box of bullets. No good giving him the gun if he can't shoot it. And I'd trust Simon with anything I own."

Ma gave a little grunt of disbelief, but did not press the matter further. Somehow the word got out. The neighbors knew that Simon was there and that he had supper with us, so they must find out what he came for. Opinion as to return of the gun seemed unanimous.

The next day when Ma sent me to the store with a pan of eggs to exchange for groceries, the spit-and-whittle row in the sun were discussing it, though I did not hear Pa's name.

"He's crazy," one said. "That's the last he'll ever see of that gun. That Indian'll lose his way back, or some of the others will get away with it. They don't often get a gun like that."

Just how long the gun was gone I do not know. It must have been early November when he borrowed it, and after Thanksgiving when I answered a knock on the door to see Simon there with his same question, "Where's Hen?"

Again Pa went outside to come back after a few minutes with his precious gun in one hand and a flour sack nearly half full in the other.

"Pine nuts!" he exulted, holding up the sack. "Real Indian roasted pine nuts!" He went on to say that the Indians had a way to cook these nuts that the whites had never learned. While we parched ours on top of the stove, keeping the heavy skillet moving slowly back and forth over a low heat, they prepared a heated pit with a baked clay bottom, fired it for a whole day, scooped out most of the coals and ashes, filled it full of pine cones, dampened them just a little, covered them with something—he wasn't sure what—and then built another fire on top. After several hours they opened the pit, took out the cones, and shook out the nuts.

At any rate, it was now our time to crow, for we not only had the gun and bullets back (except three. Simon got a mountain sheep with long curled up horns, a rabbit, and a fox) but we had these wonderful nuts. We children did not know where they were kept hidden; we must not get into them at all, but they were wonderful to us because every time Pa got them out to pass to friends they worked like magic! The people eating them at once remembered Indian stories which they were eager to tell.

One time it was Aunt Leen and Aunt Sadie, two of Pa's older sisters, who were victims of this magic. "Do you remember that first Indian dance and pow-wow at Gunlock?" Aunt Sadie asked. "Maybe it wasn't the very first, but it was the first that I remember. It was before you was born, Henry, because I was not very old then myself. But we had a good harvest, and Father invited all the tribe up for a feast—barbecued a young beef, cooked squash and corn, and had lotsa melons. The Indians danced and danced, and Father insisted that we get into the circle and go with them. Like this . . ."

And she proceeded to demonstrate. Holding up her skirt, she moved about four steps to one side and then back two steps, as she sang an eerie song without words. It was not really a song, of course, but a series of sounds ranging from low guttural grunts to high shrieks. Aunt Leen got up and joined her, and they ended laughing because they could not keep together in it. Then she continued her story:

"And after they had danced and eaten their fill, Father stood up on the wagon box and preached to them, telling them the Mormons were "too-wich-a-weino tick-a-boo" and wanted only to help them get "shaunts-a-shotcup" or lots of food. But they must not steal our cattle or hurt our papooses. If they did, the Great Spirit would curse them, and their own children would die. Then the next spring when the measles broke out in their camp and so many papooses did die, they thought that Father was a prophet."

Then they began remembering the different Indians: Tutsegavit, and Watermann, and Shem, and Queetuse, and Toab, and incidents about each until to us children these Indians became very real indeed. So it was that whenever the pine nuts were passed, we were all attentive.

One evening when I stopped to leave some fresh milk for Grandpa Dudley and Grandma Thirza, Pa was there with a bowl of the pine nuts, which they had evidently been eating at for some time. Grandpa sat studying the little blue flames on the underside of the fireplace log, like he was looking into the far past. To me he was about the greatest man that ever lived. He held his great body erect; his thick, white hair stood up like thistledown; his face was clean-shaven except for the clipped mustache and a white ruffle of beard from ear to ear under his chin.

"I was riding Old Vittick up the Mogotsu one night," he began. "It was pitch dark, so dark you couldn't see your hand before you, with a storm threatening. I was singing along and talking to Vittick to encourage him when he came to a dead stop, just braced himself and threw back his head with a bit of a snort and refused to move. Now Vittick was a smart horse, and I trusted him— times was when his judgment was better than mine. So I sat there waiting. In an instant there was a flash of sheet lightning that showed me what was wrong. Indians! Vittick had smelled them. I was almost surrounded by armed Indians, each with his bow pulled up to the highest notch. In one jump, one had Vittick by the bridle and others were pulling me off his back.

"I called out my name, Wamptun Tunghi, and tried to remind them that I had always been their friend, but they were not in the humor to talk. I didn't put up much of a fight, it was so dark and we were so far away from any help. I didn't want to risk a skin full of arrowheads for either me or the horse.

"They led me down into the creek bed and along a steep bank quite a ways, until we made a sharp turn where they had a fire going and some wood piled to keep it. They put me between the fire and the bank which curved out like a horseshoe, and the Indians ranged themselves on the other side of the fire. I could see several strange ones in the crowd, but some of them I knew. I tried to talk, but no one paid the least bit of attention. From what I could gather, an Indian had been killed by a white man—a good Indian they loved very much, and he left a family. According to their rules, the first white man they caught was to be sacrificed to even the score: I was that man. The point not yet settled was the way in which I was to be killed—with arrows, or with fire torture and then a tomahawk blow, or what.

"I stood quiet and composed, trying to figure what to do. And then it came to me! The Indians are afraid of 'talking papers,' which they do not understand. I reached into my pocket and pulled out a little daybook that I always carried—about so big, four to six inches—and took a stub of a pencil out of another pocket. Then I began to make big, heavy marks, carefully, as though I were writing an important message. I knew the Indians who stood near were watching, and soon they had signaled the others and all of the crowd was leaning forward to see what would happen.

"When I knew I had their full attention, I tore out the page and stepped to the fire. I held it out until one corner caught on, and then I lifted it as high as I could toward heaven and called out the Indian distress cry to Shanob, 'E-waki! E-waki!' They were all ears. 'E-waki, Shanob! Wamptun Tunghi heap much trouble—' and in what Indian and English I could put together I explained to the Lord that I had been the Indians' friend, and now look! see what they wanted to do to me! Help me, Great Shanob!

"I felt my guards draw away as the paper burned, and just as the flame was about to my fingers there was another flash of lightning and a loud crash of thunder. When I could see again, I was alone. Old Vittick stood on the other side of the fire with his reins hanging in front of him, and not an Indian in sight. Old Shem told me later that they were 'heap scairt of that letter to Shanob.' "

The sack of magic pine nuts did not last past the holidays, but when the squaws came begging this year, Ma was extra generous with them. The annual visits continued with little variation in pattern for several years. Then, when I was about twelve years old, one was different. The band was larger and they stayed longer and there were many children among them. As usual, they camped across the Big Ditch, but they put up more permanent tent wickiups, and some of the children had evidently gone to school, for there were some pictures on the tents and some crude printing. I rode up on Selah one evening to join some neighbor kids on our side of the river. They had been calling back and forth with the Indian youngsters on the other side, each daring the other to run across the log bridge which connected us, until some on both sides had taken the dare and gone over the deadline to scurry back with squeals and laughter.

As I sat there, I noticed an Indian boy about my age being legged onto his pony by an older man. I felt very superior, because I could get on my pony unaided. This was a point of pride, an evidence of good horsemanship. When I was too short to reach the mane of my horse, I had to lead it to the stump near the corner of the corral and climb on from that vantage point. When there were two of us, we could manage by having one lead the horse alongside a pole fence and hold it in position while the other climbed the fence and jumped on from there. Sometimes we would open the big gate just enough to let the horse through and then hold it midway so that we could get on from the gate, but this often resulted in scraped legs. One time a younger brother, unable to mount unaided, climbed onto the shed, now bare of its bagasse and straw winter cover, waited until the horse was eating at the manger, and then lowered himself onto its back from above. The startled animal jumped, turned, and ran out of the open gate and toward the river at a sharp trot, the child hanging desperately to its mane. He had not been tall enough to even get a rope around its neck, let alone a bridle on.

The usual procedure was to get the horse bridled, the reins in place over its head, to grasp the mane and say to a companion, "Gimme a leg, will you?" in much the same way that you would ask one to give you a hand up a steep bank. Real riders needed no assistance to mount, but with one bare toe against the horse's knee could spring to the back unaided. So I thought the Indian boy who still had to be legged on was something of a pantywaist.

This year the squaws made their annual round for Christmas gifts, but the camp stayed on all through the week until after New Year's. Someone said there was a man too sick to travel; someone else said they were waiting for the old year to leave or for the moon to change or for some other omen, and then they would have their regular rabbit drive.

Once by chance I saw part of an Indian rabbit drive. I had turned the stock out to the ditch to drink and then neglected to follow and check on them closely. When I came to close the gate and throw down the hay, two were missing, a young heifer and a cow that would calve in another month or so, both too valuable to let run. I mounted Selah and started toward the hills. From a high point I saw the missing animals to the west, while from the east came strange sounds of voices rising and falling, punctuated by sharp yelps and yells. Riding to the edge of the hill, I saw in the wash below a thin line of Indians a few yards apart, moving together up through the brush, brandishing long sticks and keeping up this half-singing, half-yelling sound. I watched as they passed a little way, the excitement and noise growing as rabbits leaped from the brush and ran ahead. I learned later that the real kill came at the narrow point where they had a yucca-fiber net stretched from one cliff to the other and held securely in place by several younger boys.

Friends later told of the return of the band, each man with many rabbits hanging from his waist, the estimate being anywhere from twenty-five to fifty or a hundred, depending upon who was making the report. Others told how the rabbits were cooked whole—head, feet, unbroken hide, entrails and all—in their heated pit. A row of rabbits would be laid parallel and close to each other, then another row placed on top, crosswise of the first, the whole then covered with coals and ashes and a small fire over it all. For this one night there was great feasting.

But to come back to the Indians camped above the Big Ditch, an afternoon came when the wailing and drumbeating and crying told us that the sick man had died. While we were doing the chores, during supper and throughout our evening activities we did not notice this so much, but after we were in bed in the quiet house, the very walls seemed to pulsate with these eerie cries. They went on without ceasing, one group evidently picking up the strain as another grew weary. I pulled my pillow over my head, I rolled and tossed, and finally I got up to walk around. But it was cold upstairs in our unheated bedroom. At last I went in where Pa and Ma were sleeping soundly through it all.

"Can't we do something about this awful noise?" I asked. "Can't we get the bishop or the sheriff or somebody to go and tell them that they are keeping the whole town awake and they must be quiet?"

"Don't be silly," Pa said. "That is the Indian way of mourning, and no one must interfere. Their grief is just like ours when one of the family dies, only they show it in a different way. Go back and get into bed, say your prayers over again, and you'll go right to sleep."

The next morning everything was quiet. When I went to milk, I climbed the fence and looked toward the Indian camp but could see no activity. After I had the chores all done, I hung my bucket of milk on a jutting pole and ran up to the place. No one there! Everything deserted and cleared, as if even the trash had been used for fuel in last night's campfire. They must have taken turns crying and packing up all during the night. The campfire ashes were there, and another pile where the wickiup of the sick man had stood, but there was little further evidence that a tribe had ever camped there.

Pa explained later that the Indian custom was to have the litter prepared sometimes before the person actually died, or to have the willow poles and crosspieces ready to assemble. Then after a period of mourning and some personal rites, the leaders wrapped the body in its blankets and strapped it securely in place. Four men carried it and all the tribe followed at least part way, with stops while they changed carriers. At each stop there was some crying, but otherwise the journey was relatively quiet. The body would be left in a cave or a secluded place, the personal belongings with it, some food at the head, and the man's horse killed nearby so that he would have transportation to the Happy Hunting Ground. Sometimes, if he had a special pet dog it was killed also.

No Indians came to our town the next winter, nor the next, nor the next, and we were told that for several years, at least, they would not camp on the spot where one of their number had died. In the meantime, the pattern had been changed. The authorities of the church talked to the Indian leaders and agreed that "shaunts-a" beef and food and clothing should be taken to the reservation each Christmas, and the squaws no longer needed to go around the town calling "Crees'mas geef!"

While we were glad to be through with this, our village still lost something—something of color and variety, something of depth in time, something of contrast, and our younger brothers and sisters missed some experiences which we older ones remember with pleasure. Our annual visitors left an exchange for the bits of food we gave them.

Karl E. Young

Red Magic

"You know, Karl, I don' feel pretty good las' year," Looking Elk confided to me. He paused to pin a swinging black braid against his chest with his left wrist. His left hand kept in neat control the folds of a mauve cotton blanket that looped over the top of his head and fell in a loose drape over his shoulders. In his right hand he held a birch rod, which he now cautiously extended beyond the willows flanking Taos Creek. His grasshopper dropped lightly on the smooth water, but the trout were wary. Dark shadows flicked upstream. Looking Elk shook his head. "Too many mans fishing these water," he said.

I brought him back to the confidence he had started to share with me. "What was the matter, Albert? Why didn't you feel so good last year?"

"Well I don' know, but I am very sick. I loose about two poun's every day. So the doctor send me down to the hospital at Albuquerque. An' I still loose two poun's every day. And I goin' to die. So I say to the nurse, I going away from this place.

"And she say to me, 'You better wait till the doctor come.' And I say, 'When is that?'

"And she say 'Well, the doctor coming tomorrow.'

"And I say 'I not wait for the doctor then.'

"And she say 'Well, you better wait till tomorrow anyway.'

"And I say, 'No. If tomorrow is good enough day for me to go, today is good enough. So I going today!'

"So I get out of bed and go away from there."

Looking Elk leaned his birch rod against a cottonwood sapling, rearranged the fold of his blanket over the thin hair on top of his head, swung the free end of the flimsy cloth over his left shoulder, and turned his unemotional eyes on me again.

"Where did you go, Albert?" I asked, not wishing to press him, but hoping to fan, ever so gently, the spark of self-revelation which almost inevitably extinguishes itself under the breath of a white man.

"I go to Picuris," he said.

"Why did you not come back to your own pueblo?" I asked, fearing lest the account had already degenerated into a bold question and answer interview, fruitful of nothing except perfunctory responses.

But today Looking Elk, aloof Taos sophisticate that he was, wanted to talk!

"I went to Picuris. There is medicine man at Picuris can cure everythings. He could even cure sick Navajo." A glimmer of appreciation passed over his eyes as I smiled at his tart thrust at the Navajos. Overwhelmingly outnumbered by the thousands of Navajos who come pouring out of the hills and badlands into Gallup at ceremonial time, the Pueblo Indians fortify their own egos by making sly remarks about the frequently unimpressive members of the Navajo nation who have just emerged from the "way far back" country and show it.

Without pausing, Looking Elk continued, "This man put me in little inside room and keep me there four days. Every day he brush me with prayer feathers and sing little songs over me. An' every night I go for sleep and have ver' strange dream. I dream I walking down long trail, and on each sides of trail is telegraph poles, and on each poles is eagle. These eagle peck at me when I'm go by and want to eat my heart. And next night is mountain lion following me and want to eat my heart too. And on third night I dream I am walk through ver' bad storm, and is winds blowing, and thunders and lightning striking every ground around me, and makes my heart swallow hard in my throat. And on the fourth night is poles turned into snake and eagle's neck turn into snake too."

As he talked, Looking Elk's eyes shone. His usually placid face reflected the excitement in his breast. Shrewd though he was in the jostle of daily living in the pueblo, in this state of mind he would fall an easy prey to the practitioners of Indian black magic, the medicine men.

"And then the medicine mans come to sing to me some more," he continued. "An' he take all my clothes off and stand me in middle of room. He paint me all over with color paints, an' he blow all over me and brush me with prayer feathers and put prayer sticks on me and sing this songs, an' then he put his mouth down to my side quick, and he suck there. Then he turn away to the corner to vomit, an' he vomit up a little green snake. This snake is been up in my chest, and he steal all my breath. I couldn' scarcely breathe."

Looking Elk paused. His eyes were moist and his mask of calm was gone. He was panting slightly. But gradually, as he stood there silent, the memory of that dark kiva with its skillful priest and his miraculous cures receded into the deep regions of his Indian mind. His features settled themselves once again into the placid and serene expression with which he usually faced the world.

"But when it is gone, this snake, I feel pretty good," he said.

"An' then my wife take me home to Taos. An' every day we go for little walk, and it is walk a little longer every day. An' every day I gain about two poun's. An' now you see me how I am. I feel pretty good this year."

Ann G. Hansen

Spinning Wheel Hairdo

Chief Pocatello lurked in the trees, tired from a night of fighting and murder. He had the scalps of five white men as souvenirs of his night's plunder and strands of long blond hair wound round the knife that he had used in the struggle. He would continue to fight for his people and their hunting grounds, he told himself proudly. The whites would be driven off, or he would die bravely trying. But now he must have food.

There in a small clearing stood a cabin half hidden by a large cedar whose branches, dirty at the bottom, touched the ground. Clumps of bunch grass stood up stiffly, dotting the dooryard, and a rooster high on a straw shed proclaimed the glories of the morning and another new day. Smoke came from the cabin sending little curls over the weeds on the dirt roof as it reached to touch the bright blue of the sky. It was early, and a little cold, but already the household was moving. Two little children, a boy and a girl, dashed out of the house to feed the pigs and chickens, and as they opened the door, the smell of bacon tormented the Indian's empty stomach.

He stealthily surveyed the situation. The cow had been milked, and fresh hoofprints and wagon tracks pointed to the canyon. He grinned. There would be food with no problem, and even if he did need to kill, a few more white scalps would only add to his glory. Slyly he led his horse under the cedar tree and crept softly to the door of the cabin. He pushed it open a crack and peeked in. There was a woman seated by a strange wheel that kept going round and round. He was fascinated. He stood still with wonder. Then he pushed the door inward a little more, slipped his body through the opening, and closed the door again without making a sound. He stood tall and straight with lines of bitterness and hatred showing through the war paint on his hideous face. His shirt was streaked with blood, and his coarse, black hair protruded from his war bonnet.

Sarah Jane looked up. There stood the gruesome savage smiling at her. She turned white and slumped in her chair, but regaining her composure as she thought of her children, she flashed her dark eyes defiantly at him, but could not utter a sound. The cords on her neck stood out, her thin lips moved, but still no words came. She tried to rise, but found herself too weak and faint to move.

The Indian, enjoying the misery of his victim, brandished a long, thin-bladed knife, and began to sharpen it on a rough piece of sandstone he held in his bloody hand. On the handle were bits of blond hair stuck with dried blood that showed through his filthy fingers. He sharpened the knife again, at the same time making tormenting grimaces toward Sarah Jane as she sat petrified at her spinning wheel.

He walked toward the crude cupboard, picked up a dish of cold mush, and began eating it with his dirty fingers. As the mush was not to his liking, he tossed the dish against the wall and laughed as it broke into little pieces. Turning next to the stove, he dipped his fingers in the greasy skillet, licked them, and proceeded to eat a piece of bacon left from the morning meal. As the heat from the stove warmed his body, a nauseating smell of sweat, blood, and smoke filled the room.

Sarah Jane wiped her own cold sweat on her waist apron, smoothed her dark hair, and with a prayer in her heart resumed her spinning. Round and round went the wheel as the Indian came nearer. She peeked over her shoulder and there he was, right beside her. She would die bravely she told herself, but what of her children? How could her husband stand the shock of coming home to find their butchered bodies? She prayed again as she felt the Indian's hot breath on her neck as he leaned closer to watch the magic of the spinning wheel. Closer and closer he leaned, too close! A terrified shout of pain shook the cabin. There was the chief, caught fast, his long black hair tangled with the other fibers in the spinning wheel. He stamped and roared. He swung his bloody knife, but there he was—caught fast before his captive squaw.

The baby woke and screamed with fright at the howling of the visitor, and the children came running in from outside—terrified as they saw the redskin fighting helplessly to free himself.

Thoughts raced through Sarah Jane's mind. Shall I take my children and run and leave him here? Shall I hit him over the head with the axe? No, the

Indians would kill too many whites to retaliate. Indians admire bravery. If I cut him loose, perhaps he will be friendly with the whites. She paused. I'll try kindness, she decided. "I'm sorry, I'm sorry," cried the trembling Sarah Jane, as if he could appreciate her apologies. She took her scissors and quickly cut the strands of black hair and the Indian stood up, humiliated and free.

Meanwhile, William, who had gone to the canyon for wood, had listened to an inner voice prompting him to go home. He had seen the Indian sneaking through the forest, and the thought that his family might be harmed grew until he decided to return. Shaking with apprehension, he felt more anxious each step of the way. Great boulders stood in his path that he had to wind around, and the grass was slippery and dry. Chipmunks skittered in the brush and crying hawks made him more tense than ever. He clucked to his horses to hurry them up the trail toward home. As he neared the cabin, he looked suspiciously everywhere. All was quiet—too quiet—not even the bark of the dog or the greetings of his children broke the silence. Something was wrong. He got down from his wagon and was about to enter the house when suddenly the Indian sprang from the door and made a jump for his pony, concealed behind the cedar tree. But William was too quick for him. He grabbed him by the leg and jerked him from his horse. The Indian, with the agility of a cat, dropped to his hands and tried to twist his foot away, but William held fast, sinking his fingernails into the dark skin. The Indian stood on his other foot and gave William a bunt in the stomach with his head. William staggered, but with renewed strength sent the Indian sprawling in the dirt. The savage reached for his knife. Sarah Jane and the children screamed. William, who thought he was fighting for his family, fought again. This time he caught the red man by the throat and gripped until he began to fight for breath. His hands relaxed and the knife fell to the ground. Sarah Jane grabbed the knife and stood ready to use it, but it was not necessary; the Indian lay quietly in the dirt, the hacked ends of his black hair spread out like a matted fan. William let him breathe again and gave him a blow on the right ear for good measure. Speaking in words the Indian understood, William demanded, "If I let you go, will you promise never to molest my family again?"

The Indian promised, and William let him up. The dirt and leaves fell from his shirt as he slowly mounted his pony and rode away. But a souvenir of the fight remained. Black hair was still wound in the spinning wheel.

Ann G. Hansen

"Sing, Tom! Sing!"

"Will they torture me before they kill me?" Tom pondered, as he sat on a big rock surrounded by Indians. He could see hatred, anger, and revenge in their hideous, painted faces, and he knew his fate was entirely in their hands.

Nineteen-year-old Tom had been sent by the settlers of Clarkston to Mendon to get men to help ward off an Indian attack, and now here he was—captured. What would the people do, and what would he do? Who would find his body? Agonizing thoughts raced through his mind as he more fully realized his predicament.

The Indians were determined that the whites should not settle in Clarkston. There were grassy meadows for their ponies, and plenty of wild game on the hillsides; this was their land, and if the whites would not leave peaceably, they would force them with tomahawks and arrows. The settlers were just as determined that they would stay, and the battle continued. How many lives it would cost no one knew; perhaps it meant Tom's.

Indians hate a coward, thought Tom, trying to straighten his shoulders and look composed. They must not see that I am trembling. He shoved his hands in his pockets and squirmed about on the rock. Cold beads of sweat stood on his forehead as he watched the hard and satisfied grins of the Indians.

Enjoying the misery of their victim, they sat still in the circle with no haste for his murder. The strange sounds of night filled the air. Clouds were in the sky, and the vast expanse of sage added to the desolation and loneliness of this young English immigrant. He had joined the Mormon Church and this was the result. There was only one thing he could do. He would call upon God to save him.

Humbly and fervently he offered a prayer that his life might be saved, and he had no sooner said "Amen" than he was impressed with a thought—Sing! Sing, Tom! Sing! There was no time to question. In a weak and croaking voice he sang the old English song, "The Nightingale."

He hesitated then, clearing his throat, and in his fine tenor voice—stronger now—sang "Drink to Me Only with Thine Eyes." It seemed a burlesque to sing this song to the Indians, but in his heart he was singing it for the lovely Danish girl, Maria, who had promised to marry him. He paused to think of her and then the prompting came again—sing, sing, keep singing.

This time he sang the inspiring Mormon hymn, "Come, Come, Ye Saints." But when he came to the last verse, there was a choking in his throat, "And should we die before our journey's through, Happy day! all is well!" He couldn't think of death as a happy day, especially at the hands of Indians, but regardless of his feelings, he knew he must keep singing. Finally he sang "High on the Mountain Top," looking at the mountains around him, firm and majestic, giving him the courage to continue.

Faint streaks of dawn appeared in the east. Tom knew that he had been singing for hours. Surely his father would miss him. Surely someone would come. He drew his coat around him and was attempting one more song when the old Indian chief stood up to tell him of his fate. In deep guttural tones he said, "One who can sing like a bird should not die. He should live to bring joy to his people."

Tom shuddered with relief. And then he heard something—a sound in the distance. He knew what it was and began singing again to cover it. But the quick ears of the Indians heard the hoofbeats, and they jumped on their ponies and raced away.

In a few minutes Tom's father, with a posse, arrived to find the young man exhausted, hoarse, and shaken, but unharmed. Tom rode back to Clarkston with a testimony of the power of prayer never to be forgotten.

This singing boy became my grandfather. The words of the old Indian chief were indeed true; Grandpa brought much joy to the world with his singing. He sang at parties, concerts, funerals, in the town choir, and then, as he grew older, he bounced his grandchildren on his knee, let them hold his big silver watch, and sang to them. He sang a humorous song to the teenagers about a little drummer who loved a cross-eyed cook. Then, whenever there was bickering or faultfinding among his family or friends, he sang, with an English accent:

> Always hear both sides
> Always hear both sides
> Let equal rights all men enjoy
> And always hear both sides.

Grandpa sang and led community singing until his death when he was in his eighties. He never forgot the inspiration of his youth, "Sing, Tom! Sing!"

2

Of Local History and
Reminiscence of Pioneer Days

This section deals with the oral history of small towns: Washington in Utah's Dixie, Midway in Wasatch County, Utah, the mining camps of Carbon County, Utah, Silver Reef in southern Utah, and Bunkerville in Nevada. Every community has its stock of stories growing out of its own distinctive cultural, national, and geographical inheritance. The pathetic, the tragic, the comic, the farcical—all exist in folk tradition. The miscellany which appears in a given settlement in a pioneer society in its detail is peculiar to that community; yet, in basic features or motifs it may be and usually is a part of the common heritage of larger units of society. Thus the specific items appearing in the articles in this chapter may be recognized as folklore of value chiefly when related to the larger frame of reference. For example, the tale Mary Alice Collins tells of men from Midway being "called" to serve as missionaries for their church and at once accepting the call, leaving their families financially destitute, describes a folk pattern that was followed in all Mormon settlements.

Juanita Brooks' explanation of the origin and meaning of the "wedding stake" is of value to the linguist and to the folklorist; to the former because the potent colloquial term is authentic language though it has expired, and to the latter because it contributes to the mass of knowledge of folkways and actions which helps us to better understand ourselves and others.

The historian may fail to record how Midway got its name, even though early settlers remember and tell the stories as they are recorded in the articles in this section. Many folkways which give way to other patterns live chiefly in the minds of the people, as, for example, the practice of borrowing fire, use of the tithing office for farm produce contributed to the church, races to the filing office to secure land, dude drummers' activities, economy measures, death and burial customs.

The story herein of the mysterious Eugene Levignier, who prepared himself for death and burial; William Wilson, the farmer who by his own request was buried sitting upright against a hill so he could view his fields eternally; the story of the boy who slipped a can opener in the tin burial vault of a dead man so he could cut his way out for resurrection; the four violent deaths in Silver Reef, including the story of the two who killed each other because one man told the other to take off his hat in the courtroom—all these stories have no reason for being other than personal interest. Yet they are part of a massive accumulation of stories about death common in every culture which if studied and compared fall into motifs and patterns.

References to Brigham Young's admonition to his followers to "treat the

Indians kindly" and to make agriculture rather than mining their vocation are likewise part of an oral and written lore, based unquestionably in truth, but twisted, distorted, varied in all directions, stretched to the breaking point by both purposeful and innocent truth distorters.

In my own collecting I have found a good many stories of the Butch Cassidy gang of outlaws: "Butch Cassidy tried to give me a dog," said elderly Nephi Williams of Castle Dale, Utah, in 1958. "Butch Cassidy was born and reared a Mormon; he was an adult member of the Aaronic Priesthood," said Garth Seegmiller of Provo in 1955. Stories go and stories grow about significant people whether noted or notorious. Helen Papanikolas' references to Matt Warner and Butch Cassidy are examples of that lore.

T.E.C.

Andrew Karl Larson

Ithamar Sprague and His Big Shoes

As I remember it now, I was a boy in my middle or late teens when an old man returned to Washington, in Utah's Dixie, to pay a visit to the haunts of his boyhood. He had no relatives there at this time, but he had friends and acquaintances who remembered him well enough. One of them was Hyrum Boggs, who had lived in Washington since 1861 when he came there with his father, Francis Boggs, at a time when three hundred families had been "called" to colonize Southern Utah. The old gentleman and Hy Boggs sat reminiscing after the manner of old men sitting comfortably in the sun. Every now and then one or the other would throw back his head and give way to a gust of merry laughter in which his companion heartily joined. They were reliving the days of their youth when the visitor had thrown the young settlement into such a dither as the town had seldom experienced, before or since.

Hyrum Boggs used to walk by our home in Washington on his way downtown, where his daughter Evaline Boggs Iverson lived on what has since become Interstate 15. My father and I were soaking up the wheels of our hay wagon at the ditch that ran through our lot and across the street in front of our home. Brother Boggs came striding by, waving his cane with characteristic gesture, and seeing us, he stopped to chat. His first words were, "Say, did you know that Ithamar Sprague is in town?" "No, Hy," replied my father, "and I haven't seen him for ever so long." "Well, he's here, and he's still laughing about the way he fooled the people here. I have to laugh every time I think of it myself; it's downright funny!" "Yes, it's funny," my father agreed, "but a lot of people didn't think it was so funny at the time." Hyrum Boggs agreed. He and Father talked about a number of things, and then Brother Boggs swung into his accustomed vigorous stride and was off down the street.

As he moved away, I inquired of Father what Ithamar Sprague had done that made them laugh now, this something which was no laughing matter when it happened. Father told me what he knew of it. It was brief, for he was not given to long speeches and explanations. Since then I have talked with others who lived in Washington at the time of Sprague's hoax, and from different accounts the unusual story becomes fairly clear.

One of Ithamar's duties was to drive the family cows to the fields across the Virgin River. One day he was crossing the river bottoms about a mile south of town. There had been a freshet from a summer cloudburst on the upper reaches of the stream, and it had deposited on the river bottom a film of slick, gray sediment. As he drove his father's cows across the river, one of them slipped, and in her struggle to stay on her feet, she slithered and skidded around a lot, and to his amazement left a mark that strikingly resembled a huge human shoeprint. As he gazed in wonder at this chance example of the cow's unconscious art, an idea began to take shape in his fertile imagination. With far more alacrity than he normally displayed in doing up his chores about the farmyard, he worked out his plan.

Just a day or two later some children were startled to see on the dusty streets of the village some gigantic human footprints, at least three feet long! They followed them for some distance, and then just as suddenly as they had appeared, the footprints petered out. In a state of considerable excitement the mystified children ran to their parents with the news of the oversize shoeprints. The parents pooh-poohed the idea, thinking it only the fanciful imagination of childhood. But when the young ones insisted on the reality of their discovery, the parents investigated—and sure enough, there were the tracks, unmistakably plain as day!

The news spread through the village like a grass fire before a strong wind. The whole town was goggle-eyed with excitement; everyone wondered how the tracks had been made. Some of the more mature and level-headed people refused to believe that they had been made by anyone but a prankster, while others reserved judgment, awaiting further developments; but many were convinced that some huge creature was lurking about or lying in wait, intent on their destruction.

All this, it may well be imagined, was very satisfying to young Ithamar Sprague. He made more tracks that night, and the next day more of the townsfolk succumbed to the fear that a ferocious being was about to dispose of them in some ogre-like way.

What could the creature be? The local Indians added to the growing dismay when they seemed to recall a legend of a giant who prowled the country, killing, plundering, and even carrying away the children. This giant was still somewhere in the country, the Indians claimed. Two other ideas, equally fantastic, were advanced as the hysteria grew. According to some, this unusual being must be one of the Three Nephites; to others it was likely a member of the Gadianton Robbers. To those of the Mormon faith these characters will be more or less familiar; for others a word of explanation may be necessary.

It is said that when Christ was preparing to leave this earth after His crucifixion, John, the beloved disciple, asked that he might tarry on the earth until the Second Coming of Christ, a wish that was granted (3 Nephi, 28). According to the Book of Mormon, Christ appeared among the Nephites in America right after His crucifixion and preached essentially the same message found in the Four Gospels of the New Testament. The account relates that Jesus called Twelve to lead His organization in the New World, and that three of the Twelve made a request similar to John's, which was similarly granted. Mormon folklore abounds in stories of the appearance of the Three Nephites among the faithful. Always doing good wherever they go, they are invariably described as old men with long white hair and beards, scrupulously clean and shining in their always simple clothing. Just why the folks at Washington should think the Nephites might have such big feet remains a mystery; but the tracks were there, and they *had* to be ascribed to *something*. The Three Nephites seemed to do for the moment, as did the Gadianton Robbers, a band of outlaws whose sinister and spectacular career is described in the Book of Mormon. Organized by Gadianton about fifty years before the birth of Christ, they flourished until the final destruction of the Nephites at Cumorah (in New York State) in 385 A.D. So powerful did this band of cutthroats become that at times they corrupted and even controlled the Nephite state (Helaman, 2).

In the thinking of these simple folk of Washington, some of these Gadiantons survived, and they too occasionally appear in local folk tales. About fifteen years ago I heard an old gentleman, originally from Pine Valley (about thirty-five miles north of Washington) tell such a story in a Sunday School class in St. George. A sawmill had been established in one of the canyons adjacent to Pine Valley. This particular mill—there were several operating in the area—was dogged by an endless chain of bad luck. The ditch (millrace) kept breaking for no reason at all; tools disappeared; in the morning they would find teeth broken out of the saw which had apparently been all right the evening before; odds and ends of harness vanished, and all manner of petty annoyances got the brethren so discouraged that they finally took the problem to President Brigham Young, who happened to be in Dixie on one of his periodic visits to the southern settlements. When Brigham visited the mill site, so the story goes, he soon resolved their difficulty. He told them that the place had been the burying ground of a band of the Gadianton Robbers, and that their troubles would disappear if they moved the mill to another location. They followed his counsel, and thereafter everything was all right.

Town gossip did not deter the practical joker; young Ithamar continued his pranks, and each day victims of his hoax grew more frightened. He went to the cemetery and made tracks there. He went to the two streets by Bishop Robert D. Covington's home where a dance was in progress on the upper floor of the big rock house. The sounds of the accordian and the fiddle drew him irresistibly. He made his tracks in the dust of the well-traveled dirt streets and then departed, still on the huge shoes, to the spot where he kept them hidden in the stone quarry north of the cemetery and almost directly east of Bishop Covington's home. Once among the rocks he removed the shoes and took them a few yards among the stones where he hid them in a convenient crevice. Then he went home.

Next morning the excited inhabitants found the tracks mingled with their own in the street fronting the bishop's residence. They followed them to the hill on the east and then lost the trail among the rocks, much to the relief of Ithamar, who was obligingly helping to track down the mystery.

He thought up other ways to convince the people of the reality of the gigantic presence. Across the creek south of town, on what people called the Sand Plot, was a luxuriant growth of sage. With infinite patience he made a huge bed of this soft shrubbery and pressed it down in the proper places to make it appear that some mammoth man-like creature had slept there.

In desperation the overwrought community began to attribute every little thing that went wrong to this strange creature. The hens were frightened and would not lay; the milk soured too soon, and the butter would not "come"; one good lady had a miscarriage out of pure fright! The city fathers, in the face of this dire calamity, organized a posse which went out at night—the new tracks were always discovered early in the morning—to track down this monster. Ithamar, now dizzy with the success of his project and sensing a fresh opportunity to display his genius, followed close after, making new tracks, and next morning there was the terrifying discovery that the giant had probably been right there with the posse during its search! Now invisibility was added to the giant's other frightening attributes.

Truly, young Sprague was having the time of his life. But one thing was lacking—there was no one to share his triumph, none to applaud his genius. There are different versions of how the hoax was finally exposed. One account says that Ithamar confided in his frightened wife who, while her crying babies clung to her skirts, begged him tearfully not to join the search. The wife, who had a frightened neighbor friend, whispered the secret to her; she too had a friend, and within a few minutes the story was known all over town. But I have talked with a number of old residents, my father among them, who was a boy of ten or twelve at the time, and they said that Ithamar was not married at the time of the hoax and was in fact just a big, overgrown boy. Most informers said that Ithamar was no longer able to keep his secret to himself and so let the cat out of the bag. Anyway, the story got out, and Ithamar had his brief moment of glory, and then, some say, he had to face the wrath of certain citizens who were determined to discipline him. But it is said that he ducked out of town for a while, probably finding refuge with relatives or friends in one of the nearby settlements. Within a short time people forgot how ridiculous he had made them look, and when things had simmered down a bit, he returned to Washington. Many people adopted the "I told you so" attitude. Of course, those who had been most terrified said they knew all the time that it was only someone trying to frighten them. Such are the vagaries of human nature.*

---

*Another account of this story is given in Austin and Alta Fife, *Saints of Sage and Saddle* (Bloomington, Indiana, 1958), pp. 272-73.

Andrew Karl Larson

Reminscences of a Mormon Village in Transition

I was born in the last month of the nineteenth century in the little town of Washington, Utah, and grew up in that village, where as a boy and young man I witnessed the transition that changed my birthplace from a sleepy frontier Mormon community to a spot on one of the busiest thoroughfares of the West—U.S. Highway 91. But heavy traffic through this hamlet never changed its size. It remained in many ways what it had always been, though many customs and happenings of more than a half-century ago are now but memories of an age long gone. The old grist mill was performing its last decade of service, and the old cotton factory, like a worn-out ghost, gave its last feeble gasps and expired.

Life was different then. Practically everything we bought from the old co-op store was acquired through the barter of the eggs our hens laid. From the gingham, calico, shirting, and cotton flannel received in the exchange, Mother made most of the clothing for the family on the old Domestic sewing machine. Following the custom of many of his neighbors, my father each fall loaded his double-bed Peter Schuttler wagon with produce: grapes, onions, dried fruit, molasses, etc., and took it north to Parowan in Iron County, where he exchanged his load for potatoes, cheese, flour, lumber shingles, or anything else he could use to feed, clothe, and shelter his family of nine children. The trip took from a week to ten days, depending on the condition of the roads (by today's standards impossible) and how soon he could dispose of his load.

Household furniture and other furnishings were simple. The kitchen floor was of plain wide lumber, kept clean by much scrubbing. The other floors were covered with rag carpets woven in the village. Worn-out clothing was torn into narrow strips, sewn together and wound into balls by willing neighbors at a "rag bee." My mother wove her own carpets and rugs on a loom my father bought for $5.00 from the old cotton factory when its demise was decreed by the hard logic of economic events. We slept on homemade mattresses of heavy striped cotton ticking filled with clean straw or corn husks. We walked on rag carpets padded with straw. Every spring the carpets were taken up and the ground-up straw under them gathered and burned. New straw, well sifted of its chaff, was put down and the carpets, well beaten to get out the dust, were stretched over the straw and tacked to the floor once more. The mattresses, or rather straw ticks, were refilled each year with clean golden-white stuffing.

Food was simple but ample. Most of it we produced ourselves. We raised our own vegetables, except potatoes for winter. We had an abundance of string beans, carrots, peas, beets, radishes, tomatoes, squash, and new potatoes. We bottled peaches, apricots, and tomatoes. Mother made preserves from peaches and other fruit, my father traded a ton of hay for a five-gallon can of honey from George Hall who kept bees, and when everything else was gone in the category of sweets, there was always molasses; it never failed! We produced our own meat—fowl, pork and beef—and the cows gave us milk, cream, and butter. In the spring, when the hay was gone, I had to herd the cows in the nearby hills. The plants of the wild desert often made the milk and butter unpleasant and bitter to the taste; but it served.

Every morning my younger brother and I were routed out of bed to carry the "dip-water" for the day's culinary needs. We lived in the lower part of town, and by the time the ditch water reached us it had a strong taste of horse and cow dung, particularly if the day preceding had been windy, which often enough it was. We had to carry the water from across the street where there was a water spout and a footbridge. We slung a five-gallon bucket on a broomstick and carried the bucket between us, and in our free hands smaller buckets full of water. It did not take long to fill the fifty-gallon oak drinking barrel. On wash-day we of course had to fill up all the tubs and the heavy brass kettle used to heat the wash water.

The only way to get a drink of water at school was from the ditch if the water happened to be going by, which it usually was in wintertime. But kind old Brother Neils Nisson, who lived kitty-cornered across the street from the old meeting house where we went to school, used to keep a water barrel filled just inside his gate, and when the water was not in the ditch we used to troop over there just before the recess bell rang and have a drink from a cup which he kept chained to the barrel. When the water was in the ditch, we flopped on our bellies and took a copious swig of ditchwater, well flavored in wintertime with decaying leaves. We thought nothing of it—germs were not so well known then. Occasionally there was a water bucket and cup in the window of the school-room. This really was not much of an improvement—more convenient, per-haps, but the water came from the same ditch.

At school there seemed little attempt at organized play. The girls played hopscotch, jacks, "King William," and "Farmer in the Dell," and in these games the boys sometimes joined. The boys' old standby was base rounders. We made our own ball by raveling out old worn-out home knitted socks and stockings. Wool was better than cotton because it was more resilient and elastic; cotton became very soggy when wet, with no "bounce." We also made our own bats, usually from straight young cottonwood limbs. On rainy days the favorite games were "pomp-pomp-pullaway," and "dare base." In the spring we sat on the green ditch banks and played mumble peg.

The water barrel played its part in the celebrations on the Fourth and Twenty-fourth of July. Usually the barrel was brought into the rear of the meeting house and filled from the ditch across the street. Then into the water were poured the ingredients of homemade lemonade—tartaric acid, lemon ex-tract, and sugar. This mixture was stirred up by continuously dipping a bucket of water from the barrel and pouring it back until the sugar dissolved. But I remember that when I helped once to make the lemonade—I was about six-teen—one of the boys borrowed Willard Nisson's irrigating shovel and stirred it with that. The lemonade, cooled by a chunk of ice, was passed to everybody during the program until none was left. Usually about a half-dozen boys using a pitcher and glass passed the lemonade. Again the germ concept had little sup-port. It was a proud day when I grew old enough to pass the lemonade; the passer could pour himself all he could drink, and did so unfailingly.

The arrival of the mail and its distribution was an event of considerable social as well as practical importance. The post office was located in the post-master's house in a room which had an outside door and window. There would usually be a good-sized crowd assembled outside the window with its sliding panel. After the postmaster had finished sorting, he opened the window and began calling out the names of those who had mail. When one heard his name called, he answered "Here!" in a loud voice, and the postmaster then passed out the letter to the crowd where it went from hand to hand until it reached its addressee. Often one took his neighbor's mail when no member of the family was there to receive it. Newspapers were distributed in the same manner—there were no carriers, and a daily paper was unknown. There was the inevitable complaint if an expected letter did not arrive, and the harassed postmaster, who somehow was held to blame by those who received no mail, would petulantly retort that he was being held responsible for letters that never had been written! If it seemed a bit long before the postmaster got the mail sorted, some wag was always ready with the crack that "they're taking a lot of time to read the post cards today!"

During this waiting time the farmers talked about their crops, housewives about the kids' illnesses and the proper remedies for them, and the little children chased each other in and out among the crowd in an improvised game of hide-and-seek. Choice bits of gossip were exchanged. Men who engaged in occasional freighting of wool at sheepshearing time or bringing in stock for the local store from Milford (later from Modena and Lund), sat around regaling each other with impossible tales of the loads their teams were able to pull up Cottonwood Hill without doubling. Or, if there was a lull in the conversation, it gave J—— H—— a chance to tell one of his stories in which he always played the principal role.

The excitement engendered by the possibility of a railroad coming to Dixie gave J—— his opportunity. The crowd in front of the general store and post office was indulging in wonderful daydreams of how life would be when the Iron Horse arrived. Two or three in the crowd claimed to have worked at railroad construction in the outside world, and the group was properly impressed by the air of authority with which they detailed the advantages which the railroad would bring. Then came a lull in the conversation, and J——jumped into the breach. "I was an engineer on a railroad once when I worked in Nevada and Californy," he said with a fine air of nonchalance. The crowd, sensing one of his tall yarns in the offing, gave him their attention, tribute for his recognized genius. "Yes, sir," he went on with a reminiscent note, "I made some long runs with that old locomotive of mine. In fact, they claimed that I made the longest run in railroad history. I took that train fifteen hundred miles without a single stop!" Dead silence greeted this tale of herculean effort, until someone exclaimed, "Oh, hell, J——, why that's half way across the continent! You couldn't a' gone half that far 'thout stopping for coal an' water!" For a second it looked as if J—— had been trapped by his own cleverness. But his wit was equal to the challenge. Quick as a flash he retorted, "Oh, you bet your life I did! It was all downhill!"

There were other times when storytelling was welcomed. On one of those rainy days in wintertime, when it was impossible to do outside work, a crowd of men and boys, myself among them, had gathered around the potbellied stove in the main room of the store. I was about fourteen or fifteen at that time and was just beginning to go to the dances. The conversation centered about an episode involving two or three young fellows from St. George who had been put off the dance floor on the previous evening for "ragging." J—— came in just as the details of the story were unfolded. Raggin, as it was called, was quite a daring feat in those days of the waltz, two-step, schottische, and quadrille. It involved considerable body contact and much shoulder and hip movement, and only the most daring spirits risked the disapproval of the dance manager by indulging in its risqué wigglings. J—— was by now in middle age, and this was probably the first time he had even heard the term "raggin." But his eyes lighted up, and he took opportunity by the forelock. "When I was a young feller," he began, "there was trouble about this raggin." The spectators leaned forward attentively. "A bunch of us young bloods went over to The Clary (Santa Clara) to a dance. All of us was having a real gay time, when the bishop got up and said, 'I been told that some of this raggin is going on. Now, I don't know what raggin is like, but if any of it is going on, it's got to stop!' Now, I was dancing with a real pretty girl who was a swell dancer, and I says to her, 'Let's rag!' She was game and away we went at it, with all the other dancers following suit. We ragged the whole evening and the bishop didn't even know it!"

On another occasion there was conversation concerning the new dentures that one of the villagers had recently acquired. J—— was quick to see an opportunity for one of his stories. "Once a few years ago I worked as a traveling salesman," he announced. "I traveled all over the country, selling things from here to Mexico City. Well, I was down there in Mexico when I decided it was time to go home to see Mother, who was getting old. I thought it would be nice to take something from Mexico to her for a present, but I couldn't find anything that suited me. Finally I stopped before a dentist's shop, and there in the window was just the thing for Mother. It was a set of false teeth, uppers and lowers. Mother had lost all her teeth, and it was hard for her to eat. I went into the shop to bargain for the teeth and succeeded finally in trading some of my stock for them so that I did not have to pay any money. When I got home, I slipped up behind Mother without her seeing me, put my hands over her eyes and said, 'Mother, open your mouth and shut your eyes, and I'll give you something to make you wise.' " J—— paused here to note the effect of his tale on his appreciative audience. Then he resumed. "I was just a bit worried for fear the teeth might not fit very well. But she shut her eyes and opened her mouth as I told her to, and I plopped in the teeth, just like that. And what do you know? It was a perfect fit!''

The post office had been moved to the co-op store in 1913. Its location on Highway 91 made it more central, and the crowds grew at mail time, especially with the passing of the parcel post law. When the mail arrived from the north late in the afternoon or early in the evening, the whole town literally presented itself at its distribution. Carried in a light buggy or "buckboard" and drawn by a nervous team of small "buggy horses," the mail came dashing up at a rapid pace and came to a stop with a grand flourish. Mail sacks were quickly exchanged, and with a crack of his whip the driver was once again on his way, his horses rearing and plunging until he gave them the reins as off they went in a cloud of dust. The crowd loved this bit of "grandstanding."

I remember the weddings and the funerals. Weddings offered entertainment for old and young. In many cases, at least, the whole town was invited to what amounted to a great community feast. For days, it seemed, the bride's household was converted into a pastry bakery in preparation for the great event. When one went to a wedding he expected to be fed, and rarely was he disappointed. At an earlier day than my own childhood, "Dixie wine" was served to all who wanted it, but as time went on the evils of this potent, locally-manufactured beverage led to its falling under the ban of the Church. At about the turn of the century the groom was expected to give a dance and a keg of wine to his cronies. One of the songs still sung during my boyhood concerned the marriage of Charles Knell. Knell got married, but failed to follow the town custom of giving a free dance. In retaliation the boys gave him a shivaree at the home of his in-laws, where he was temporarily housed. R. J. (Rube) Jolley and his associates composed the following song to commemorate the occasion. It was set to the music for "Whoa, Mule, Whoa!"

CHARLEY KNELL'S WEDDING

'Twas in the month of April when our youngest widow wed,
And it was almost eight o'clock before they went to bed,
The boys, they thought they'd shivaree and that they'd have some fun,
And so they got their cans and bells, and this is what they sung:

> Chorus
> "Oh, Knell, Oh! Don't you hear us holler!
> If you will get the dancing hall, we will get the caller.
> Why don't you say you'll give us a dance, and then we'll all go home."
> But all in the world the poor man said was, "No, boys, no!"

We went upon the doorstep then and played our music sweet;
Nellie came out into the door, all in his stocking feet.
He said, "Now, boys, I'm much obliged, I tell you that was fine!"
And then the boys, they all yelled out, "Why don't you get the wine?"

　　Repeat chorus

The old lady gave it up right there, and she went back to bed,
And Frankie Barron, he slept so sound, they thought that he was dead.
Huldy, she of course was mad, and this is what she said,
"I wish them bells were all in hell and all the boys were dead!"

　　Repeat chorus

Rube and his cronies composed a number of songs having to do with weddings and other subjects. One of them not only told of a wedding, but lampooned the city officials as well. Mac Nor and Old Lady Larson, mentioned in the last verse, had been selling wine in violation of a town ordinance. Arthur A. Paxman was justice of the peace, a fearless and talented young officer with little sympathy for those who sold wine to young men; hence the reference to the forty-dollar fine and the wish to consign Paxman to the nether regions. The song went as follows, to the same tune as "Charlie Knell's Wedding":

JULIUS HANNIG'S WEDDING

Now white folks, your attention, and I'll sing to you a song
About Julius Hannig's wedding, and it won't detain you long.
He's been a-getting married now for six or seven years,
But he couldn't get the girl's consent till April did appear.

Now when he got the girl's consent, why he began to prance;
He went and got a keg of wine, but he wouldn't give a dance.
The boys, they thought it pretty good, and Julius thought it fine,
So they all went up to Boggs's, and you bet they had a time!

Now where they got that keg of wine, this is just what played hell,
They fixed it so the boys, they could neither drink nor smell.
They fined Old Mac so very high, they thought they'd done him well,
And all the boys in Washington wished Paxman was in hell!

Ed Van Orden is the Mayor, and of course you all know that
He always prowls around the town, just like an old stray cat.
I think he'd better stay at home, or else down to the store,
For there he has plenty o' clothes, and don't need any more.

Randolph Andrus is the Marshal, and he's got a brand new hat,
He wears a white silk handkerchief, likewise a new cravat;
He has a pair of brand new pants to ornament his frame;
You bet he'll trig himself right up, if he gets back again.

If you want a drink of wine, boys, you mustn't go to Mac
Nor to Old Lady Larson, for they'll say to you, "Go back!
Forty dollars is too much to pay for every little fine
For selling, boys, on wedding days, a little keg of wine!"

The funerals of my childhood made a deep impression on me. There was no mortuary. The dead were laid out by local people who had practical experience in these things. The funerals had to be held no later than the day following death because of the speed of putrefaction. People "sat up" with the dead, constantly wringing out wet cloths to put over the face and keep it from discoloring. As I recall, they used a formaldehyde solution for the face. The casket was made of native pine lumber by local carpenters and then covered and lined by the Relief Society sisters. The body was transported to the cemetery (always called the graveyard) in a white-topped Studebaker buggy, with two men squatting on their haunches on either side holding a quilt or other covering over the casket to keep off the dust. The casket was lowered into the grave by means of ropes passed under it and held by two men on each side. Then the box was closed and the dirt carefully placed in the grave by men with irrigating shovels. They tried not to let the clods fall on the box in a way that would disturb the mourners, but occasionally a loud thud brought forth a hysterical cry from an overwrought loved one. The men worked fast in relays after the box was covered until the grave was finished and all mounded up. Then the flowers were laid on—not the hothouse varieties of today, but the flowers from our own gardens, or perchance lovely sego lilies from the hills if they were in season. During all this ceremony no one left the graveside. When everything was completed, the people began to drift to the graves of their own loved ones to relive the tender memories of dear ones gone to rest.

Perhaps the thing about funerals that remains most vividly with me was the tolling of the bell. As the time for the funeral drew near, the old man who rang the bell let its mellow tones fade away completely before again pulling the rope. As little boys we used to whisper among ourselves that the bell tolled one stroke for each year of the deceased's age. I don't know how true this was; it may have been so for old people but certainly not for babies and young folks. The bell kept up its melancholy message right to the time the funeral began.

In regard to amusement and recreation, there were, of course, the usual things which one would find in an isolated village of four or five hundred people. The events I remember most were those at Christmas holiday time. It seemed that almost everyone tried to get home for the holidays. There were those fortunate young people, most of them males, who had been away to high school either at the Branch Normal School at Cedar City or the Murdock Academy at Beaver. Men who worked at the mines—Pioche, Nevada, the Grand Gulch in northern Arizona, and the Apex Mine fifteen or twenty miles west of Washington—always tried to spend a few days at home. There was a dance every night except Sunday, and numerous daytime activities, most of them spontaneous.

Washington's main street ran north and south, intersecting what became U.S. Highway 91 at the point where the schoolhouse now stands. During Christmas holidays it was converted into a race track for boys, men, and horses. Nothing much happened until the sun warmed things up on the short winter days. People out late the night before slept late and ate their breakfast around ten or eleven o'clock, then went to Main Street to see what was at hand to make things lively. Usually the footraces came first. Someone would say, "I've got four bits says Rass Cooper can outrun Roy Pectol in a hundred yards." Like as not Roy would say, "Make it seventy-five yards and I'll run him." And then he would hand a quarter to a friend, saying, "Bet this on me. I think I can outrun Rass." So the bets were on, the men pulled off their shoes and socks, judges and starters were posted, and the runners were off to the cheers of the crowd. Afterward others were matched and the mild betting continued. No one had much money to wager, but the betting of a fifty-cent piece could create the excitement of gambling added to the natural excitement of the race itself. A few of the men who had been away to school were pretty fleet of foot. The Cooper brothers, James and Sherman, could run with almost anybody. Sherman was the fastest man in town. I remember when he was matched with Hy Thompson of St. George in a race that brought a great crowd of people from that town to Washington to see their favorite take Sherm to the cleaners. There was considerable St. George money went begging that day, not because people weren't sold on Sherm's prowess as a footracer, but because they had little money to bet. The outcome gave our town a great deal to boast about, for it wasn't often that Washington could crow over its larger and more sophisticated rival. But the St. Georgers returned home that afternoon, if not wiser, at least sadder men; Sherm beat his rival by a good ten yards. The contestants in this race wore running trunks and spikes, something I had never seen before. My dad thought such thinclads scandalous!

During the intervals between races the kids played around at marbles. The older youngsters had going a little gambling game of their own, pitching pennies. It took little equipment. You simply stuck a pocket knife upright in the ground and then pitched pennies at it. The one closest to the knife got the first chance to "shake-'em up." He could take all pennies that fell heads up; then the second closest got his turn to shake, then the third, etc. Those like me who had no pennies had to be content with playing "walnut keeps." We used small black walnuts for marbles. The game was none the less fascinating even with walnuts. Of course we had marbles for taws.

But the horse races were the best entertainment of all. The horses were not really race horses but saddle horses, kids' ponies, and even an occasional nimble workhorse which usually doubled for his owner as both saddle horse and work plug. The stakes were not high—a quarter, a fifty-cent piece, a dollar. But when some of the better saddle ponies were matched, the stakes went as high as five dollars; and in one grudge race, a rerun brought about by charges of unfair play in the first contest, the stake was twenty dollars! The whole town was worked up to a high pitch of intense excitement and partisanship.

The fanning of quick tempers wrought by these races was frequent enough, generating an occasional fight stimulated, usually, by liberal helpings of Dixie wine. All sorts of people rode in these races, young, middle-aged, and some fairly old. Of the many such races I witnessed, none remains so vividly with me as the one in which Old Brother C—— tried the role of jockey. The race ended in near tragedy, although in retrospect it remains hilarious comedy.

Now Brother C—— was a Southerner. He always said "cain't" for can't and "daince" for dance, and for that matter he put the southern twist in all his words. He was jolly and good-natured, and it took a lot to upset his naturally blithe spirit. Among his other accomplishments was pulling teeth. He was not a professional dentist by any measurement, but he owned some wicked forceps which he used to banish toothache. Practice had given him a modicum of skill in the use of this formidable weapon, but like many others of his kind in isolated communities like Washington, his only qualification for the job was a certain confidence in his ability and faith in his strong right arm.

In late middle age Brother C—— had finally departed from Washington to live in what he felt was a greener pasture elsewhere. But occasionally he made his way back to visit his cronies and to be with a married daughter who still lived in the town. He always came to Sacrament Meeting and bore a strong testimony of the truthfulness of the gospel. And he never missed a dance. Age had not withered nor had custom made stale his love of dancing. Never, I think, have I ever seen anyone who loved to "daince" more than he. Lively as a cricket, he stepped nimbly about in the polka, the schottische, the Danish slide-off, the two-step, and the quadrille. He was a marvel of grace and energy who never showed any signs of "running down."

Brother C—— liked Dixie wine too, and it flowed rather freely during the holidays. Well, on this particular occasion he was pretty well tuned-up with Dixie wine, and in this condition he attempted the role of jockey for a horse raised by Lafayette Jolley but now owned by someone else. Brother C—— was not drunk—just felt as if he could conquer the world. He must have been approaching seventy at this time. The course could accommodate any race from a quarter-mile to a mile. This race started one block below Highway 91 and terminated just above Lafe Jolley's house, a distance of about three-eighths of a mile. Both horses were a little too heavy for the saddle and a little too light for draft work. But they were both surprisingly nimble. Brother C—— had taken a notion to the Jolley plug, said he knew good horseflesh when he saw it, and was ready to place a bet on him as well as riding the animal himself.

A few friends tried to dissuade him, but he waved them off; so one of them helped him to mount and he rode off down the street to the takeoff spot, smartly tapping the horse's flanks with a mulberry switch and holding him in just enough to make him restive and impatient.

The two horses came pounding up the street, making a real race of it. Brother C——'s mount seemed to catch the spirit of the occasion, and, with ears laid back, he forged slowly ahead, urged on by his rider's excited exhortations and switchings. The old gentleman was a sight to behold. His necktie stood straight out over one shoulder, his coattails flew in the breeze generated by the rather creditable speed of his awkward mount. Both Brother C—— and his horse sensed the heady excitement of victory as they galloped on two good lengths ahead. And then fate threw both jockey and horse for a loss.

Back in the Jolley lot about forty yards stood the hay barn and horse corral. The Jolley horses, hearing the pounding of hoofs, ran to the corral fence where they saw their old friend racing up the street. Recognizing him, they set up a great whinnying which could be heard all over town. Brother C——'s horse heard it too, and forgetting everything but the joy of happy reunion, sent forth a loud nicker in answer to his brothers' greeting. As luck would have it, the Jolley gate was open and the horse, like a homing pigeon, jumped the ditch and dashed through the gate over to the corral where he received a most heartwarming welcome. The prodigal had returned.

And Brother C——? He lay sprawled on the sidewalk moaning in pain. Right by the Jolley gate there grew a huge cottonwood tree, probably as old as the town itself. It had great gnarled roots, some of which, half buried and half surfaced, crossed the sidewalk. When the horse saw the open gate and abruptly changed his course toward the Jolley barnyard, the gallant rider lost his balance, flew feet-first (fortunately) at the base of the big tree, his foot striking with great force upon an exposed root. His ankle was badly wrenched in this unfortunate mishap, and as he writhed in pain his despairing cries were added to the neighing of the horses and the uproarious guffaws of the large crowd which enjoyed this tragi-comedy far more than the horse race itself. "Oh, now I cain't daince! Now I cain't daince!" he moaned distractedly. Cronies commiserated with him, but he refused to be comforted. Friends got him home and summoned a physician from St. George to treat his wounds.

Next day he was back with the crowd, hobbling about on crutches, holding his well-bandaged ankle off the ground by crooking his knee. He had partially regained a semblance of his naturally ebullient spirits, but there was something missing. He could still mingle with his friends, bet sparingly on the races even if he could not ride, and there was still Dixie wine to console him. But life had suddenly become pretty drab, almost cruel. "Oh, now I cain't daince, I cain't daince!" he kept repeating after every sympathetic acquaintance's greeting. If he had made comedy for others, to himself he had brought only sorrowful limitations.

Mary Alice Collins

Midway, a Town Still Sleeping

I remember that even as a child I was impressed by the peacefulness and quiet charm that always prevailed in Midway, near Heber in Wasatch County. Once each summer we joined our Salt Lake cousins to spend a day at the Hot Pots, a resort in this sleepy village. We splashed and swam in the naturally warmed water of the pools and as we later devoured our picnic lunch, Mother and Aunt Marge reminisced about the days they had spent at the Cannon Summer Ranch in this community.

Midway's history seems to be one of peacefulness and beauty; the people telling stories of the past remember no particular violence. And so Midway has dozed and nodded from earliest times right up to the present day, apparently escaping the bustle that is constant along the highway. In doing so it has held fast to a charm I'll never forget.

Midway was settled about 1853 in compliance with Brigham Young's request that pioneers begin settlement of the valley. Additional settlers followed in the next few years. Most of them became situated in either the Upper Settlement, which was later called Mound City because of the numerous limestone formations in the region, or the Lower Settlement. Though these settlements continued to grow, they were too small for the organization of a ward and so a Presiding Elder of the Church was supplied them. After he was sustained by Church members he exercised political, judicial, military and religious authority. The settlements grew independently until Indian trouble threatened in 1866. Church leaders decided that the families who were settled all along the creek were too vulnerable to Indian raids and so advised them to abandon their homes and join in building a fort. The location of the fort caused much controversy because the people of both settlements wished to remain in their homes. However, they finally compromised and built a fort midway between the two; thus the town of Midway got its name. Even though Indians never attacked the fort, the pioneers of Midway deserve a great tribute for their ability to cooperate in overcoming their common difficulties.[1]

Cooperation was the pattern in daily living as well as in seeking protection from the Indians.

Fireplaces played a great part in pioneer lives in Fort Midway. Since matches were unavailable, the evening fire was covered to retain a few live coals for morning. Borrowing fire became a ritual, and the first rising smoke always attracted someone with a fire shovel.[2]

Though Indians never caused any severe disturbance, the Midway pioneers were always ready to heed Brigham Young's advice to treat them with kindness. When the fears of the settlers were aroused

> Chief Tabby of the Utes was invited to come to make peace. He accepted. A month later he came riding across the ridge with all the Indians under his rule—bucks, squaws, and papooses. It was a gala day of momentous hilarity and rejoicing. Women bustled about preparing a feast. Each woman in the valley was asked to bake one dozen loaves of bread. The item on the menu that really gladdened the heart of the Indian was beef. They ate in high good humor and did impressive justice to the viands. What was not consumed was tucked into sacks and baskets by the squaws. After the meal the redskins and whites smoked the peace pipe. Chiefs Tabby, Towintey and Moroni responded in the Ute tongue, saying they were all good Indians and were willing to lay by the weapons of war.[3]

The peaceful spirit of the pioneers apparently was contagious and the Indian trouble subsided. Settlers then began venturing from the fort and building other dwellings and developing their own farms. William Wilson, like others, became very much attached to his homestead at the lower part of Snake Creek. One day while he was plowing his field, he said to his wife, "When I go, I want you to see that I'm buried where I git a view of this beautiful valley, where I can sit all day and look." Later it took a yoke of oxen two days to clear ground for the grave which was situated on a mound overlooking his farm. In accordance with his request he was buried sitting upright in a huge casket. Residents looking at that mound today entertain the thought that William Wilson is still sitting enjoying the view of his beloved valley and farm.[4]

The nearest thing to violence came when squatters' rights gave way to the Homestead Act. Surveyors were unschooled and unskilled and discrepancies in boundary locations caused some heated arguments. In one particular case several yards separating two farms were in dispute. Mr. Winch thought the land rightfully his, but his neighbor disagreed. He said he was going to drive his new yoke of oxen into Salt Lake City to file his rights under the Homestead Act. Since poor Mr. Winch had no oxen, he thought he would surely lose the ground. One morning very early as he watched his neighbor preparing his oxen for the journey, Winch decided he would try to reach Salt Lake first. He began walking. He trudged over the mountains, then hiked down Cottonwood Canyon to the land office where he filed his claim. He had been in town two days before his neighbor with the new oxen even entered the city.[5]

Several men from Midway were called to serve missions for their church. The "calls" came abruptly and always left a young family temporarily fatherless and often in dire need. Still the call from their leaders was always obeyed. Reed Kohler remembers his father's mission call. He left behind a wife, a son two years old, another baby on the way, and aged parents-in-law. This young mother was all alone at the deaths of her parents, which meant that she had to lay out the body on the board, wash it, and clothe it for burial. This had to be done before the body cooled and became stiff. She placed coins on the eyelids and called for Mr. Blood to make a pine-box coffin. Her brother-in-law was finally hired to run the farm, which under his care supported the wife and children, the husband on a mission, and produced enough to pay off the mortgage on the farm.[6]

These hardy, uncomplaining pioneers survived the mission trials and were well repaid by conversions which resulted in several Swiss families coming to America and settling in Midway, which reminded them geographically of their native country. Among these converts was a family named Abplanalp. Guy Coleman, who has lived his lifetime in Midway and now runs the community grocery, married one of the Abplanalp girls. Her family name has an interesting origin. The small village of Briends, Switzerland, was completely wiped away by an avalanche. When searchers went to the former site they could find nothing, not a building of any kind and not a human alive. Then someone uncovered a small cradle holding a baby. The baby lived, and not knowing to whom it belonged, the foster parents named it Abplanalp, meaning baby from the Alps. In tracing their genealogy, the descendants of this Alp baby can follow family lines back to the cradle and the avalanche, but there further clues are buried forever.[7]

Even as these early pioneers followed Brigham Young's counsel in directing the settlement of Midway, so they continued to follow Church direction as the years went by. The major part of each day was involved one way or another with the Church and its activities.

In 1873 a Pot Rock tithing office was built across from the meeting house. Bins were built in the huge cellar to hold produce; these they often over-filled until the produce spoiled. Then the deacons were called to clean the cellar out. These perishables were often a total loss because the items couldn't be transported and couldn't be exchanged for money. Yet it is claimed the Saints never failed to bring one tenth of all they owned to the tithing office. Mr. Kohler remembers always setting the tenth pile of hay aside and then at the end of the day taking these piles to the tithing office. Likewise, when ten pounds of butter were churned, one went immediately to the bishop, with one egg of ten set aside in a special dish.

The tithing office was also used for the socials which have always been an important part of Mormon living. Mr. Epperson says these occasions were "The real Johnny McCoy, the joy of our lives."

> The upper part of the tithing office had a stage used for shows, home concerts and other amusements. The main floor was used for an assembly hall and dancing. Here the happy pioneers tripped the light fantastic toe. The old time quadrille was their favorite, with George Wardle calling off and others playing Buffalo Gals or Hell in Snake Creek. You should have seen the dancers sasha and swing on the corners. They sure knew how to do it. Everyone came in for their share of the good old waltz.[8]
>
> Dancing was very popular. An orchestra usually consisted of a fiddler and another stringed instrument. Sometimes a dulcimer. The whole family came. The children would eat then be put to bed in one end of the hall. Popular dances included the mazurka, schottische, polka, and the Brigham Young dance, designed so that a man might dance with two partners.[9]

Sunday meetings were announced by ringing bells. A colorful person in the valley was Jesse Bond, an early pioneer, who was the bell toller for all Sunday meetings and special occasions. He was a professional bell toller from England and knew how to toll for each occasion. He could even toll the bells mournfully for funerals.[10]

Sunday morning, when these bells announced Sunday School, the faithful Midway residents all attended.

> Sunday School began at 10:00 a.m. The meeting was devoted to religious instruction in classes arranged according to age groups. Children were rewarded for attendance with Sunday School tickets printed with Biblical quotations. After a number of tickets had been collected they could be turned in for a "chromo," a highly prized picture of one of the characters from the Bible.[11]

Pioneers in Midway were never wealthy, and when news came that rich ore had been found over the mountain in Park City there was a great stir in the community, but again the Saints listened to Brigham Young who cautioned them to leave the mining to the Gentiles and spend their time tilling the soil.

There is a story told that Porter Rockwell brought news to Brigham that he had seen fabulous amounts of rich ore up Little Cottonwood Canyon and wanted to rush back to take these minerals from the earth before others did. Brigham told him that he wouldn't find this ore again, but that neither would the Gentiles get wealth from it. Porter didn't find it, but others did and sold it to England at a great profit. Ironically, after the sale the ore vein ran out immediately. Some people in Midway think that the tailings from these wealthy ore deposits caused a movement in the earth which pushed up the big mound in the middle of the town.[12]

The mining history of Midway is a story in itself. The men who drifted over the mountains from Park City provided much color in the lives of the Midway pioneers. One very intriguing character was an elderly Frenchman, Eugene Levignier. He was from Paris and very well educated. He had brilliance and wealth—enough money always reached his hands that he never knew poverty. He stayed at the mine in the summer and rented a home in Midway in the winter where friends took care of him. One night when his friends visited him, he asked them to help him shave and to open a trunk and take out a fine white shirt. After they had complied with his request and set a candle on the table, they left with his assurance that he would be all right. When a neighbor saw the candle still burning before daybreak, he went to the house; the door was unlocked and Mr. Levignier was in his fine shirt with his head in his arms at the table, dead. Men went through his belongings in the trunk and found letters that indicated he had a wife and child in France. Nobody knew why he had left France and his family. Henry Coleman wrote to Levignier's son in Paris and the son sent money for a beautiful monument which can be seen in the Midway cemetery today.

Mr. Axtel and Mr. Bowen were two younger men who prospered as miners in Snake Creek and Pine Canyon. They thought one day that they had struck it rich. To celebrate their good fortune they went to Park City where they both enjoyed beverages from the saloons. After many drinks they decided that only one of them should own the mine to avoid their having to divide the anticipated wealth. The bargain was made that the one returning to the mine first would become sole owner. In the race Mr. Axtel returned before Mr. Bowen, but to insure his claim he killed Bowen with a blow of an ax as he entered their cabin.

It appears that Mr. Axtel escaped and was never found. Residents of Midway decided that these men must have been from wealthy families because those sent to take care of the body found among their belongings jewelry, fine linens, gold cuff links, books, and other costly items.

Another ending to this story was related by Reed Kohler. According to his account, Axtel, after killing his partner, was full of dismay on the morrow and gave himself up in Park City. His subsequent fate is not clear for it is told many different ways. The mine they discovered failed—it was soon found to comprise only a small pocket of ore. [13]

The mining era passed without great incident to Midway, and the pioneers settled down to their own domestic problems. The *Wasatch Wave*, a newspaper still being printed in nearby Heber City, records these solutions for the trials of cattlemen:

> August 10, 1889—A short time ago a cow belonging to a Heber lady got too much lucerne and became bloated. A neighbor said he heard that gunpowder burned under the animal's nose was a sure cure. He accordingly got a plate of powder, tied the cow up by the head with a good strong rope, held the plate of gun powder under her nose and put a match to it. Result: a puff of smoke, a blaze somewhat resembling a flash of lightning, a broken rope and a man with burned hands, singed hair, beard and eyebrows, thrown about ten feet by reason of his coming suddenly in contact with a portion of the cow. The cow got better and it is undoubtedly an excellent remedy, but we suggest that the next time the operator get a piece of fuse about three feet long and watch developments from behind the barn.

> March 23, 1889—This remedy for animals afflicted with alfalfa bloat is a sure cure. Get an ounce of colocynth: drop six drops on a teaspoon of pulverized sugar, for horse or cow, place it well back on the tongue and if not relieved, repeat the dose in twenty minutes. With this remedy at hand there is no need of losing any stock from bloat.

The happy ways of these people are also revealed in this humorous report:

> October 12, 1889—Last Saturday evening a man on his way to Park City saw the hind wheels of a wagon, some quilts, etc., at the foot of a dugway and looking about he saw a man lying dead by the side of the road. He rushed to Park City to report what he had found. A coroner's jury was summoned and taking a bottle of whiskey and some cigars the jury and justice of peace repaired to the spot. They found the mangled body. From appearances, it seemed the team had run away throwing the man out and probably running over him. The jury concluded to take the body to Park City before making a thorough examination of the corpse. Two men took hold of the body to lift it into the wagon when the dead man opened his eyes and said, "Can't you let a feller sleep?" One of the jurors said, "Aren't you dead?" "Not by a d——n sight," was the reply. The justice and jurors didn't propose to be fooled in any such way as that though and took the man to Park City anyhow and placed him in the cooler till morning to sober up. He was tried Monday and found guilty of—well now we are unable to say what, but we

understand he was fined for something. They wanted the dead man to pay for the expenses of the inquest, but he demurred, saying it was bad enough for a man to pay for an inquest when he is dead, but he wasn't dead and the d——n fools ought to know he wasn't.

And now though the years pass on, Midway, Utah, remains just about the same. You can still hear the Swiss cowbells jangle as Mr. Gertsch herds his cows home for the night; you can still see horses, cattle, and sheep grazing in verdant meadows; you can still enjoy a leisurely swim at the Hot Pots resorts; you can still visit with happy, unruffled citizens, who add charm as their ancestors did to this sleepy, lovely community of Midway.

NOTES

1. Kate Carter, Daughters of the Utah Pioneers, *Under Wasatch Skies* (Salt Lake City: Deseret News Press, 1954), pp. 22-23.
2. Ibid., p. 33.
3. Simon S. Epperson, *Sidney H. Epperson, Pioneer* (Acorn Publishing Co., 1941), pp. 50-51.
4. Reed Kohler, interview. Mr. Kohler is a lifetime resident of Midway.
5. Ibid.
6. Ibid.
7. Guy Coleman, interview.
8. Epperson, *Sidney H. Epperson, Pioneer*, pp. 59-60.
9. Carter, *Under Wasatch Skies*, p. 86.
10. Ibid., p. 63.
11. Ibid., p. 62.
12. Kohler, interview.
13. Lethe Toleman Tatge, interview. Mrs. Tatge is a lifetime resident of the community.

Juanita Brooks

Pranks and Pranksters

Always, in every town, there are those who delight in the practical joke—the rose filled with cayenne pepper, the tulip connected with a squirt-bulb of water, the horned toad placed in the teacher's chalk box. Likewise nearly every town has its own time when pranks are expected and condoned—New Year's Eve, April Fool's Day, or Halloween.

In our town of Bunkerville, Nevada, it was "New Year's Eve, do as you please," the idea being on this, the last night of the year, the youngsters might have their last fling of devilment before they turned over their new leaf. We learned to expect outhouses to be tipped over, cattle turned out or put into other corrals, wagons dismembered and scattered. At one time the gate from the front of the bishop's home was found crowning the church steeple, placed there at some great expenditure of energy and with some engineering skill if one were to judge by what it took to get it down whole and back into its place in the fence.

There were spontaneous pranks as when one man was long inside the local wine-merchant's cellar and boys outside turned the saddle around on his horse. The owner, unsteady but happy, untied the horse and proceeded to mount.

"Hey, Ben, you're going the wrong direction," a boy called out.

"How do you know what direction I want to go?" Ben answered, and jogged along, face toward the horse's tail, while the faithful animal took him safely home.

At another time a group of boys had decided to have a chicken supper. One, knowing that his neighbor's chickens roosted out of doors in a pear tree, went there to secure one. He climbed the tree and caught his bird, but not without a lot of squawking and flapping. The owner, hearing the commotion, came out to investigate.

"Hey, get down out of that tree!" he ordered. "What are you doing up there?"

"Sh-h-h! Quiet!" came a loud stage-whisper. "We're playing run, sheep, run, and they'll find me."

"Oh, I beg your pardon," said the man. He returned to the house leaving the boy to pull off the chicken's head and so make his contribution to the party.

Another good man had a tree of early apricots, which in this land of little fruit was a sore temptation to young people. No one meant to take them all, but by the time enough had each taken a few apricots there were none left for the owner. So one year he issued a public ultimatum.

"Every year you boys have eaten my apricots," he said. "This year I plan to have a few myself. I warn you, I'm not going to put up with your foolishness. I'll fill your backsides with buckshot if you try to get my apricots this year."

So he moved his cot out under the tree and set himself to guard it. For a few nights nothing happened. Then, when the fruit was almost at its best, the boys waited until they could hear his regular, steady snores, and, slipping to the tree, they began to eat the fruit. They saved pits enough to fill both his shoes. Then while he still slept on, they picked up the cot, two at the head and two at the foot, and set it out on the sidewalk.

Many pranks grew out of our marriage customs, or perhaps the customs were shaped by the pranks. No one ever announced an engagement; no one ever set a definite date. This would be decided by time and circumstance. People would generally know when a young man had his eye on a special girl. She might accept some dates and favors and then finally "give him the sack," or he might be dropped by the girl for another special friend in which case he was said to be "cut out." But if they continued to "spark," it was assumed that they planned to be married, and in this case it was always quite necessary that the young man go away to the mines or the freight road to earn his wedding stake.

The term "pulling up stakes" derived from moving a tent, gradually changed to mean moving, and "putting down your stakes" meant establishing a new home. So a "wedding stake" was enough money to buy at least a bed and a stove as the first two essentials of a home. No one spent money for a ring, either an engagement ring or a wedding ring. A good piece of furniture seemed a better investment.

Most weddings were performed in the St. George Temple, which meant that a Bunkerville couple must take a two-day trip in a wagon. They usually left long before daylight in order to make a good day's drive the first day and arrive in St. George before the courthouse closed on the second. Otherwise they could not get a license in time to attend the Temple ceremony that day. To get a few miles on the road and have one of the wheels leave the wagon and go careening out through the brush would be a frustrating experience indeed, yet it occurred. Some prankster had taken the burr off the spindle in the hub, or had worked it loose so that it fell off. What to do? Try to hunt for so small an object over several miles in the dark? Unharness the team and ride one horse back to town to find another burr that would fit? Bring the team back, get another wagon, transfer all the load, and go on? Any course would mean a full day's delay unless the young man should know that according to the custom, the burr should be left in a prominent place where the wagon had been loaded, the idea being that no teamster should become so excited at the prospect of setting out to get married that he would neglect to check the wheels of his wagon before he left. Usually when he got back the burr would be quickly produced by friends, ready to joke at his discomfiture and yet drink to his successful trip from that point on. His only revenge would be to pay in kind when the tricksters planned to get married. Thus it was that the man who had lost his wheel might help to kidnap a later groom, carry him blindfolded into the country, take away his shoes, and leave him to pick his way back to his bride barefoot.

The newlyweds were supposed to bring back a keg of good wine to serve their friends at the wedding dance, or at a shivaree. Young men who did not drink were sometimes taken advantage of by those who did. For example, one was persuaded to drink a glass of Dixie wine and, finding it good, tried another. When finally his young bride came to look for him, no one knew where he was exactly, but one had seen him enter the back room of a neighboring house. Following this lead, the girl opened the door to see him asleep on a bed, a young squaw sitting beside him fanning him and brushing the flies away with a leafy branch—a situation carefully arranged for the bride's benefit.

There were times when situations had tragic rather than funny results. At one time a preacher came into Silver Reef hoping to teach religion there and to help some of the men live better lives. He was a serious, earnest young man who rented a hall and advertised a series of meetings to be held each night for a week. For some of the young men this was an opportunity to test him.

On the first night a fair crowd attended the service. The song and prayer and Scripture reading went on very well and the sermon was moving toward its climax when a donkey underneath an open window brayed so long and loud that it seemed a direct derision on what was being said. A ripple of laughter passed through the audience, and the speaker brought the meeting to a rather abrupt end.

The next night someone put a cat through the open door and set a dog after it, and by the time the two had scurried up the center aisle, across the stage, and out the window, that meeting was ruined too.

That night the young preacher had a heart attack which kept him down for some time. Once again he announced a meeting, but when he arrived to see some grinning boys around the door, and when a couple costumed like an old man and woman solemnly followed him up the aisle, he sat down heavily and did not even try to go on with a meeting. Within a short time he died of his heart condition.

Full of remorse now, some of the pranksters were humbled as they learned of the preacher's past and found that he had really been a martyr to their gross rudeness. His body was to be carefully prepared, sealed into a galvanized tin box within the casket, and shipped back to his home for burial. One boy stood looking at him, so still and peaceful, and as the tinsmith arranged the lid to be soldered into place, he said suddenly, "Hold everything! Wait just a minute till I can get back!"

He ran out as fast as he could and soon returned with a large can opener, which he placed on the dead man's chest.

"Now go ahead," he said. "That will help him cut himself out on Resurrection Morning. He can't say that I didn't give him a break. I might-a bothered him some, but maybe this'll help to make up for it."

This time he wasn't trying to be funny.

Helen Z. Papanikolas

Greek Folklore of Carbon County

In the early 1900's when coal veins were rapidly opened in the mountain draws and slopes of Carbon County, young men from the Balkans and the Mediterranean swarmed into the coal camps. Some had worked their way across the country on labor gangs building roads and bridges and laying track. Some had come directly from their villages with tags in their coat lapels. Other countrymen and labor agents, mostly disreputable *padrones*, had contracted for their work. The new immigrants were "cheap" labor; they worked for wages few native Americans or older immigrants would tolerate. The notion was widely held that they had inferior blood and deserved no better.[1]

Around each mine, boardinghouses shot up, and near these saloons, hotels, and company stores were hastily built. Gamblers and prostitutes followed. On Saturday evenings the young "foreigners" rode trains and twelve-seat stages from the camps to the towns of Price and Helper. For the first time in their lives they could jingle money in their pockets. Wearing their black Sunday best, shouting, shooting off guns, they jarred the towns. There was something wild about them, the natives said indulgently.

When labor troubles paralyzed the coal camps, the natives wanted them "sent back where they came from." They had taken jobs from "red-blooded Americans." They were "biting the hand that fed them." There was something peculiar about them, especially those Greeks, the ringleaders. None of them was married. They should all be locked into a railroad car and sent flying down the grade as the Chinese had been in Scofield during the Yellow Peril Scare.[2]

What did those Greeks think of the natives, those bland people who when they were angry were never horrendously angry, when they laughed were never ecstatically happy, and when they lost someone in a mine accident or explosion could stand at the graveside and shed a tear or two at the most? The Greeks had a word for them—"unsalted."

The natives knew nothing about the historical forces that had molded the Greek character. They saw the men as unpredictable, violent, "unassimilable aliens." The Greeks were perplexed by the natives' revulsion. They made light of the stories of hardships and sporadic Indian massacres on which they based their claim to the country. These troubles were insignificant compared to the barbarous four-hundred-year rule of the Turks over Greece and the Revolution of the 1820's. Captured guerrilla *klephts* were roasted alive on spits, tied to four horses and quartered, impaled, cut into small pieces slowly. Entire villages of women and children were slaughtered in abominable ways. Children were conceived and raised to fight the Turks. They were taught that heroism and life were one and the same.

The stories the natives told of the enigmatic bandit Matt Warner and Butch Cassidy's Robbers' Roost Gang were pale in comparison to those of their own *klephts* and rash warriors, the *palikária*, who with great flourish harassed and robbed rich Greeks as well as Turks. Yet the young Greeks admired Butch Cassidy. He had some of the audacity of their own heroes. They liked the story of Cassidy confronting Tom Fitch, the despotic justice of the peace of Helper. Fitch had jailed a Price lawyer with whom he had been feuding and set bail at the improbable amount of $20,000. Cassidy came out of hiding to post bail. "Here's the bail," he said, and took out his guns. Fitch quickly unlocked the jail. The Greeks loved guns, which were precious in their impoverished land. Guns and skill in using them were signs of manhood. Charon (Death) respected guns.

Because men emigrating to America followed relatives and villagers who could help them, the entire young male population of villages often came to the same city or town. In Carbon County this produced an unusual circumstance. Almost all of the Greeks were from Crete and the province of Roumeli in northern Greece. Cretans and Roumeliots were among the poorest of Greeks. In Crete poverty was legendary. People often owned not one goat and lived on berries, nuts, and greens picked on the mountains. Among the Roumeliots was a saying concerning their Agrapha Mountains and the town of Karpenision: "In the Agrapha and in Karpenision, not even the ovens will smoke this winter." There would be no fires; there was neither wood to burn nor food to cook.

The Cretans and Roumeliots greatly prized *leventía*, that zest for life, that quickness to act regardless of danger, that gaiety and generosity of possessions and self, that championing of the less strong.[3] They were also the most warlike of Greeks. Cretan heroism was unmatchable from ancient times to the German occupation. As for the Roumeliots, their mountains were called the Agrapha, the "Unwritten," because soldiers refused to accompany Turkish tax collectors into them. These *klephtic* strongholds remained "unwritten on the tax rolls."

For both Cretans and Roumeliots family honor was the highest virtue. An outrage against it had to be erased at any cost. This vengeance was developed to the highest degree among the Cretans. (It is not to be confused with the extortionist methods of the Sicilian Mafia.)[4] Carbon County was rife with affairs of honor that are remembered today as if they happened only months past.

One of these began in Crete fifty years ago. A young man killed another as the victim left his house to bring the midwife to his wife. The young Cretan fled to America and Carbon County. Not long afterward a cousin of the murdered man also came to Carbon County and feigned friendship with the murderer, by then married. At the moment the murderer left his house to bring a doctor for his own wife's delivery, the cousin of the murdered man stepped before him and killed him. He was caught and convicted by American justice, not so sensitive to crimes of passion in the name of family honor as Cretan justice. The murderer did not consider himself a criminal; he had vindicated his family's honor.

A final characteristic made Greek immigrant life turbulent in the county. The Cretans and Roumeliots were convinced that they were superior to each other. Only when the "Americans" attempted to lynch one of them or when they put on Ku Klux Klan robes and burned crosses did the Greeks unite.

By the time the young men had been in the new country a decade or so they were ready to marry. They had followed the custom of their people; they had sent back dowry money for their sisters. Now it was their turn. Picture brides came in weekly from Crete and Roumeli.

A generation before, many Carbon County natives had also married women they had never seen. A scarcity of women in the county had sent men scanning pink matrimonial bills. Women "desiring matrimony" advertised themselves as "refined young woman," "willing and able to work," and "small nest egg." The Greek picture brides, however, were always sponsored by someone related to them. It was unthinkable that a woman would come to America without the protection of a male relative. Such women were suspected of having sinned and been abandoned by their families.

The brides brought with them the folklore of their country. If the natives

had known the elements of this folklore, they would have been even more inflamed at the continued influx of Greeks. They would have had the ultimate
proof of what they already expounded: "Like oil and water. They don't mix."

In arranging marriages, families were guided by two unbreakable rules.
The Greek Orthodox Church forbade two families to marry more than once
into each other. Two brothers, then, could not marry two sisters of another
family. This was considered incest, as was marriage between first, second, and
third cousins and unions between a man and woman who had a mutual god-
parent. Baptism conferred a divinely sanctioned blood relationship.

Male relatives then arranged the marriages. All male relatives had to be
consulted. If this honor, a man's *filótimo*, was ignored, he often took a knife or
gun to redeem it. The newspapers of Carbon County reported several killings
over this matter. The betrothal then had to be approved by the parents. Disaster followed a marriage that parents did not want. Two young Cretans from
Helper eloped and were cursed by the bride's mother. On their honeymoon
they drowned; the mother's curse, the worst of all *katáras*, had done its work.

Usually men arranged their sisters' and cousins' marriages with men from
their own village or province. Sometimes, though, a casual conversation with
new-found Greek friends from other parts of Greece resulted in a *synekésio*, a
marriage bond.

The Cretans were exceptions. Only Cretans were worthy of marrying their
sisters and cousins. Turkish rule lasted a hundred years longer in Crete than in
the rest of Greece. *Enosis*, union with Greece, was achieved in 1915. This long
isolation made the islanders Cretans first and Greeks second. In their talk they
differentiated themselves: "There were six of us. Two Greeks and four Cretans." Several Roumeliot *palikária* eloped with Cretan girls and had to be
guarded by their friends wherever they went. The hazards were so great that the
Roumeliots returned to the expense and long wait of bringing picture brides
from friendly provinces.

The weddings took place the moment the preparations for the celebrations could be made and according to the customs of the brides' and grooms'
provinces. When a woman from one province married a man from another, the
customs of his village prevailed if he had a woman relative or villager to remind
him of his prerogatives as a male. Men usually were less rigid in following custom, and their brides eventually had their way.

There were certain periods when marriages could not be performed. If a
death in either family occurred, one year's mourning was necessary. A church
dispensation was often granted when the bride was left in a precarious position.

During her brother's night shift, for example, a miner working the day shift could take advantage of her. Marriages were not solemnized during the forty days of Lent, nor during the fasting periods before the great church feasts of the Repose of the Virgin on August 15 and Christmas.

Although May was a good month for weddings in most parts of Greece because it was the month of germination, in Samarina, located in the northern Pindus Mountains, and in Anatolia of Asia Minor, it was also considered the bewitching month, and weddings were avoided. The word for the month, *Maíou*, has the same derivation as the word for magic.

After all the rules and customs had been satisfied, the mystery (sacrament) of marriage took place on Sunday, the holy day for burials, weddings, and baptisms. The ceremony was heavy with biblical references and symbols of fertility. The best man, the *koumbáros*, three times interchanged the flowered wedding crowns worn by the bride and groom, queen and king of the new household. With the priest they made three circles before the altar in the Dance of Isaiah. The *koumbáros* had taken on a kinship more binding than that of blood. It had been witnessed and blessed by the Trinity. It was the *koumbáros'* duty to uphold the family, rear the children in the Greek Orthodox faith and provide for them in the event their father died.

The guests kissed the wedding crowns and threw rice on the bride and Jordan almonds, a symbol of fertility, on the hapless groom. The wedding feast was held in backyards if the weather was good. Lambs turned on spits, bread came warm from domed mud ovens, goatherders from the mountain draws brought fresh *feta* cheese, and wine was plentiful.

When appetites were sated, the bride led the first circle of dancers. The groom led the next dance. Dancing feats began. As each man led the dancers, he tried to outdo the others, leaping, slapping his ankles in mid-air, shouting a triumphant *Hopa!*, making backbends with a glass of wine on his forehead, picking up a chair with his teeth and twirling about. For hours the men danced and sang. For the Cretans the revelry lasted three days.

The brides looked on with traditionally modest glances. Some of them from lands where Turks were as thick as Greeks and whose customs had left their imprint, were surprised that they were participating in their own wedding celebrations. They had expected to be sitting in their wedding finery in a back room.

None of the brides could escape a terrible anxiety. Their virginity had yet to be proved. In a country as poor as Greece, a man's only true possessions were his honor and his daughter's virginity.[5] In America the Roumeliots preferred the bride's state to be secret, but for the Cretans it had to be known. The first brides who came were spared the ordeal of having the bridal sheets examined, but as soon as a cluster of women, all safely married, formed, the new brides had to suffer in America as did those in Greece. There were tales of gallant men cutting themselves to provide the necessary blood, but these were women's fictions—Greek men considered it unmanly to marry a "soiled" woman.

In Price and in the mining towns the Greeks lived in sporadic clusters called "Greek Towns." In Helper, the Roumeliots lived by the grade school and the Cretans on the northern limits of the town.

All the while Greek laborers were leaving the mines. Many bought sheep and returned to the occupation of their fathers. Others opened markets, cigar stores, restaurants, and hotels, and a few became farmers. This activated the hostility of the natives. They had expected the "foreigners" to fight in World War I, but they also expected them to remain laborers.

Cretans remained longer in the mines than the rest of the Greeks as they had come to America later. Hordes of them had arrived dressed in the baggy black breeches, boots, and bandolier vests of their island. Two hundred and more of them in one labor gang was not unusual.

Children were born. There were no grandmothers, great-grandmothers, elderly aunts or midwives to preside. When labor began, the young husbands called the camp doctors to their houses, and this shame was added to the women's pain. Helping the doctor was a neighbor who noted the conditions of birth. If a veil, the placenta, covered the baby's head, it was a sign of good luck. Women remembered their labors. An easy birth could mean an "easy" child, a hard birth a "hard" child. "He tyrannized me at birth and he's still at it!" mothers said.

The child's fate was decided the first three days of his life. A gold coin was placed near the child because this would please the spirits who decided the future. Visitors brought gold coins or silver dollars for good luck when they saw the baby for the first time.

After delivery, the woman was "freed." Now for a week, if she was fortunate and had neighbors to come in, she could rest. If there was no one to help her, she had to do the best she could alone. Husbands were not expected to help. They were a *város*, a burden. On a farm outside Price a Cretan woman went into labor. Her husband set off for the town to bring the doctor. There he stopped at the coffeehouse "for a moment." When he returned home late that night, he found his wife at the stove cooking. She had given birth alone.

Following the biblical injunction, women were considered unclean for forty days after birth. Other women could visit the new mother, but she could not leave her house. When the forty days had passed, she went to church to be "cleansed" by the priest. Soon afterward the baby was baptized. What happens to a child dying without the ministration of this mystery is still an unsolved theological question in the Eastern Orthodox Church. An early Church Father, St. Gregory of Nyssa, believed they became angels. The prevalent view is that they exist in nothingness and to the Greeks this is a most terrible fate. For parents, baptism, rebirth into the Christian community, was a great joy and worthy of the best in food, drink, and music; it was also a great relief.

Hair, fingernails, and toenails of babies were not cut until after baptism. Bad luck followed a child if this rule wasn't heeded. During the baptismal ceremony, the priest made small crosses on the child's forehead, cheeks, chin, palms, and soles with cotton dipped in consecrated oil. This gave the child strength; the crosses on the palms, specifically, insured the ability to do hard work. The priest also cut three strands of hair and dropped them into the baptismal urn. The meaning of this, as with other church drama, was unknown to the participants and even to most priests. It was a Christian replacement for Judaic circumcision and also represented a symbolic gift from the child to God; the cutting off of one's hair as a sacrifice was a tradition from biblical times.

The mother was not present during the ceremony. She stood in the narthex, the entrance of the church, while the child cried and screamed. When the godfather pronounced the name (the privilege to choose was his alone), children rushed back to the mother. The first to tell the child's name was rewarded with a coin.

Hundreds of children were born and grew up in the Greek Towns. They chattered in Greek as they played and ran in and out of each other's houses calling all mothers *Thítsa*, Auntie. Some were in truth aunts; others were called aunts out of respect; many were called aunts (the men *Théo* or *Mbárba*) because their parents or grandparents had been nursed by the same woman. This relationship was as deeply familial as one of blood. In days when a child would have died if his mother had not been able to nurse him, the giving of nourishment was the giving of one's own body and soul as well as life to the infant.

The ceremonies of birth, marriage, and death could be conducted properly only by an Eastern Orthodox priest. Within a few years of their emigration, the young immigrants had brought priests to America. The only church in the county was built in Price and consecrated August 15, 1916. The Sunday liturgy and officiating at the mysteries were only a small part of a priest's many duties.

More often than not, the priest was poorly educated. Burdened with the superstitions of his own village, he was constantly called to cleanse houses of real or imaginary sins. In black robes, rimless black hat, full beard, long hair knotted at the base of his neck, he swung his smoking censer and intoned prayers and incantations in houses where a child had been born dead, illnesses or accidents abounded, or mice defied usual means of extermination.

Sometimes the priest was called to dispel the Evil Eye, but it was usually done by a woman possessing special powers. The formula could never be taught by saying it aloud. The magic would be lost. It could be written on paper and thrown in a spot where it would be "found" by the aspiring practitioner or it could be overheard, but supposedly without the practitioner's knowledge.

A simple ritual was often all that was necessary to cure the spell of the Evil Eye. Three drops of olive oil were placed in a glass of water while the magic formula was repeated. Difficult cases required finer points. The afflicted person's clothing was folded three times while a dark song was sung of boats whose black sails had been charmed by witches so they could not move.

Because a person, usually a woman, could have the Evil Eye and not know it, women often counteracted its power themselves by using a charm, spitting at the recipient. "A beautiful child, may he live and give joy. Ptt. Ptt. Ptt." The spitting was more a blowing, but the intent was accomplished. Children wore amulets around their necks to keep the Evil Eye away. A small piece of garlic or a sliver of the True Cross—the most prized of all ingredients for amulets—was sewn inside a piece of cloth.

Children wore amulets to protect them from other dangers besides the Evil Eye. During the Ku Klux Klan attacks against the Mediterranean immigrants and Catholics in 1923 and 1924, children wore amulets around their necks and slept with them under their pillows to keep away nightmares.

A giant cross was burned in the railyards at Helper. The Catholics answered with a circle of fire on a mountainside. Greek and Italian stores were vandalized. The letters KKK were splattered on cement retaining walls, buildings, and mountain boulders. An Italian farmer, hearing noises at night, picked up a shovel and went out. He surprised men painting the letters on his barn, chased them, and fell dead of a heart attack.

Nick Jardine, an Easterner who had tried but failed to make his fortune in Alaska, told his employer, George Zeese, a Greek-born businessman, that the Klan was "out to get" him and Joseph Barboglio, a prosperous banker and native Italian. "Tell the Greeks and Italians not to buy any new cars or property or build anything for awhile. The Klan says you're taking over and they're going to drive you out."

The Greeks, Italians, and Irish railroad men armed themselves. Greek bachelors deserted the coffeehouses and patroled the Greek Towns. Young godfathers and uncles stationed themselves on the streets of the town and, unknown to the children, watched until they reached the schoolyard.

The excesses of the Klan throughout the country and the united strength of the immigrants sapped the Klan movement of its momentum. Mothers believed their children had been spared by supplications to the Virgin at their family icons, by prayers and lighted candles to saints on the icon screen in the church, and by the children's amulets.

As the children grew, the Greeks' obsession with their being taught so that they would "not grow up like crooked sticks" led to the establishment of Greek schools. This attitude toward learning was a heritage, not from ancient times, but from the Turkish occupation. The remarkable survival of the Greek language and faith, the teaching of which was prohibited by the Turks as their empire weakened, was accomplished through schools held at night in caves and cellars.

In Carbon County, as elsewhere in the country, children attended "American" school and Greek school afterward. Priests and fathers added to their education with proverbs: "Stars fell and pigs ate them." "The beautiful is destroyed by the beastly."

Mothers taught the children the necessity for faith through folklore. "In our neighboring village long ago, there was a man who ate meat on Good Friday. The next day he was walking down the road. The ground opened under his feet and swallowed him up."

> In our village there were termites eating away. The priest was called. He went from one house to the other sprinkling them with holy water and saying "Termites, termites, to the mountains!" There was one man who wouldn't pay the priest to bless his house because he didn't believe. All the houses touched with holy water were freed of termites, but the house of the man who didn't believe collapsed.

The mothers whose husbands had been killed in mine explosions had to make their growing sons aware of the dangers of becoming involved with *poutánes*, prostitutes. Shamefaced, they would whisper at the sight of a certain crippled man, "See old man ———. You see his twisted legs and arms. He was a strong fine man until the night he went to the *poutánes* during Holy Week." The mothers knew the *poutánes* were bad, but necessary. Abstinence made a man sickly. They could only hope their sons and brothers married early.

Other than not smoking in the presence of their parents and other elders and being expected to marry Greek girls because only they could make good wives and mothers, boys were free of the many restrictions custom placed on girls. A menstruating girl was not allowed to attend liturgies. To take communion at this monthly time was a special sin. During Holy Week, the great climax of each year, the forty-days' fasting and confession went in vain for such girls and women. They sat home conspicuously absent, deprived of participating in the inevitable journey of Christ to the Cross, his Passion and Resurrection. In afternoon and evening services each step of the journey was intoned. On Great Thursdays a flat wooden figure of Christ was secured to a black wooden cross and venerated. On Fridays children were herded beneath His flowered tomb to insure their health for the following year. The Lamentations were keened around the bier in the evening. The next day murmurs of excitement shimmered in the Greek Towns. Scents of roasting meat and honeyed delicacies wafted over the houses, whose window blinds had been drawn since Great Wednesday evening. Sweet Easter bread baked in mud ovens.

At midnight the congregation, no longer in the somber clothing of mourning, the children in bright colors, waited in darkness and silence. Then one small candle flame appeared inside the altar. The Resurrection Hymn began softly, tentatively: "Christ is arisen, truly arisen. By death over death He has trampled." Other candles took light from the one and the hymn grew louder, more joyful until hundreds of candles glowed in the dark and the singing vibrated against the stained glass windows.

As the people left the church, they cupped their hands about their candle flames. If they succeeded in lighting the vigil tapers of their family icons with the Resurrection candles, the following year would be a safe one for them.

Often the moment of Resurrection was the time for people to fulfill their *támas*, pledges they had made to a saint, a martyr, but most often to Christ and the Virgin. In return for health of a child, the passing of a crisis, relief from pain, a *táma* was pledged—money for a new icon or other church ornament by the rich, a simple act of humility by the poor such as coming to church shoeless or in old clothing.

An oath spoken in the name of a saint, the Virgin or Christ and later regretted required confession and a *táma* decided upon by the priest. An anonymous gift of money to an unfortunate person was a common *táma*. The priest also ordered a reconciliation. Following the Resurrection, old enemies and new found each other, embraced and forgave with the kiss of *agápe* (the brotherly or spiritual love of one Christian for another).

All this was missed by the unfortunate women whose physiology had been untimely. Only after the Sunday Easter *agápe* service were they allowed to appear. In the church basement or a civic hall they joined the rest of Greek Town in the feast of *agápe*. Roast lamb, eggs dyed red for Christ's blood, goat cheese pastries, honey and nut sweets, *retsína* wine and *mastíha* liquer rewarded the faithful. Songs of *xenetía*, foreign lands and the bitterness of them, of love and of longing and of the revolution were sung. Dances from all of the provinces were performed. The forty days' restriction of certain foods, pleasures, and conjugal relations was over.

Next in importance to church ceremonies, food, and shelter was the curing of sickness. Few immigrants had ever seen a doctor in Greece. They depended on folk cures, the *praktiká*, the practical. In America when the *praktiká* failed, they called a doctor. If his medicines were not effective, they tried other folk cures. Sometimes a doctor's prescriptions and folk cures were used simultaneously, the doctor unsuspecting.

If the doctor was Dr. Charles Ruggeri, the mothers went about their work fearfully. They were afraid of him, but also respected him. Dr. Ruggeri was a "xeno like us"; whose parents were immigrant Italians. For this reason Dr. Ruggeri knew them as native American doctors could not. Charging into their houses upon discovering they had not followed his orders, he shouted, threatened, and subdued. He was as awesome a figure to the mothers as St. George with lifted spear poised at the dragon's heart or St. Demetrios with the Anti-Christ under his horse's hoofs.

Cupping was the pan-Greek cure for most illnesses. Water glasses, heated with a tuft of burning cotton, were placed on the patient's back. When the flesh swelled from the heat and suction, the glasses were removed. If the patient was very sick, small crosses were cut into the skin and then covered with the glasses. Another bleeding cure was with leeches found in stagnant pools.

Vizikánti (cantharides) was another favorite cure for illnesses. The theory was the same as that for bleeding: impurities had filled the body and had to be drained out. Plasters made of powdered Spanish flies were placed on the body. Dollar-size blisters formed that were deftly twisted and broken. Pleurisy, pneumonia, bad coughs, and kidney disorders were treated with *vizikánti*.

To prevent infection from a rusty nail, hot olive oil was dripped over the wound. Black pepper sprinkled into hot wine was used for coughs as was a mixture of honey and lemon juice. Garlic was a cure for almost everything. For influenza, tea with whiskey was drunk as hot as could be withstood. During the influenza epidemic of 1918 that killed thousands of people, heroic measures

were needed. Many Greeks believed they were spared because they chewed garlic throughout the day, drank whiskey liberally, and did not go to bed when
chills took hold of them. "Once in bed, you were as good as dead."

For sties and to prevent gangrene, the victim's urine was used. A badly
injured person was wrapped in the pelt of a freshly killed sheep. A child who
suffered often from the Evil Eye was cured by laving his head with the blood of
a rooster. A sheep tuft tied to a wound stopped bleeding. Shavings from a
leather belt also promoted coagulation. Immigrants from Arcadia sometimes
spread chicken droppings on the throat for mumps and soreness. Poultices of
boiled mustard greens were used to draw out "cold," and boiled onions to draw
out infections. A silver coin or knife pressed on a bump reduced the swelling.

For a tonic the immigrants went to Alex Rizos, a Greek druggist in Salt
Lake City. The tonic was called *manjoúni* and was a liquid made of quinine
sulphate, powdered Peruvian bark, a laxative, honey, nuxvomica, rhubarb powder (herb) and cinnamon. Long after his retirement, the quiet druggist mixed
manjoúni for Greeks throughout the mountain states.[7]

There was not an illness that did not have its cure. When there was doubt,
Mbarba Yianni was paid a visit. Mbarba Yianni, Uncle John, was John Diamanti, a sheepman of Helper with overhanging eyebrows and luxuriously
curled mustaches. Uncle John had come from the Roumeli province of Greece.
He arrived in 1903, the first Greek in Carbon County. Most of the young men in
his village Mavrolithári (Black Rock), followed him with a tag in their lapels—to
John Diamanti, Helper, Utah, U.S.A.[8]

In all villages in Greece there is a man like Uncle John. He can read a little
better than others; he has a certain way with people and animals in illness.
Uncle John was also intuitive. He had *hárisma*, charisma. The sick and grieving
felt better after he visited them, although he merely sat and said little.

Uncle John had delivered all eight of his children: "It's no different than a
ewe and a lamb." Pregnant women came for his verdict: "Would it be a girl or a
boy?" Barely glancing at the woman, in deference to her modesty, he made his
pronouncement. Legend has it that he never made a mistake.

For more than sixty Easters, he read the shoulder blade of the paschal
lamb. Peering at the bone, feeling the bumps and demarcations, he foretold,
accurately, it is said, what the coming year would bring.

Uncle John also had a dream book, and many came to consult him about
their dreams. With ceremony, while the traditional spoonful of preserves and
mastíha were served by his wife, he would put on his glasses and look into the
worn book. Nothing was missing from it. Freudian images and fantasy mingled.

A dream of a brother's death was a sign of good tidings for the family. A dream that one's stomach had swelled meant great wealth and good fortune. If one saw himself as a youth in a dream, and in fact was one, he would win the beautiful girl he desired, but if he was old and dreamed he was young, an old mistake or sin would stir and bring grief.

Uncle John mused over the dream book's words. Sometimes he changed the interpretation slightly; sometimes he discarded it and gave his own view. Whatever he said was satisfactory to the people who came to him. Greeks wanted their dreams interpreted. They wanted to know their fate. Those still doing immigrant labor, the Cretans, were especially sensitive to what that fate would be.

"American" miners stayed away from the mines when they had premonitions and bad dreams. Often they heard voices warning them away from the entrance to a mine, or saw ghostly miners at their bedsides, or some small change in their morning routine was an ominous sign. The Cretans were not so encumbered. Whether they had bad dreams or not and even if the sense of doom was inside them, they reported for their shifts because Fate could not be cheated; one's fate was determined at birth.

This belief, both harsh and comforting, was as strong among the Greek immigrants in America as it had been for them in Greece. In America, however, the immigrants were freed from the terrible fear of the *vrikólakes*, vampires, and the nereids, the young women who sang and danced with evil seduction in the forests at night. Rather than pass through after sundown, a person remained on an open plain until morning, when the nereids vanished. Bridges, too, were not crossed at night. Dead men inhabited them.

The immigrants told tales of the *vrikólakes* and nereids, but such creatures had remained in their native country. Why didn't they follow the immigrants? In frustration the old-country Greek shouts, "Because! Did Christ cross the ocean? No!" (They had not heard of the Latter-day Saint dogma, and those who had could not believe it.)

The reason for the absence of *vrikólakes* in America might also have been the burial customs of Greece. Because of the extreme lack of tillable land, bodies were, and are, unearthed every three years, cleaned, blessed and stored in wooden boxes. Often bones still had flesh clinging to them. The people shrank back in horror; vampires had possessed such bodies. Incantations and storing under the altar for forty days were necessary and again burial for another three years.

Legends grew about the dead whose bodies had been invaded by the *vrikólakes.* Either they had been evil to the very core, or vampires had gained entrance through cunning. The lives of such dead were interminably discussed for final evidence. In America, where bodies were not dug up, no one knew whether the *vrikólakes* had claimed them or not.

Even though Fate determined when death would come, life was too precious to allow it to come quietly. The women relatives of the dead railed against Fate in their keening of the *mirológia*, the words of Fate. While the dead person lay in an open casket in his living room, women intoned in high-pitched undulation his life, wishes, triumphs, and griefs. For hours the keening wore on, interspersed with long, eerie wails. Traditional *mirológia* were also sung:

> Only for this I grieve for you, I pity you,
> how will you live your first night in the earth?
> You will find snakes embraced, vipers entwined.
> A snake, a black snake, a two-headed snake,
> has nested on your joined brows.

For a small child:

> You did not deserve it, a bed in the earth was not for you,
> you belong in the garden of May,
> between two apple trees, under three bitter orange trees,
> blossoms gently falling, the apples on your lap,
> carnations a red circlet round your neck.

In the 1924 explosion of the Castle Gate Mine in Carbon County, 172 miners were killed, 50 of them Greek. (According to the Cretans, there were "48 of our boys and 2 Greeks.") *Mirológia* pierced the air for the ten days it took to recover the bodies.

If a dead man had not been married, he was buried with a wedding crown on his head, a white flower in his lapel, and a gold band on his wedding ring finger—the third of the right hand because that is the hand that makes the sign of the cross. Young women were buried in wedding dress and veil, with gold band and bouquet of flowers. The unmarried dead were lamented not only for having died, but for having gone without the mystery of marriage.

At the funeral the priest gave supplications that the soul be like good wheat that is sown and sprouts again. Following the chanting of the dirge for the dead—"Eons live your memory"—the casket was lifted onto the men's shoulders. The bells tolled as it was carried out to the steps and set down again. The casket was opened and relatives and friends in black crowded about it. A photographer took pictures. The bells tolled again as the casket was closed and taken to the graveyard.

At the burial the priest sprinkled olive oil and dirt on the casket. Then the mourners each picked up a bit of earth and threw it into the grave. Afterward the people returned to the dead one's house where someone had stayed to prevent his soul, unwilling to begin its journey, from entering. A dinner of fish, symbol of Christ, was eaten. Stories and laughing followed, lessening the burden of death.

After forty days, commemorating the forty days that Christ walked the earth after his Crucifixion, wheat was boiled until plump, then sweetened, mixed with nuts, pomegranate seeds, parsley, Jordan almonds and raisins, then mounded on a platter and covered with powdered sugar, silver dragées, and green gelatine fir trees—symbols of eternal life. Again family and friends gathered at the dead one's house and ate the *kólivo* as a sign of mutual forgiveness. The soul had now finished its wanderings and was ready to meet God.

Deep mourning lasted for forty days. The mother did not leave the house; fathers returned home immediately after work and children came directly from school. All clothing was dyed black. Mirrors, symbols of vanity, and photographs, a source of pleasure, were turned to face the wall or covered with black crepe. Church attendance was viewed as a social activity and was avoided. Women remained away from Sunday liturgies for a year. Some never went to church again except for funerals, family weddings, baptisms, and Holy Week, excluding the Resurrection service. As lifelong mourners, they felt it improper to join in the communal happiness.

At the end of the year's mourning another memorial service was held. Children took off their black clothing; fathers removed the black bands from their sleeves, but mothers continued to wear black until the third-year memorial service. If husbands, children, or parents had died, the young mothers grew old in black.

The numbers three for the Trinity and for the days between Christ's Crucifixion and Resurrection, and forty from the many Old Testament references were favorite numbers in everyday talk. "Give me your answer in three days' time." "Come back in forty days."

Wheat, olive oil, and bread were sacred to the immigrants. If bread was dropped, it was picked up, the sign of the cross made, and then it was kissed and eaten. If it was dirty it was burned, but it was never thrown away. If any bread remained after the meal was finished, it was kissed and put away.

On Sundays and saints' days only work that was a true necessity was done. Assorted miseries and crises were blamed on women who washed or baked on holy days. Men and boys who were named after the saint of the day received visitors who wished them *hrónia polá* (many years). Food and drink were laid out in their houses. If the saint was a popular one such as Demetrios, Constantine or Nicholas, with many namesakes, one day's visiting was not enough; people needed several days to pay their name-day respects. For women and girls there was no celebration, only *"hrónia polá"* called over the fences.

Most of this folklore is no longer practiced. The children of the immigrants are now in their forties and fifties. They scoff at the Evil Eye; they long ago rebelled at the keening of the *mirológia*. The immigrants themselves began to see the impropriety of it all, and shamed the later immigrants who came after the second world war. These outwardly dropped what they could still secretly believe. American-born priests have ruthlessly cut out the lore calcifications attached to their religion, and icons, vigil lights, and memorial wheat (now in sanitary, stapled plastic bags) are all that remains of the immigrant years.

With the passing of the old-country folklore, other changes have come. A grief-wounded patriarch commanded his children as they left for the funeral of his wife of fifty-five years, "Now watch. Control yourselves. We mustn't make a spectacle of ourselves."

During a recent liturgy an old man suffered a seizure. Those near him attempted to help him while the priest went on with the liturgy. Only two people stood up to stare, a man and his wife who had just emigrated from Greece. Old women who had once torn their hair as they keened the *mirológia*, although anxious for the stricken man, looked at the immigrants disapprovingly. Old men who fifty and sixty years earlier had risked their lives over affairs of honor stared straight ahead and wondered which of the old *palikárs*, which of the old *levéntis* had been struck down. The recent immigrants looked about and slowly sat down.

The first Greek immigrants have been American citizens for more than sixty years. They have shared Carbon County history with the native Americans—strikes, labor wars, attempted lynchings, the Ku Klux Klan attacks, the sadistic lynching of a Negro, mine explosions and accidents, the Depression, war, prosperity and again depression.[10] When Uncle John Diamanti died a few years ago, his obituary was on the front page of the *Helper Journal*. He was called a pioneer.

NOTES

1. For an analysis of the unsound methods used by the Immigration Commission's report of 1910 and the Laughlin Report of 1922 to support this theory see Oscar Handlin, *Race and Nationality in American Life* (New York: Doubleday Anchor, 1957), ch. 5.
2. Source: Lynn Fausett.
3. For a non-Greek view of Greek characteristics see Patrick Leigh Fermor, *Roumeli* (New York: Harper and Row, 1962, 1966); *leventía* pp. 133-35, *palikária* p. 141, *filótimo* pp. 110, 115.
4. Louis Adamic, *A Nation of Nations* (New York, 1944), p. 273; Fermor, *Roumeli*, p. 127.
5. Shared by other Mediterranean countries. See F. G. Friedmann, "The World of 'La Miseria,' "*Partisan Review*, March-April 1953.
6. Although women interviewed professed no belief in the Evil Eye, they refused to reveal the magic formula.
7. Carbon County Greeks were unfortunate in not having their own midwife like the celebrated Magerou of the Magna-Salt Lake area (see Helen Zeese Papanikolas, "Magerou, the Greek Midwife," *Utah Historical Society* 38 [Winter 1970]). Mrs. Haralambos (Angheliki) Koulouris, however, selflessly and without pay cared for newborn babies and their mothers.
8. The following people and families in Carbon County had their roots in Mavrolithari: Shilaos, Gust Pappas, Pete Pappas, John, Nick, and George Diamanti, Steve Diumenti, Pete, John, and Ted Jouflas, James and Haralambos Koulouris, Gus and Jim Kaddis, Draggatis, Mahleris, Sampino, and others.
9. Rae Dalven, ed. and trans., *Modern Greek Poetry*, rev. and enl. edition (New York: Russell and Russell, 1971), p. 45.
10. For documentation see Helen Zeese Papanikolas, "The Greeks of Carbon County," *Utah Historical Quarterly* 22 (April 1954).

Jessie K. Empey

George Miles' Reminiscences of Silver Reef

I went to Silver Reef in September 1880 and worked there most of the time until 1889. It was early fall, and I would be fifteen in December, and I had taken a man's job. Barbee and Walker had a system of bringing the wood to rick quite a way back because there was no room near the mill to stack it. They'd haul it in with a wagon. We used to handle five cord of wood every day—three times. I thought it was a good job because in those days we couldn't get anything to work at here in St. George, and had to work for "chips and whetstones"—that is, take anything we could get for pay.

Now, the people in St. George were very poor. They had very little money and nothing much to eat or wear. Wages were $1.50 a day. But at Silver Reef they were $4.50 per day for miners, $3.50 a day for laborers. Loose hay sold there for forty dollars a ton. The people of St. George, Washington, and Santa Clara sold hay and all their other products at good prices. Many of the men found work there for good wages and did well, some of them going into business and really prospering.

A man by the name of John Kemple, with others from Pioche, Nevada, discovered Silver Reef, or the White Reef. Another man who came from Pioche was John Barbee, and he discovered the Buckeye Reef. A man named Tom McNally, a spiritualist, told Barbee where to find the ore vein. Barbee worked there and found it and got the Walker people of Salt Lake City interested so they formed a mining company. There were two main ore bodies in Silver Reef, the White Reef and the Buckeye Reef.

Four mining companies were formed: The Barbee & Walker, the Leeds, the Stormont, and the Christie, sometimes called the California Company. Each of these four companies built mills; two of them built five-stamp mills and two built ten-stamp mills. They did a lot of work there, and brought out millions of dollars worth of silver ore.

Some peculiar characters of Silver Reef were John Rice, James N. Louder, George Miller, Doctor Cooper, Hal Fortman, Captain Lubbert, and Nigger Johnson.

John Rice built the finest, most splendid building that Silver Reef ever had. He came to Silver Reef penniless, and was a good man in many ways, but he had done a lot of wrong. It was said that he had killed a man in Pioche and was afraid of being killed himself because of it. He lived in a 'dobie hut just east of the John Rice Building. No windows in it. He wouldn't have windows for fear someone'd get into the house, but there were transoms over the doors.

He lived there with a squaw known as Sally Rice. Her husband, the Indian, was there, round about, but he put up with it. I guess John must have kept him, looked after him or something. As I said, this squaw lived there and seemed quite a decent sort of woman. John lost everything in that big building, and finally went away, down into Arizona and around Colorado and in the White Hills there. We got word finally that he was working in the mines there, and had later died.

James N. Louder was a peculiar man in his way, too. He could do most anything. He was a lawyer and editor of the *Silver Reef Miner*. Finally he became postmaster. There was an old gentleman working in the Christie Mill by the name of McClosty. The post office was in the northwest corner of the John Rice Building. When he came in he would stand way back by the door and he'd say, "Any mail for me?"

Louder took exception to it. Finally he shook his fist at him and said, "If you ever say 'Any mail for me?' and don't mention your name, I'll paste your mug all over the wall of this post office."

The man must have forgot—he was getting to be an old man; his hair was quite gray. I knew him. He came into the office one day, stood off, and said, "Any mail for me?"

Louder opened the post office door and rushed out, grabbed him and jammed him up against the wall. Then he shook his fist in the man's face and said, "If you ever say that again without giving your name, I really will paste your mug all over this wall." And he bumped the old man's head against it a couple of times.

Then a man came to Silver Reef, a Cornishman by the name of Painter. He had the reputation of being a prize fighter. Louder, as editor of the *Silver Reef Miner*, put a piece in the paper that read, "We have here an erstwhile Pug, per-ambulating the streets of our fair city, and someday he'll wake up to a realiza-tion of his own insignificance by finding a square inch of cutical taken off his uninviting mug."

People thought Painter'd go in there and challenge Louder to fight, but the man never did a thing about it. Louder said he'd been in the ring himself, and didn't care what he said.

Speaking of violent deaths, there were four while I was at the Reef: John Truby, Jack Diamond, Mike Corbage, and Tom Forrest. John Truby was an Irishman and Jack Diamond a Cornishman and they hated each other. Court was being held in a room off George Miller's saloon. John Truby was constable of the court. One evening when court was in session Diamond came into the courtroom with his hat on.

Truby said to him, "Take off your hat!" Diamond said, "Try to make me!"

Then Truby grabbed hold of him and took him out. When they got out-side, they took hold of the lapel of each other's coat with their left hand and drew their guns with their right hand and both fired at once at close quarters. Both fell back and died instantly. They lay there on George Miller's porch with their feet joined.

Then we had Mike Corbage who was foreman for the Stormont Company mine, and Tom Forrest, who was a miner, a worker there. Corbage discharged Forrest over some difficulty, or supposed wrong, and Forrest brooded over it until he got desperate. He lay in waiting along the trail and, as Corbage came along, stepped out with a big knife and slashed him across the abdomen, cut him almost in half and Corbage died on the spot.

Tom Forrest was arrested by Sheriff Gus Hardy and his deputy, Joe Hoag, and was brought into St. George and put into the jail in the basement of the Washington County courthouse. The night after Corbage's funeral a band of horsemen came down, took the keys from Gus Hardy and Frank Bentley, his deputy here, got Forrest out, put a rope around his neck and dragged him to George Cottam's corner, where they hung him on a big tree and left him there. When George Cottam came out the next morning to do his chores, he saw the body hanging there, and that was the first thing he knew about it.

I didn't haul wood long in Silver Reef but became instead delivery boy for the Woolley, Lund & Judd store. I also took all the dead people to their graves. My wagon was built just right for a hearse, with a long bed up at a pretty good height and long slats along the bottom so that one could slide a coffin easily onto it. So my outfit was used as a hearse, and I was always the driver. The cemetery had been built by the Ancient Order of Odd Fellows, a very fine little cemetery, with the letters A O O F placed over the gate on the circle.

Now for a Chinese funeral—but first I must tell you about Sam Wing. He was a Chinese mandarin and ruler of China Town, a good, educated man who seemed well liked and able to handle his people quite well. China Town was located east of the John Rice Building. Sam Wing would come to the store, get his mail, and sit outside in front to read his paper. I used to talk to him as I watched him reading from right to left and up and down the columns—hen scratching it looked like to me.

But about the funeral: When a Chinese man or woman died, they were buried in a graveyard east and a little south of Bonanza Flat, right in the corner of where the mountains came together, but there was a canyon between the two. The Chinese graveyard had no fence that I knew anything of. When they took a person to the graveyard, they carried him on a litter and two Chinamen would go ahead, carrying a lot of pieces of paper about two inches square—a lot of them—which they'd throw in every direction, in front and at the sides.

Someone said, "Why do you do that? Why do you throw that paper?"

"Why," they were told, "if the devil would get to the grave as soon as we do, he'd take the body. But he's got to gather up all those pieces of paper, and he can't do it because we can get the body buried before he gets there."

They had another idea. They thought that if the dead person was going to heaven, he'd need to eat and drink on the way. So they'd leave a lot of nice aromatic roast pork and other delicacies and a bottle of liquor, and go away. In the evening the Indians would come and eat the roast pork and all the delicacies and drink the wine. And they'd have a high time among themselves, those that didn't drink too much.

Enough things went on in Silver Reef to make a book. But I believe that God placed that silver in the sandstone—and it is the only place in the world where silver has been found in sandstone in paying quantities. When his people were in dire poverty, God made it possible for the silver to be discovered, and it was a great blessing to all of Southern Utah. There may be a lot more silver that is yet to be found. I believe there is, myself, and it will be found when the right time comes.*

---

*This reminiscence was recorded in St. George, Utah, August 11, 1959, when George E. Miles was ninety-two years of age.

3

Of Folk Experience and Family History

his section is a potpourri, each item a savory bit of lore; it is borderline, peripheral to established traditional lore. Yet it can be defended through the principle of the indigenous emerging as inherent patterns.

Such folk and family experiences are more valuable as history than history itself if one interprets them as accurate accounting of folkways and customs, for surely to reveal folkways accurately is to reveal the true life of the folk.

Like Frank Robertson, I am dyed in the colors of the multicolored West. The coyote has yapped at my door, stolen my lambs, outwitted me, and caught my .22 shots in his head. I, too, think of him as a legend of the West, western as sagebrush, with talkative cunning, sense of humor, a danger only when cornered, uncommonly smart. To many of us whose ears have heard two coyotes yapping night after night, sounding like a pack in their rapid-fire yelps, these stories are legend. The grey ghost of the desert is personalized for us as was Reynard the Fox a millennium ago. In his book *The Folktale* (New York: The Dryden Press, 1946), Stith Thompson says of legends: "Whether a story-teller has recounted the long . . . adventures of a dragon-slayer, a joke about a stupid married couple, an anecdote of an embarrassed parson, or a shrewd trick of the fox or has successfully threaded the mazes of a cumulative story, he is seldom under any illusions that his story refers to actual events. He knows well enough that his characters live in a world of make-believe." To this he attaches a footnote saying, "This remark must be taken with some caution, since there are undoubtedly story-tellers who believe in the reality of their stories."

Robertson, in his article "How To Grow a Legend," nostalgically recalls his youthful acceptance of the belief in the legends of the Three Nephites and of Mormons with horns. The supernatural was a very real part of his youth, a wonderful and harmless part, a legend. Karl Young explores the origin of the Mormons-with-horns legend.

When a father leaves his barber chair and scissors each summer to "go on the road" with an amateur theatrical troupe composed mostly of members of his own family, the group is set for some interesting experiences. Dean Farnsworth presents many of these, and throws a spotlight upon the entertainment of rural folk of the Great Basin and Snake River communities just before the advent of radio and television.

Something must be said about two other folk patterns presented in this section which are part of the inheritance of people reared in the Mormon tradition. The theology of the church, through its demand for genealogical research, promotes an interest in ancestors so potent in its intensity as to be unique.

Through a phenomenal religious drive, ancestors are disinterred and born again to new life in family histories. The article "Woman-heart Is Many Voiced" belongs to the cult of ancestor study; it is stylistic, poetic, sentimental family history, and sentimentality being of the nature of the folk demands no apology. Though more literary than most family histories in the genealogical mode, it finds place in this work as representative of the folk interest in preserving a favorable image of our forebears.

The folklorist need not be an interpreter; he is a collector and recorder of the work of the folk. It is not his business to say that beliefs are based in truth or in falsehood: the existence of the belief is what really matters. Thus, the prophetic power of the woman presented in "A Strange Gift" could be a "faith promoting" story to lead others to seek the Divine. But, regardless of purpose, accounts of premonitions and divining and unknown are the essence of folklore. This piece is typical of much that can be found in oral circulation and in written diaries and journals, and is again part of the inherent lore that makes Mormon society distinctive.

T.E.C.

Frank C. Robertson

The Gray Ghost of the Desert

The coyote will soon be only a legend of the West; indeed he already is but as a legend he will be even harder to exterminate. This gray marauder is an animal whom people seem to instinctively hate, and since the beginning of the West as we know it, killing coyotes has been a favorite sport. Until hunters began to take unfair advantage by using airplanes the coyotes more than held their own, and I have confidence that some will still have cunning enough to survive.

I owe my writing career to a coyote, and I am a friend of the species. When I was about to lose hope of ever selling a story, I wrote one about a coyote called "Three-Foot's Little Game," which was published in a New York magazine and which changed my occupation from sheepherder to writer, at least good enough to get my name in *Who's Who in America.* I couldn't have written it if I had not known considerable about coyotes.

The only trouble with coyotes is that they refuse to recognize property rights as people refuse to recognize the coyote's right to live. The late Frank Hale of Grantsville, Utah, a professional hunter and trapper all his life, who killed hundreds of coyotes while in the employ of stockmen, always maintained that it was a mistake to kill off the coyotes since they alone kept the balance of nature by destroying the rabbits and rodents which devoured the vegetation.

In my years as a sheepherder I have been outwitted by them many times. At the insistence of my employer I occasionally carried a rifle, but I seldom saw a coyote when I was carrying one, and never close enough to get a good shot.

When I left the gun at camp, I would often see them laughing at me from a nearby ridge. They had learned to associate the smell of powder with danger.

I have spent weary hours putting out lanterns by night during the lambing season because my employer hopefully believed the lanterns would frighten the coyotes away. To the contrary, the coyotes, whom I firmly believe have a fine sense of humor, would often kill a lamb and drag it under a lantern to eat it.

On the ranch we would carefully conceal traps around the carcass of a dead animal, but we would nearly always find the traps sprung, and the only thing we ever caught in any of them were some of the ranch dogs.

A favorite pastime of coyotes is luring ranch or camp dogs a mile or so from home, then chasing them back with painful nips at their hindquarters. Unlike their big brothers, the wolves, coyotes are never dangerous unless cornered. One time my brother Obe was herding sheep on Caribou Mountain in Idaho, and there was a nightly game between his two dogs and a couple of coyotes. The coyotes always stopped before they reached my brother's bed and the dogs would try to get into bed with him, but one night the dogs leaped over the bed and raced on. A moment later Obe saw an animal that looked to be as big as a yearling calf standing on his chest for a fleeting moment. That was a wolf, and Obe made sure it was long gone before he came down from the nearest tree into which instinct had propelled him.

The only account I ever heard of anyone's life being endangered by a coyote was told to me by my friend Frank Hale. Frank was hunting out in Nevada when he saw a coyote moving straight toward a group of children playing in a ravine near a country school. Fortunately, Mr. Hale recognized by its actions that the coyote had rabies, and he brought it down with a single shot fired directly over the heads of the children. That coyote was not responsible for its actions.

Another friend of mine had a hair-raising experience with a coyote near Leadore, Idaho, but the fault was clearly his. Riding the range one day, he saw some coyote pups playing around the foot of a large pine tree. When they saw him the pups disappeared into their hole underneath the tree. My impetuous friend dismounted and without waiting to tie his horse, decided to go into the den in search of a considerable amount of bounty.

The tunnel had been dug between the roots of the tree and was longer and smaller than my friend had counted on; but being a determined man he kept on crawling until finally he could see several pairs of eyes shining in the darkness and could hear the snarls of the mother coyote, whom he hadn't anticipated finding at home to receive callers. Suddenly, deciding that he had not lost any coyotes, he started to worm his way back—only to discover that when he crawled backwards his heavy coat didn't go with him, but bunched up around his shoulders and wedged him tightly in the tunnel.

Just what his reflections were no one will ever know, for the only thing he remembers is thinking that he was going to die, and that his horse would soon weary of waiting for him and would go home, and nobody would ever know where to look for him.

Bob admits to knowing an hour or so of panic while his coat grew thicker and tighter until it held him like a vise. Finally realizing that the only thing to do was conquer his panic, he began to inch his way a little more forward, risking the slashing fangs of the she coyote, until he could find room to peel his upper garments off over his head and then back out in his bare skin. By peeling himself like a banana he was finally able to extricate himself, find his horse, and go home. When he went back to the tree the next day he found that the coyote family had moved elsewhere in search of greater privacy.

My first experience with a coyote occurred down in Dog Valley, west of Nephi, Utah, when I was a boy of sixteen. I was working on a dry-farm owned by a group of Brigham Young University professors. The valley had been named because of the coyotes that had held undisputed possession of it until that summer. We saw coyotes every day, but the largest group we ever counted was sixteen, and they never allowed us to get too close to them.

Early in the fall my job was to ride a brush harrow where the sagebrush had been pulled up by a large machine and left lying on the ground. As I rode the back of the harrow the brush would collect underneath to a depth of two or three feet. When I reached the windrow, I would jump off the harrow and it would dump itself. Each time there would be a great scampering of frightened mice picked up in the harrow.

One day I noticed an old coyote following along behind, catching what mice he could. He was poor, his fur was ragged, and he seemed half-blind and toothless. Wishing him no harm I ignored him, and each day he got a little closer until he was following only a few feet behind the harrow. When the bewildered mice ran out he was usually able to gobble up a few, though for quite a while he eyed me warily while doing so. Convinced at last that I didn't intend to fight him for the mice, he would sometimes get so close that I could almost reach out and touch him, though I never tried to do it.

I think we got to be pretty good friends by not crowding each other, and when my job was finished I was happy to see that his eyes were less dull, and his fur was sleeker than it had been before.

There began my friendship and admiration for coyotes, a feeling shared by my range-raised wife. Once we visited the zoo in New York City, and when I noticed that my wife was spending more time looking at a pair of captive coyotes than all the rest of the animals, I realized that she was homesick and that it was time to get her back to the West.

Others, I know, feel the same as I do. Herewith is a letter I received many years ago from a long departed friend, a poet by the name of George F. Hibner:

Homesteading in Idaho, a brother and I made the hunting of furs our winter work through several years; the high altitude making for excellent furs. In white duck suits and caps that made us all but invisible against the snow, and with high-powered telescopes on our rifles the work was pleasant, and often we met interesting nature things.

The furs we sought were coyote and wolf. We worked our way northward from our cabins upon a morning early in winter—a foot of new snow not yet deep enough for web-footing over the sage and buckbrush—we planned on working lines some three hundred yards apart.

With the white suits, along with a here-and-there service bush we could easily lose sight of each other. So it was that, arrived at the edge of a draw leading up to Lucky Canyon, I found myself a considerable distance in advance of my brother, and sat down upon a bush to wait.

I had been there but a little while when I saw three coyotes, far down the slope and on the north side of the draw; and did they hold to the course they were following, would soon come in fair distance of my rifle.

Soon I saw that, unaware of my presence, they were keeping tab on brother Lon, but, not worried, were holding to their course, sometimes hidden in sagebrush, again in a bit of open ground. Finally, they entered a wide expanse of sagebrush where they would not be visible to me until they were very close—if at all.

Just northeast of me, its wider end nearly breaking into the far side of the draw, lay a pot-hole—very like the shell of the great egg that had been halved lengthwise and pressed some five feet into the stony ground. Every foot of the floor was in plain view of me. Into that bowl through the narrow end, after a suspense of waiting, spilled the three coyotes—no other word would fit that entry—and at once, as silently as though they were shadows, the trio raced, tumbled and wrestled upon that white floor.

For five minutes they played. Then as though there were some bugle note I did not hear, or waved signal I did not see, the three lined up toward the southeastern side of the bowl, motionless as marble statues as they peered through the brush on the bowl's edge at the oncoming hunter. No drilled soldiers in line could have been more perfectly upright. The backs of all three were a perfect line. Not even the tip of a tail showed above the rim; tails, like braces, straight-lined down into the snow.

For perhaps three minutes they stood there; a mother and her two nearly grown pups. Then again, as at an unheard signal, they executed a right turn in unison, and the carefree, romping, shadow-silence was resumed.

Three times they lined up so, equal distance apart; fore-feet so snugged that no line was broken. Each time, as though an electric button had been pressed, the right turn down was executed and the no-care-in-the-world play was resumed. And slowly brother Lon was drawing nearer.

Then, suddenly, the mother stood at the rim alone; the pups equally motionless, watching the face of that gray-marble mother. For minutes there was no least whispering of movement; I wondering what Lon was doing. Then once more the right turn down, a few carefree leaps and turns about the bottom of the white bowl, then out the narrow end, turning to the left this time to disappear into a sea of sage as brother Lon came into view.

And I did not shoot! Who could there in the frozen silences of the hills, with so much grace and joy and beauty spilling out to him, blast it all with a rifle shot?

Unfortunately for the coyotes, not all hunters are poets like my friend Hibner. The coyote is as Western as sagebrush. To me he is a living legend, and I shall always be on his side in his battle with what we sometimes erroneously call progress. The last time I saw a free coyote we were driving across the Nevada desert from Tonopah to Ely, and one loped across the road ahead of us, paused for a moment on top of a knoll to watch us, then went on about his business.

As I gave him a farewell salute, I said, "Peace go with you, brother!"

Dean B. Farnsworth

Barber on the Boards

Nothing is more commonplace today than the observation that change is rapid, but a particular application of that observation sometimes serves to underline, to capitalize, to print in dark red ink what is said every day. For example, the question asked the other day: "What did you do, Daddy, before television?" Television seems to me to have come only yesterday. "Why," I answer, "we listened to the radio (as sometimes we still do) or went to the movies (as, less often, we still do also)." A man doesn't have to be more than middle-aged to remember when his folks first bought the beautiful Atwater Kent radio, or the excitement of the first talking short at the little Avalon movie house, or even earlier the Victrola playing Sir Harry Lauder "Roamin' in the Gloamin'." Besides reminding one of how fast the changes have come, such reminiscing also reminds him that movies and radio have lived on into the age of television and that although Edison's cylindrical phonograph records are now collectors' items, their grandchild or great-grandchild, the stereo recording, is today's home entertainment status symbol. Similarly, as movies gave way to talkies and the spiral of spectacular technical innovations spun wider and brighter, the stage was not suddenly abandoned by the stock companies, the vaudevillians, and the "legitimate" actors, but it became a smaller stage in more and more isolated areas.

It is about one of the little acting companies whose history is enclosed in the parentheses of the two world wars that I want to tell you. My first knowledge of this company came to me almost as obscurely as a boy's first initiation into the world of sex. I heard hints, intimations, half-finished conversations, indirect warnings, that my charming and lovable Uncle Dennis, with the handsome mustache, the beautiful voice, and the courtly manner, was not only a barber—he was also an actor. This placed him for me in the magic company of Hoot Gibson, Ken Maynard, and Tom Mix—my movie idols, for I had never seen real actors except those in the amateur community and church theatricals in a small Utah town. But I heard that Uncle Den traveled with a troupe of actors, sometimes for months at a time, when—his sisters sometimes intimated—it would have been better for him, certainly better for his family, to stay at his razor strop and not be gallivanting about putting on plays.

I never got to see one of Uncle Den's plays, but all my life I have been asked if I knew the Farnsworths who came to Rigby, or Enterprise, or Parowan putting on plays "when I was growing up." I always planned to ask Uncle Den to tell me about those days when we both had the time. He stopped touring before World War II. His troupe had all married and had families of their own; they had roots, and like the old nomadic peoples, had finally assumed settled ways. But before I got around to it, Uncle Den died. Finally, too late to interview the impresario, the entrepreneur, the manager, I wrote to Aunt Venola, his wife, to ask about those times flying so swiftly into the past. She wrote, "I am very happy that you are interested in getting a record of the plays and will be very happy to have you meet with us. . . ." In my cousin's home one evening we cousins and aunts and in-laws spent some unforgettable hours trying to "summon up remembrance of things past," but there was no wailing of "dear time's waste." The memories now seemed all to be happy ones or humorous ones. As Aunt Venola had written me: "Our family did travel around a lot. They didn't make much money but did get a lot of experience that they will always cherish." There on that warm summer evening were gathered from Uncle Den's company five daughters and three sons, his wife, and a dear friend, whose fine voice still speaks in accents meant to be shared across the footlights.

I guess no one now living knows when or why Uncle Den became an actor, but family stories indicate it was early. As a youth freighting between Beaver, Utah, and the rail terminal at Milford, Den was stage-struck. He pictured himself as playwright and actor, and with a friend named Gentry he wrote and staged an original play that did not show evidence of great literary merit. Years later he told his children that the producers were practically run out of Beaver and that a druggist in Milford, where they tried again, told them that "it was so bad it was funny." Still, as an actor Uncle Den showed promise. Acting seemed to be natural to him—"He could improvise anytime." Moreover, the theatrical urge was soon shared by his growing family, for his daughter Venice and his young half brother Howard made up and presented plays and charged admission to them. Thus the beginning goes a long way back.

The existence of the traveling company, however, dates from the early twenties off and on to 1938. Before 1920 Uncle Den's first wife died; he had become a barber, and his older children were old enough to act with him. Most important of all, his second wife, necessarily long-suffering and tolerant, knew that he had acting in his blood. She bore with it as one learns to live with incurable allergies. Yet why did he love it so much? Perhaps he simply felt like Dickens' actor-manager Vincent Crummles, who told Nicholas Nickleby, "I am in the theatrical profession myself, my wife is in the theatrical profession, my children are in the theatrical profession. I had a dog that lived and died in it from a puppy. . . . I'll bring you out, and your friend too. Say the word." Uncle Den "brought out" his children in turn as they got old enough, his wife as the babies grew big enough to travel, and his friends, too.

Perhaps Uncle Den dreamed of making money in the theater, but this seems most unlikely. The tours seldom more than broke even. "Dad spent till we were broke," writes his daughter Beth, "then traded tickets for supplies." Still he did expect to break even, though the expectations often proved too sanguine. For example, one summer he subleased his barbershop and left Aunt Venola with a new baby and a garden in the care of son Larry, still a small boy. The new barber, a stranger to Uncle Den's clientele, had too little business to pay the utilities, and the water was shut off, forcing him to close the shop. Then began an exchange of tragi-comical letters, each received with the expectation that it contained much-needed money and each containing instead an affectionate request for money. Fortunately Venola had the garden, the cow, and boundless forgiveness.

No doubt touring gave the family a chance to travel. A barber's income alone would not have provided this, especially during the depression years. The itineraries took in Yellowstone Park, the Utah parks, and many out-of-the-way places from the remote Uintas to the Salmon River country. Still, there must have been in Uncle Den, as in Vincent Crummles, something of the gypsy besides, for as we shall see, the travel was rarely easy and comforts were few. Uncle Den's adventures are suitably described by Dickens' phrase as a "course of wandering speculation."

The name of the troupe varied from The Farnsworth Players to the Farnsworth Metropolitan Players. The second name may have meant to imply a certain sophistication to the small-town audiences, but it may have been a fair attempt to distinguish this troupe from another, older, and more illustrious company, called Farnsworth's Imperial Players or, under canvas, Farnsworth's Imperial Stock Company. The existence of two companies over the years helps explain how it is that so many people from so many scattered places remember their plays. Possibly one group profited from the good reputation of the other. In my own case, I was unaware of the existence of two groups until I was told by Aunt Venola: "You know, O. L. Farnsworth was more active in theatrical work than Den was." This doubling helped explain many things in the questions put to me over the years by their former fans. My cousin Venice explained further:

> There were two troupes of Farnsworth players active at that time, the "O. L. Farnsworth Players" and dad's group, called the "Farnsworth Metropolitan Players." The O. L. Farnsworth Players had been active longer than we had and were probably more experienced and a little better financed than we were. They left a good reputation wherever they played, as I hope we did. We covered very much the same territory—the small towns that didn't have much by way of entertainment—very often we were mistaken for each other, one reason being the similarity of the girls' names; theirs were Melba and Verus, ours were Mildred and Venice. I have never met any of them.

Leaders of the two troupes were distant relatives, but I have found no indication that their dramatic interests did not develop independently. Despite Venice's individually missing contact with the other troupe, on occasion they must not only have crossed paths, but met, for Marlow Callahan, one of Uncle Den's young friends and an actor on the earliest ventures, recalls that one time they "joined up with the O. L. Farnsworth troupe. After the play, they got a band together and danced." In contrast with Uncle Den's one-night stands, the O. L. Farnsworth group, Farnsworth's Imperial Players, often played several consecutive evenings, had its own eight-piece orchestra, and kept careful records both of its income and its repertory, which included several original plays by O. L. Farnsworth and Joseph F. Catmull, who is still a distinguished actor and director. Farnsworth's Imperial Players leave a well documented story and it deserves telling at length.

Uncle Den kept no records. Some of the children's scrapbooks include a handbill and snapshots, but nothing like the two carefully typed and bound volumes of the other troupe.

The personnel of Den's troupe always included Uncle Den and several of his children, and occasionally Aunt Venola. The other members each season were friends who wanted to act or travel and who had demonstrated their capacity to act in a local play directed during the winter by Uncle Den. Some thirty individuals appear to have made up the casts over the years, several of the men having fine singing voices to complement their acting ability. Only one of the actors appears to have been professional all winter as well as during the summer tour. This was Melvin Jensen, who played with the Wilkes players at the Lyric Theater in Salt Lake. To the younger members of the troupe Mr. Jensen seemed irritable and crotchety but always did well in performance. Perhaps he suffered from the feeling, so often documented in theatrical biographies, that he was superior to his fellows and had simply fallen on evil days. Local people were not used by Uncle Den even for bit parts due to the one-night stands, but were sometimes used as stagehands and passed out handbills for tickets to the show. "Once in a while," writes Venice, "we used local musical talent between acts but usually took our own." Unlike the life in fictional narratives of traveling shows, the general behavior of the company was carefully supervised. "We were always in good company and well chaperoned," Venice recalls. "The only times I remember Dad being annoyed with me was when he wanted me to do something and I would be backstage practicing the 'Black Bottom' or the 'Charleston' or the 'Flea Hop' or whatever the dance trend was at that time. I loved to dance!" Still, great informality is suggested in the leisure time activities of the group, who stopped to swim (and perhaps bathe?) at every swimming hole along the way. On one occasion two young men and two young women made a raft and nearly became marooned on Koosharem Reservoir.

If money was not the motive for traveling with the troupe, neither was "culture" the basis for the selection of the repertory, which was made up entirely of farce, romantic comedy, and melodrama. The plays selected were good vehicles for the actors and "good entertainment" for the audience. Of the plays remembered by the actors, about half may be found in play indexes, such plays as *It Pays To Advertise*, *My Dixie Rose*, and *Safety First*. Others seem to be mysteriously missing from play lists. As I mentioned earlier, Uncle Den had decided on the basis of youthful experience that acting, not writing, was his forte. The mystery of the sources of his plays disappears, however, in light of the practice—reputable among the Elizabethans and disreputable in the days of the modern copyright and royalty—of adapting plays to fit a troupe (and to avoid the royalty, which was quite beyond the means of many companies). Among the plays so adapted for the Farnsworth troupe, apparently, were *The Mender*, *Love Germs*, and *Whittlin'*. The nature of the last-named play may be inferred from a handbill kept by Doraine (reproduced here with original spelling intact): "A Three Act Comedy Drama, Full of Heart Interest." The dramatis personae: "Dr. Adam Good, Mrs. Wilson (a Widow), Ruth Wilson (A

Sweet Country Girl), Jimmie Edwards (Dopie), Gip (Dopie's Pal), Alma Dee (Not all there), Johny (A coming kid)."

> The PLAY: Act I. The widows home; Foreclosing Mortgages, The Arrival of Dopey Jim, Just A Bum: Love and Kindness starts to work, You mother him and I'll doctor him, "Gee it's great to have a mother."
>
> Act II. Same Scene, next morning: The Dr. tries to propose to the widow. Whittlin. Ruth Looses her job. The widow's faith, we still have ONE who watches over us; The widow's son died over there in France. Going to give up the old home; Jimmie starts thinking; Whittlin out toys. Dave told to beat it.
>
> Act III. (One month later.) Gip tries to take Jimmie back to the old life. Dr. tries to propose again. Jimmie likes to wash dishes, now; Paying off the mortgage.
>
> Scene II. (next morning) Jimmie skipped out. Dave's money gone. Telegrams; Dr. and the widow plan to elope. Could you give me a kiss to bind the bargain. Jimmie's return. Success. Just one thing more to make me happy. Dr. says: "Don't let Mrs. Jones name any of yours!"

FINALE

* *

SPECIALTIES, VAUDEVILLE BETWEEN ACTS.

CURTAIN 8:30 P.M.

POPULAR PRICES

This plot seems to embody all the devices of farce and melodrama, including the topically appropriate allusion to the dead hero "over there in France." Despite the adaptation preceding the casting of the play, further temporary alterations were sometimes dictated by circumstances. For example, Beth reports, "We cut out Johnny if we didn't have a door for him to go on." Sometimes the circumstances forced more serious alterations. In time all the company knew all the parts. Of the play just discussed, John Farnsworth, listed on the surviving handbill as "Dr. Adam Good," says that he played "every male part and one female." Such substitutions in the bit parts probably caused no serious difficulty, but when the leads failed, the quality of the substitutions could be the salvation or the ruin of the production. Two such episodes Venice recalls. The first involved a rare winter tour taking the troupe into Idaho:

> We took the train up to Alexandria, Idaho, high in the mountains; just a small depot was all that we could see. It was wintertime; the mountains were covered with snow.

We arrived sometime around midnight, but the moon was shining brightly. A covered wagon type sleigh pulled by a dog team was waiting to take us to Shelley and Grace, Idaho, where we were scheduled to play.

I believe it was here that our leading man became indisposed and couldn't go on. Dad seemed to have no other alternative: so he gave me a man's haircut, put a suit on me and sent me in to play the part! Now, you just don't do this to a well developed girl of 17 and expect to fool an audience! When I went on stage they just "hooted, hollered, and laughed like anything!" I couldn't help but laugh with them; it was truly comedy that night.

Venice also records a second substitution which ended in something of a success:

The last time I played with the "Company" was when I was a senior in high school. Dad was barbering in Park City and had a group up there ready to perform. They had been selling tickets all week and expected a big turnout. Something had happened that the leading lady quit—so Dad sent for me to come up and play her part, which I had played so many times. The theater was packed and it was "curtain time" and no leading man! It seemed that because the regular leading lady wasn't playing he wouldn't play either. Dad had scouts out looking for him; finally they located him and got back to the theater about the time the audience was getting rather impatient. We were introduced and didn't have any trouble. I wore a cute pink sun bonnet type hat—the "ohs" and "ahs" when I went on stage were very gratifying. . . . I made $13.00 for the performance—the most I had ever made.

The specialties and vaudeville between the acts mentioned on the handbill depended necessarily on the nature of the theater and, from year to year, on the talents of the troupe. There was usually a competent male singer, accompanied on the piano, if there was one, and occasionally on the accordion, harmonica, or ukulele. Marlow Callahan remembers singing "For You," "I Will Gather Stars," "Isn't This a Night for Love." Others remember him singing "Waltzing in a Dream with You Dear," and "Try a Little Tenderness." Earlier Lucien Bates sang, sometimes unaccompanied. Venice writes of him, "I particularly enjoyed hearing Lew Bates sing 'Roses of Picardy' and 'Roses of Yesterday' and 'Let Me Call You Sweetheart.' " Still earlier Bill Pratt sang "Gold Mine in the Sky" and "An Old Straw Hat." Thus their songs span nearly two decades of American popular songs. On the last tour the youngest travelers, Beth, eleven, and Nolene, nine, danced and sang to Doraine's piano accompaniment. The dancers still recall that they felt themselves at their best, rivals of Shirley Temple, and made a good thing of their act outside of the theater in a little town in the Uinta Basin when they discovered they could dance and sing for candy, chewing gum, and soda pop at the local service stations where their car was parked. The vaudeville, beyond what is suggested by the dancing children, seems to have consisted of such acts as a dialogue between Uncle Den as the straight man and Johnny as a "nut" with blacked out teeth and stage freckles. The nature of their dialogue has been forgotten but is not hard to imagine. Uncle Den also told stories and jokes such as the following barbershop joke, probably culled from his winter experience: A man came into a barbershop for a shave. After the barber had seated the customer, he went into the back room for some clean towels, leaving the customer with the barber's pet monkey, which proceeded to lather his face. The monkey then picked up the razor and was about to shave the customer as well, but the latter sat up and said vigorously, "Oh no, I'll wait for your father." Younger members of the troupe also gave readings, such as Beth's "There's a Little Brown-eyed Boy," which the whole family can still recite. As with the repertory, the *entr'actes* seem to have been designed to please more than to elevate. At least no one reports emulating Twain's Duke of Bilgewater training the Dauphin in delivery of Hamlet's soliloquy "with involuntary variations."

Preparation for the tour, which was usually from mid-June to mid-September, took place during the preceding winter. The plays were cast, rehearsed, and produced locally, often in the recreation hall of the neighborhood church. Transportation was provided, preliminary booking was begun, and the tour was launched.

Itineraries varied from season to season. Sometimes Uncle Den and a member of the troupe went ahead to book the show; other times the booking and performing seemed to be done in a series of loops. The outside limits of the company's activities seem to have been Fredonia, Arizona, Southern Montana, the Salmon River territory in Idaho, and most of Utah. One year, the advance men went as far as Las Vegas, not then the glittering desert gambling resort of today, planning "to book the old theater off Fremont Street," but they never did. They did perform in Bunkerville, Mesquite, and Junction, Cannonville, and Marysville that season. Names of some circuits are as picturesque as the Old West itself: Kingston, Koosharem, Pinto, Kanarraville, Tropic, Newcastle, Hurricane, Ophir, Stockton, Mercur, Heber, and Coalville. One year the season began with a week in the Uinta Basin followed by a swing into southwestern Wyoming and up to Yellowstone Park. When the profits were nearly used up, the troupe turned into Montana. They had, in fact, overstrained their means and had to exchange some carpenter's tools for gasoline in West Yellowstone.

Yellowstone seems to have been a favorite stopping place, and was included in the itinerary of another tour, partly recorded in a letter full of youth and nostalgia written by Doraine to her leading man of the preceding summer:

Hello, There!

As you sit in your camp in the twilight, I'll tell you a story of a little caravan of one Hudson car, six or seven suitcases, boxes, bedding, etc., and seven passengers which left Salt Lake Monday morning and now slowly wends it way across the western states to a corner of Nature's Paradise, called Yellowstone. 'Tis evening now, and after driving over 150 miles and engaging a house at a little town called Franklin, Idaho, the little caravan stops in a secluded grassy valley some few miles from town. Of course the occupants of the car were not hungry, but just as a result of habit, the grub box was brought out and a nice lunch consisting of cold meat sandwiches, boiled eggs, *milk*, peanut butter and honey sandwiches, and cake was enjoyed by all; even the countless number of mosquitoes were all well fed. While the girls washed up the few dishes, the fellows spread beds around the merry bonfire. The evening work thus being completed the little band circled themselves around the sparkling fire and listened to the harmonious strains of a ukeleyly [*sic*], occasionally joining in on some old familiar melody. It is a pretty picture, but somehow there seems to be something missing. An elderly gentleman [She is referring to her father, still under fifty] lying thoughtfully on the blanket near the fire is thinking longingly of a woman who tenderly tucks in her new born babe and wonders where the rest of her family is, wishing she might be there beside him on this lovely night.

The next paragraph shows graceful loneliness for the young man who had the summer before whispered "My Dixie Rose" "when the curtain falls on the end of the play." It continues:

Even to you, who have seen so many types of show houses as we, this one in which we are going to play tonight, at Ucon, Idaho, is a novelty. The building is a large, barnlike frame structure which has never seen a coat of paint and probably never will. The stage will be made of planks placed over saw horses. We won't have to use blankets for the scenery, however. There hasn't been a show here for a long time and things look rather favorable. We play at the Royal Theatre in Rigby two weeks from yesterday in connection with a movie. They do all the advertising, furnish the movie, and we get 40%. That, however, will be on our way back. We expect to be at Yellowstone at least by Sunday; we're only 150 miles from there now, but we've just 50¢ in the treasury, so luck had better fall our way. Does this bring back any memories?

The makeshift theater (as at Ucon) and the low cash balance were repeated fairly often. Luck did not always fall their way. One night at Radersburg, Montana, a heavy rain drove away all but about ten valiant enthusiasts. Money was short—the play went on, illuminated part of the time by candlelight. Sometimes the rain came inside. Though the place is forgotten the actors remember an audience sitting with umbrellas up while the rain dripped down the leading man's face until it soaked off his mustache.

Nevertheless, Uncle Den maintained an effort at professionalism. "We always practiced on each stage," writes Beth, "so that we could know the layout. Many times we had only one exit and no backstage."

Beth describes further the booking and advertising:

> During the day Dad would canvass the town for a spot. We put on a play every night but Sunday and tried to keep ourselves dated up. Upon getting a date, he would leave posters with the local businesses and a few free passes. The morning of the play handbills were passed around door to door to encourage a good turnout. Also we usually drove through the town with flashy signs, sort of parade ourselves to get people interested. . . . [We] usually got one-third of the house and we had to do our own advertising, setting up stage and furnish scenery.

Handbills were printed before the tour began, a space left at the bottom being filled in by hand to indicate time and place in each new town. The places ranged from theaters to ward houses and barns. Besides the writer's cramp occasioned by filling in the handbills, the girls objected in time to distributing them, for they picked up a crowd of children like Pied Pipers and the children were mostly little boys. The popular prices mentioned on the bill were usually ten cents for children, twenty-five for adults. During the Depression, even these prices were not easily paid and payment in kind was common. Marlow Callahan remembers receiving at Toquerville corn, butter, milk, and eggs, an acceptable variety to hungry actors. Sometimes meat was fortuitously provided. One night at Loa, a turkey, caught by pranksters from some vulnerable flock, was flung from the rear of the hall onto the stage, where in landing it broke its wing. The alert actors hurried the prize into the wings and trussed it up for a fatal trip down Sigurd Canyon where it was plucked and roasted after the show.

Other meat was procured during the nighttime travel from stop to stop, wild game, you might say. At least all along the road jack rabbits were picked off with a .22 and eaten at the next camp. Beth and Nolene report that one night when hunting had been particularly good they discovered that they were boasting of their kill right to a game warden who informed them that hunting "jacks" was illegal. He told them that if they gave a good show he would not fine them. After the show they waited until they had left the county to cook their rabbits. As jack rabbits have been a range land pest for many years, it is more likely that the handling and eating, rather than the shooting of the animals was against the law. It was already known that rabbits carried tularemia, a highly contagious disease, popularly called then simply "rabbit disease" or "rabbit fever." The danger that they faced and fortunately avoided is suggested by this excerpt from *The Roosevelt Standard*, June 28, 1934.

Mrs. C. B. Bartlett and her grandson, George O., 9, . . . of Tridell were taken to
Vernal last Wednesday, ill with what is commonly known as rabbit disease.

The boy had killed a rabbit while his father was away from home and after cleaning
it asked his grandmother to cook it for him. Mrs. Bartlett cut up the meat for frying.
Each of them became infected by the disease with a high fever, suffering for several
days.

Spared from the disease, the actors were not always lucky enough to have
enough rabbits. They remember one night when, having used all but one shell
without success, their hunter fired the last round at a rabbit and only wounded
it. Lanky as a jack rabbit himself, he took off on foot after the wounded animal
which he finally chased into a shallow hole and desperately dug out with the
now useless gun. His triumph was hollow—the rabbit was inedible.

Other dismal recollections stimulated by the sad rabbit hunt include the
taste of biscuits during a serious shortage of flour and an abundance of baking
powder. Still, hunger was usually cleverly checkmated if not actually avoided.
For example, on an evening promising more fasting than feasting the box office
would open early enough for a few early customers to be admitted before the
local grocery store closed. As soon as enough money for the price of bread and
milk had reached the till, it was rushed to the store in the hands of the youngest
performers to provide at least a late supper. From midsummer on, payment in
kind usually included sweet corn; at one last engagement it amounted to a full
bushel. Tired to death of corn, the troupe still feasted that night on corn and
headed homeward. Their loving mother, by means of late planting and diligent
care, had managed to save a special treat for her returning family—yes, sweet
corn! Sweet corn and fresh air produced other surprises. Unlike Vincent
Crummles' daughter Ninetta, who was kept the age of ten for a good five years
"because she had been kept up late every night and put upon an unlimited al-
lowance of gin-and-water from infancy, to prevent her growing tall," the last
season of touring, Beth, admittedly eleven when the season began, was well on
the way toward twelve when it ended and had nearly grown out of her clothes,
costumes and all.

Equipped with clothing at the beginning of the tour, with some food usually purchasable or taken in lieu of cash, the troupe still faced the remaining
major problems of housing and transportation. In good weather the sky was
their evening canopy; in bad weather, the stage paraphernalia. Strange halls,
often untenanted except weekends for Saturday socials or Sunday worship,
seem eerie and noisy in the dark. Such a hall, sometime before adapted for
movies, was the company bedroom one stormy night. Aunt Venola, this time
among the actors herself, woke from a sound sleep on the creaky stage to see

lights seeming to approach and withdraw from the far end of the hall. She feared that someone was approaching, possibly to rob the company of their hard won cash. Yet the lights would approach and withdraw, approach and withdraw with the distant noise of a motor. When morning came the lights proved to have been only auto headlights shining through the projection holes at the far end of the hall as the vehicles approached the town and descended the hill at its edge. Even during good seasons hotels were a luxury beyond the budget of the troupe; besides, most of the towns had none.

Except for the last season on the road, the troupe never possessed new cars. Besides the Hudson mentioned in Doraine's letter, members recall and snapshots confirm the possession one year of a sedan, identified as a Studebaker by Marlow Callahan, converted into a pickup. Banners announcing the forthcoming attraction could be unrolled along its side. Props and luggage could conveniently be stowed in it. But where did it hold the six to eight actors? Earlier vehicles have been forgotten, but journeys in them remain vivid, such as driving by night over the newly completed Teton Pass. Still earlier journeys over the same country, probably in winter, involved both car and train. Venice writes,

> We put our car in storage for two weeks at Lava Hot Springs, Idaho, and took the train up into Driggs and Victor, Idaho. The "Teton Pass," joining Wyoming and Idaho had not been built yet and this was a beautiful, lonely remote country on the Idaho side. We advertised at both places and played at Victor. We had a good turnout and afterwards they had a dance in our honor. When we left some of the young men on horseback raced the train until we outdistanced them.

The last season began with a new symbol of prosperity. The transportation was luxurious—a new 1938 Dodge, bright red, and a newly-built house trailer, bright red to match. Still, hardships did not end with a trailer and new car. The first night on the road a wheel came off the trailer, which settled to the road with sufficient balance that at least one of its sleeping occupants did not awaken. Before the first week was over, car and trailer were stuck fast on a Uinta Mountain road while rain washed over everything. Almost reconciled to spending the night where they were (provided the road did not become a river and move them itself), the company was happily overtaken by a truckload of about twenty men from the Civilian Conservation Corps who formed ranks on either side of the marooned car and pushed it forward to more solid ground. Then the travelers were told that they had the choice of more muddy road where they would undoubtedly be stuck again or a circuitous mountain dugway descending in hairpin curves to more open country. The latter seemed the only choice, but Johnny insisted on taking the curves with the car door open, determined to leave the car should it leave the road. "This time," he says, referring to the beginning of the tour, "was the only time we left in style."

"Once we came home in style, too," adds Doraine. "One night we came home pushing the car as we came around the point of Parley's Canyon into sight of the city." No doubt that night they felt the same relief as had the Mormon pioneers overlooking the same area from a nearby spot many years before.

Memories such as these among a close-knit family and their friends are surely a large part of the "experience that they will always cherish," as are many other memories of the plays themselves. There is the time when Uncle Den was playing the part of a man on the verge of suicide in *It Pays To Advertise* and was caught at the climactic moment by the cry of "Daddy!" from his youngest child in the audience; or the times when children on the front row begged the villain not to foreclose in *Whittlin'*; or the time in the same play when young John, acting the part of the old man asleep at the opening curtain, was found truly asleep, and later realistically cut his finger "whittlin' " and was forced to suck it until the act ended; or the time that the danger of the collapse of their romantic love seat in another performance threatened to distract the lovers into completely forgetting their ardor; or the time when the stage in a town west of Ogden was so narrow that when the title character stooped over in the stage business of *The Mender*, he knocked down the set; or the night that the college boy hero, demonstrating to his girlfriend a golf drive, hit the single light globe hanging down to illuminate the stage in a church basement and "sparks flew—people screamed and all went pitch black . . . [and Uncle Den] in his most soothing manner assured them everything was all right and the show would go on." And it did go on, illuminated by a spotlight from a nearby garage. Then there is the time at Gray's Lake, Idaho, when the troupe learned that the community assembled only on Sunday from their scattered farms and ranches and that if there was to be a play it had better be between Sunday School and Sacrament Meeting *in* the church house, and then sure retribution for desecrating the Sabbath appeared, or at least arrived, in the form of an activated skunk under the stage.

All of these experiences and many more crowd the memories of the Farnsworth Players and their children. Like the strolling Italian players when belles-lettres were dormant during the Dark Ages, or like the Elizabethan acting companies which fled from London during the plague, this little troupe toured the mountain and desert villages of the Great Basin because Uncle Den loved acting and adventure more than he did security.

Frank C. Robertson

How to Grow a Legend

All childhood is a legend. Realities are a myth, and myths are realities. As a child I lived in a sort of dream world. My parents lived in the big timber of northern Idaho, and, having no playmates of my own age, I had to fall back on fantasy.

I was eight years old, and the Spanish-American War was on. Though I hadn't been to school I could read the newspapers, the *St. Louis Republic* and the *Spokane Spokesman Review*, and I "remembered the Maine" every day. The timber became Cuban jungles and I commanded the armies of liberation, except sometimes when white clouds floated across the sky I lay on my back and they became battleships of which I was the admiral.

My life changed abruptly when some Mormon elders came into our community and found my parents' sheaves ready and waiting for the sickle. The elders had a song which began, as I remember, "We are the fishers and the hunters; Jeremiah said should come . . . ."

Overnight I became a mighty hunter and fisher for the souls of men. Although my Gladstone missionary bag consisted of nothing more than the iron gooseneck from the end of an old wagon tongue with a leather shoelace for a handle, I toured the woods as diligently as Peter did the Sea of Galilee, saving countless thousands of sinners from utter damnation. The tree stumps were my pulpit, and chattering pine-squirrels and magpies my only audience; it was easy for my imagination to transform them into eager searchers after truth—and that was a commodity I had in abundance.

One missionary in particular, Elder Henry W. Talbot of Lewiston, Utah, took note of my zeal and conviction. There had been talk that the Mormon elders were going to be tarred and feathered unless they left the country. But word spread that two-hundred-pound Elder Talbot was a pugilist who had been imported for mob-fighting purposes, and peace prevailed.

There were rumors among the small fry that Mormons had horns, and I thought that if any of them possessed such weapons Elder Talbot should have them. One day I asked, "Elder Talbot, where are your horns?"

"Why, my boy, I left them home," he replied. He ran a huge hand over my head and clucked solemnly, "I'm worried for fear you are already too old to sprout a pair. You had better get baptized and see if you can't get them started. You'll feel lonesome when you get to Zion and find that you are the only Mormon lad without horns." Another elder added, "If you don't have horns you may never see one of the Three Nephites."

I was already familiar with that legend, that the Three Nephites, along with St. John the Revelator, would never die, and as they roamed the earth one might encounter them anywhere—if one were worthy and happened to need help. I knew that they might appear out of thin air and disappear the same way.

I was eager to see one of them, but that horn business bothered me. My mother told me that the elders were only joking and that no Mormons had horns, and it eased my worries on that score, though she wouldn't commit herself about the Three Nephites and warned me not to expect a visitation. Since there were millions of other people, I didn't count on being a favored one. However, after reaching Zion I met a boy some years younger than myself to whom one of the Nephites had appeared to help him catch a recalcitrant mule, and my hopes rose again.

Faith in miracles died slowly and I was able to scoff when I first heard the legend of Paul Bunyan and his great blue ox, but I still find myself wondering whether, if the Three Nephites had appeared to me, they would have been wearing long white robes or Prince Albert coats and derby hats like my heroic elders wore.

I no longer believe in legends except for the very young, but for them they are wonderful—and harmless. I am sure that if legends are not told to them they will invent legends of their own.

Every family should have at least one legend. Mine comes from those wondrous days when young Mormon elders were like gods descended from Mt. Olympus. Once I read about four young missionaries who were mobbed down South. Two of them were killed, and the other two narrowly escaped with their lives. The late, great Mormon historian, Brigham H. Roberts, risked his life to rescue the living and bring out the bodies of the dead. That, too, has become a legend—a true one.

Years after that happened I met one of the two survivors on the Idaho range and found him to be just another sheepherder like myself. I neither knew nor cared what kind of sheepherder he was, but I shall always remember him as part of the folklore that made my boyhood worth living.

Karl E. Young

Why Mormons Were Said To Wear Horns

I remember how frustrated I was as a boy whenever I heard the oft repeated rumor that "Gentiles" all believed Mormons wore horns. The most maddening aspect of this calumny was that it provided not the faintest glimmer of reason for its existence. Usually, I felt, a person could find at least one fact, however frail, upon which a charge might be founded. But no one I ever questioned could suggest how the rumor might have been started. Perhaps I should have decided, like Lincoln, that there are some fleas a dog can't reach. But the problem continued to plague me. The only conclusion I could reach was that this obloquy must have sprung from sheer malice.

Naturally, it was a great relief when, years later while I was in graduate school, the solution suddenly occurred to me. In my studies in medieval and Elizabethan literature I had frequently run across the term *cuckold*. A cuckold was, of course, a man whose wife was unfaithful to him. Explanatory notes in the texts usually mentioned that the word was probably a corruption of *cuckoo*, a bird which lays its eggs in other birds' nests and thus lets some innocent bird take on the duties of rearing its offspring. I also discovered that familiarity with the lore attached to *cuckoldry* was so commonplace that men were supposed to be annoyed at hearing the song of the cuckoo in the spring. One detail of the tradition fascinated and puzzled me: the man cuckolded was supposed to sprout horns.

The more I read in the field, the more frequently I found reference to the tradition. For example, even in that most intense of tragedies, *Othello*, one exceedingly important link in the chain of circumstantial evidence which

Othello accepts so unquestioningly is taken straight from the materials of their folk tradition. When Othello taps himself on the temple and says to Desdemona, "I have a pain upon my forehead here," he is actually accusing her of making a cuckold of him, for, he intimates, he is beginning to sprout horns. Of course, Desdemona, who is wholly innocent, fails to catch the innuendo and hence does not blush or give herself away as Othello had expected her to. In frustration at being thwarted in his little attempt to trap her into a confession, Othello gives her a rude push and so startles her that she drops her handkerchief without noticing it. The consequent disastrous results are familiar to all of us.

I still pondered the horns. Perhaps in the popular mind of the Middle Ages, any man whose wife gave her favors indiscriminately was looked upon as transforming her husband into a creature no better than a beast of the field—a bull, for example.

Then the light dawned on me. If Mormons had a number of wives, would not cynical non-Mormons expect that at least one of the wives would be unfaithful to her husband and make a cuckold of him, thus bestowing upon him a pair of horns? My belief that this explanation must account for the traditional charge gains some support from my boyhood memory of the epithet which adolescents sometimes used to identify girls who were loose in their morals. The word was "horny," surely a derivative of the tradition of cuckoldry.

Claire Noall

Woman-heart is Many Voiced

As I watch two candles burning in the polished brass holders that my grandmother brought to Utah from the Isle of Jersey in 1854, I hear the song of her heart; I hear the song of her mother's heart. The base of one of the candlesticks has been welded to the stem. The lead does not match the original metal, but it serves its purpose.

Up-borne from the room's darkness the points of flame summon the multiple voices of women who helped to colonize the streams that veined the far reaches of the Great Basin desert. Along these thin lines of fertile green, women settlers rose above their hardships by conjoining the sometimes bitter realities and the mystical events which leavened their lives. The welding of seemingly miraculous occurrences with practical incidents served as a vehicle to carry the women over their rough road. Yet there were times when even this quality failed.

The stories were told from community to community. One woman's mystical experience might become a population's solder to fuse the spiritual essence of life with the down-to-earth trials of daily existence. The seldom-doubted religious stories were readily absorbed. The Mormons teach that miraculous events would appear natural if mortals could but understand the working of God's laws. Church doctrine does not support the term *supernatural.*

Mormon women had to approach the day's work on a practical level. But within their realism lay an abiding faith that the Saints of Zion existed within the special sight and care of God. For instance, Augusta Dorius Stevens—"Aunt Gustie" to friends and relatives—endured the trials of the West with this in

mind. At the age of fourteen, she left her family in Copenhagen to come to
Utah. On the plains she met thunder, lightning and flood such as she had never
seen at home. A buffalo stampede excited the oxen and cattle of the wagon
train almost beyond control. The Indian raids terrified her. She could speak no
English. She felt terribly isolated from her friends. She looked to God for comfort. Gustie later wrote in her memoirs that "Heavenly Father was mindful of
the needs and protection of his Saints."[1]

In this concrete expression of faith we see the ensign to her ever-present
mystical belief. As she traveled she began to fear that her elderly parents could
never survive such experiences. She prayed constantly for them, and felt that
God had indeed been mindful of all of them when later they arrived in Utah
with her brothers. She became so proficient in English that she was officially
appointed interpreter for the Sanpete Scandinavians. And thus she earned her
pay in kind for the first clothing she received in the new land.

Gustie served for a year in Salt Lake City as a domestic, refusing several
offers of marriage, for she considered herself too young. Then, at age sixteen,
she accepted Henry Stevens of Sanpete. He was thirty-eight years old. She
wrote "[He] was a good man . . . . I became his second wife . . . . We made a
trip to Salt Lake City and were married in the endowment house. There was
little, if any, courtship in my marriage. . . . His first wife proved to be a good
kind mother to me. She was not a strong woman . . . and after we had lived
together for ten years, part of the time in Ephraim, part in Spring Town [four
miles north of Manti] , she died from pneumonia."[2]

Two years before this, Gustie and Henry had moved to Southern Utah for
his health. She writes that the first wife was buried in Ephraim before she and
Henry had received news of her death. Gustie took the four sons left by their
mother into her home and heart.

On the Virgin River she faced the usual trials of that area: flood, famine,
lack of clothing, and ceaseless work, such as picking cotton boles and seed,
spinning, dyeing, weaving, cutting and tailoring her husband's clothes. The
daily toil was altogether incidental to the deaths of several of her children. She
experienced childbirth with flood waters pouring onto her bed through the
mud roof of the cabin. Moreover, her husband's incurable asthma was no better
in the heat and drought of Dixie than in the snows of the north.

Nevertheless, she continued to look to the Lord for comfort, as she had
done on the plains and on the divide above the Sanpete valley. There she had

seen the mutilated bodies of four Mormon men, killed by the Indians in "Chief Walker's War." Their wagons had been overturned. The wheat not stolen had been scattered over the ground, together with whatever belongings remained on the scene.

Upon her return to Ephraim Gustie became a midwife. With her husband an invalid, she largely supported the family on her income. Her practice brought from $2.50 to $5.00 a case in the homes where she stayed until both mother and child no longer required "special care." But her life had become glorified through her handling of the newborn. Her niece, Mrs. La Verne Stallings, describes her aunt as a pioneer who believed that the choice for mortal fulfillment is made in the premortal existence. Gustie's faith in God never faltered. She spent her life in praise of the Lord, not in complaining about her hardships. At eighty-two years of age—proud to have been a colonizer for the Church—she enjoyed dancing and singing with friends and relatives.

Through the flames of my candlesticks I hear a chorus keyed to the mystical experiences that tempered the fierce winds of the pioneer life in other areas. All mothers shrank from the possibility of abnormal childbirth, and disease, hunger, and death for their children. Mary Ann Swenson, an Idaho midwife of Dutch origin, expressed the fear in its extreme form. "When the Angel of Death appeared," she told her daughter, Mrs. Inez Allen, "he always seemed to take unto himself the most talented, the most beautiful, and the most beloved of the children."[3]

Mary Ann firmly believed that the laying on of hands had saved her young son from peritonitis. He was dying when the patriarch of her stake said, "At this moment there is an angel administering life unto you. You will live to enjoy a life of usefulness." And at that very instant the midwife saw a light over the boy's bed. She bore testimony to this mystical experience, as she later did to a visit from one of the Three Nephites. Mrs. Allen said, "Mother was up after having a baby when he came . . . dressed in white overalls, and everything about him was just as clean and neat as a pin. He said, 'God bless you, woman!' He was going to go, but Mother said, 'Won't you . . . have something to eat?' . . . 'Well, since you insist, I will have some bread and milk.' After he ate . . . he disappeared just as mysteriously as he had come. It was a little town. Everybody could see what everyone else was doing, but no one saw him go, except Mother and the children with her. She went into the house and there was the bowl just as he had left it. She never forgot his words. I think they helped her to stay alive."[4]

In opposition to the good influences to which the Mormons responded so eagerly, they had also to contend with many an evil spirit. The Church defines such a spirit as one who can assume the body of a man but who can himself never possess a mortal body.[5] Therefore, how could one deal with such an amorphous being except through the power of the holy priesthood? In 1935 I heard a conversation between my mother (Elizabeth Stevenson Wilcox, then in her seventies) and Mrs. Nancy Smith, a long-time resident of St. George. "Oh yes," Mrs. Smith replied to my mother's question: Had she ever heard of the Gadianton Robbers molesting the people of Southern Utah? "Our men tell us how they ride up and down at night in the canyons of St. George and prey upon the folks. They cast spells and cause death and accidents. A horse will run away. A cow will kick over the milk . . . . The robbers . . ."

My ear quickened. I jotted down her words and later I read the Book of Mormon references to the robbers. The folk belief, as well as the Scripture, supports their presence on earth.

> And . . . those murderers and plunderers were a band who had been formed by Kishkumen and Gadianton. . . . And they were called Gadianton's robbers and murderers.
>
> And it came to pass that the wicked part of the people began again to build up the secret oaths and combinations of Gadianton. . . . And . . . that the robbers of Gadianton did spread over all the face of the land . . . .[6]

My mother drew immeasurable comfort from her personal experiences with the mystical side of life. One of these was hearing the "heavenly music" at the dedication of the Manti Temple, May 31, 1888. Since her marriage, December 25, 1884, she had been teaching in the Fourteenth Ward School, where my father was principal. She had borne two children during these years and she and Father were skimping to the last penny for their journey to New York, where he would study medicine. Mother had sacrificed to save the necessary funds. Still, poor as they were, she longed to attend the dedication. She remarked when telling me the story, "Papa knew how I also longed to see Sister Helena and Sister Maria. They had been so good to me in Gunnison." Before her marriage she had taught in this town, only a few miles from Manti, and she had lived in the home of Bishop Madsen and his two wives. With an air of pride she told me how my father had encouraged her. "Of course you must go," he had said, and her eyes shone as she recalled the words.

In his book *The House of the Lord*, Dr. James E. Talmage has described the morning of the dedication.[7] The thunder and rain of the night before had given way to a clear morning. The sun was bright. The quarry-whitened hill was dark with horses, buggies, and wagons. Cattle were lowing, sheep bleating. Above the quarry the wild shrubs had leafed, and beyond the square of the oolite masonry the towers of the Lord's house reached toward the heavens.

At the appointed hour more than twice as many people as could be accommodated in the assembly rooms arrived on the hill. The ceremonies had to be repeated the next day, but, to be sure, Bishop Christian August Madsen and his party were admitted to the original rites. The temple was charming with Old World craftsmanship: light-colored, intricately carved woodwork of lecterns, choir stalls, gallery railings, and spiral staircases. The opening music, the Mendelssohn Voluntary, must have lifted my mother's heart. "I was one of those," she said, "who heard the music of the heavenly choir during the dedication."

As we visited together, I looked up in amazement. True, with her first earnings in Gunnison she had bought a Mason and Hamlin organ. She had sung in the Tabernacle and the ward choirs. She sang alto to Father's tenor when friends and family gathered about the organ in their home. She was a practical woman of good common sense, and the statement took me by surprise. I had never before heard of this "celestial music." Raptly, she said, "It sounded like the voice of angels from above our heads and over our shoulders. It surely came from some ethereal distance. After the ceremonies several people spoke to me about hearing the music."

As I now see her story, it demonstrated not only her faith in the intuitive, mystical side of life, but also the love that united men and women as brothers and sisters, and which made of many voices one chorus. As we toasted ourselves at the sitting room hearth, I could not help sensing the mitigating influence for her in the experience. Extremely hypersensitive in nature, she suffered both physical and mental pain over the trials and tragedies of her workaday life. But in moments like this they faded and were offset by the importance, peace and beauty of the mystical event which moved her.

My mother's tone and expression were equally rapt when she continued our visit with a story of *tongues*. Devoutly acceptant, she said, "Aunt Zina [a term commonly used in reference to Zina D. H. Young, wife of Brigham Young] had risen to address a group of sisters in a private home. She began to speak in the usual manner. But suddenly no one could understand her except the sister who acted as interpreter. She said Aunt Zina was speaking in tongues, and that she was using the Adamic language."

Once more my incredulity cropped up. I did not ask what had been said. But I suppose this was of small importance in comparison with the spiritual communion that took place among speaker, interpreter, and the sisters in that room, for again my mother had demonstrated the faith that could heal the ache of the heart. And even though she was at the time young and unenlightened, I found in her account the soul-satisfaction that characterizes the Church today in regard to the mystical experience. Still, her stories pale in the light that influenced her mother's life.

Again a glance over the shoulder reveals the beginning of Elizabeth Jane Du Fresne Stevenson's story: During the French Revolution, Grandmother's grandmother, Esther Renouf, made her customary journey from her home in the island of Jersey to Normandy. She stopped in Coutances on her annual shopping tour. All about her was the destruction of the cathedrals and the uproar of the revolutionaries. Sympathetic to law and order, she carried a basket of food to the prison, where she met Philip Du Fresne, a young aristocrat. He was twenty years old. She was forty. When telling me the story my mother declared that it was a case of love at first sight between them. Legend has it that she helped him to escape. At any rate, as a matter of fact they were married, and they returned to her home in St. Helier, the harbor city on the southwest coast of Jersey.

Though she had worldly means, he learned a trade and set up a booterie in St. Helier. Here he made and sold fine shoes and slippers for women and children. As a matter of background, the *Jersias* were mostly plain folk. Largely bilingual, they were loyal to the French monarchy, even though subject to England.

Strangely, the women of the Channel Isles were allowed to retain in their own names whatever means or inheritance they possessed or received. The privilege appears still more astonishing when one realizes that only since 1967 has this state of affairs been true in France. The couple had three children. Esther then found herself the elderly widow of a young man.

Her son, Philip II, married Mary Remon, my grandmother's mother, as independent in spirit as in means. She and Philip II had eight children. Two sons died at sea, captains of their own ships. Another died in infancy. The fate of the fourth was unknown to my mother. The family resided in a large stone house above the harbor, where the son carried on the father's trade. Fuchsias grew to the eaves, ivy covered the wet stone walls. In Elizabeth Du Fresne's day the family were Methodists, but they probably absorbed the highly mystical lore of the island. The land was tightly enclosed by an ocean which in certain seasons washed the north coast with thirty-foot waves, crashing out dark caves of mysterious light. The narrow roads formed aisles in cathedrals of green forest, whose depths exuded their own gothic mystery. Two prehistoric cromlechs inspired a web of fantasy. The people generally believed that the granite monoliths could have been fetched to their location, placed on end, and capped by nothing less than daemonic spirits of supernatural strength.[8]

In 1850, when Elizabeth Du Fresne was twelve years old, she walked with her three sisters and her parents down the stone steps from the manor to the sea. John Taylor, who had converted them, baptized the group into the Mormon Church. He promised Mary Remon Du Fresne that if she would contribute a substantial sum to the Perpetual Emigration Fund the money would be returned to her in Salt Lake City. "A loan," he said, and she took him at his word, as she did in his denial of polygamy. Wild rumors were then flying from England to the continent; however, the Church made no official announcement in Europe of the practice until 1853. Mary believed the apostle. She started for Utah in all innocence. Her husband and one daughter had preceded her by one year in order to establish the family home.

Mary and daughter Elizabeth arrived in Salt Lake City on October 24, 1854. They had buried two of the four sisters on the plains. The two girls had contracted cholera from contaminated water as they traveled by ship up the Missouri River to Kanesville. In Salt Lake City, Mary and Elizabeth received no welcome from Philip II or daughter Ann. She had married in polygamy and had quite lost her peace of mind in tragic unhappiness. Philip II had been assigned to take charge of a molasses mill in Southern Utah, and had been asked to take a second wife. Desperately unhappy herself, Mary went to Brigham Young to request the return of her money so that she could build a home. He told her that her contribution was a gift. No money could be returned until the fund itself had accumulated the means. She soon learned that the revolving account was top-heavy with unpaid debts that would probably never be extinguished. No spiritual comfort could offset the hard facts of her arrival in Zion. She frankly told Brigham Young that her proud Norman blood would brook no such treatment, and back to her island home she went.

In better days missionaries traveling between England and France had frequently stayed overnight at the manor. Meetings and conferences had been held in the large home. In Jersey the Du Fresnes had been Church leaders. But never again did Mary hear the voices of elders, husband, or children in her house.

Young Elizabeth was sixteen years old when she chose to stay in Utah.

She found a home with Nancy Stevenson, whose husband was on a mission in Gibraltar. But now in order to see the incandescence of the belief which shaped her life we should take a look at Edward Stevenson's story: He was born in Gibraltar May 1, 1820, the son of an English cooper assigned to the colony to supervise the building of powder kegs for the British Navy. But he too was a man of spirit. He made a bass viol, which he played in the Methodist Church of the fortress. He looked at his five sons and desired to increase their opportunities to earn a livelihood. In 1828 he emigrated to America, where he bought a 240-acre farm in Pontiac, Michigan, on the shore of Silver Lake. But in 1832 he died and twelve-year-old Edward, the fourth of his five sons, was apprenticed to a doctor across the lake.

At 3:00 a.m., November 13, 1833, after returning from his work for the doctor, Edward was standing beside the water. Suddenly he was amazed by the great fall of the Leonids. In his old age he wrote in his memoirs that it was "a sublime scene . . . the whole starry heavens in commotion . . . shooting this way . . . that way . . . in a fiery stream . . . nearly into the silvery lake."[9] In 1832 he had heard two Mormon missionaries speak in Pontiac. Though favorably impressed, he had not asked for baptism. But after witnessing those fiery streams of light in the heavens, and after seeing the "gifts follow those who had believed" the missionaries, a dream prompted him to enter the water. On December 20, 1833, he was baptized in Silver Lake. The following January he rejoiced in a blessing from Joseph Smith, the patriarch, who with his wife was visiting her brother in this town. Enormously impressed by the occult, Edward named in his memoirs four friends who spoke in tongues during the patriarch's visit to Pontiac: Elijah Fordham, Mary Curtis, Mary Brent (who was only twelve years old, just younger than Edward), and Joseph Wood. Of these experiences, Edward wrote:

> The power of the priesthood rested mightily upon Father Smith. It appeared as though the veil which separated us from the eternal world became so thin that heaven itself was right in our midst. It was at one of these meetings . . . I received my patriarchal blessing under the hands of Father Smith.

> [He] laid hands on me, and said that I . . . was one of the sons of Jacob through the loins of Ephraim, and one of the horns spoken of [cf. Deut., 33:13-17], and that I should do so [as Joseph of Israel had done with the horns of the unicorns] by pushing the people together . . . .[10]

In October 1834, when the prophet himself dined at the Stevenson home, the family felt both proud and humble to entertain him. Edward's elder brothers doubted his testimony that he had seen and heard God the Father and his son Jesus Christ. Nor did his blessings impress them. But when Joseph laid his hands on Edward's head the young man became unalterably convinced that of his father's boys he was the spiritual heir, the birthright son and bearer of the seal. The meteor fall he had witnessed the year before now impressed him even more than when he had seen it. From Joseph he heard how this heavenly display had turned back the mob from pursuing the hapless Mormons across the Missouri River. The Saints had been driven from their homes to the autumn woods, and their pursuers were armed with guns and bowie knives, intent upon the lives of the banished. The psychic bond young Edward now felt with Joseph so supported his faith that he could walk hundreds of miles on his religious missions and travel without purse or scrip, strong in his belief that the Lord would never forsake him.

His understanding of the mysterious gift of the Holy Ghost supported him when he was a Captain of Ten in the second 1847 pioneer trek to Utah. He was a very young man, but he was convinced that he was "pushing the people together," for so he wrote in his journal. In April 1845 he had married Nancy Porter. In 1852, on one of the nine or ten missions he filled for the Church, he left for Gibraltar. In April 1853 Nancy joyously described for him their healthy 9½-month-old baby girl, who was running about. Two weeks later she wrote to Edward, telling him the child was dead.[11]

After her mother left for Jersey in 1854, Elizabeth Du Fresne went into Nancy's home as a helper. There she must have heard of the mystical experiences which guided Edward's life. When gazing at his photograph she shared his pride in his refusal of his elder brothers' offer to educate him handsomely if he would renounce his new religion and return to Michigan. As she studied his eyes an intuition took possession of her heart.

On September 11, 1855, he walked up the path to his home, bearing in his spiritual portfolio his most recent miraculous experience: He had been the only one of three elders allowed to remain in the fortress of Gibraltar. Because of his origin the government had not banished him; but now he had been ordered to leave, and he was entirely without funds. A woman in Portugal, having heard of his success in curing a man in Gibraltar through the laying on of hands, wrote to beg him to come to Lisbon to bless her daughter. She sent funds for the journey—to Edward a gift from heaven. In Lisbon he blessed the daughter, and according to his record she began immediately to improve in health. With the money he had received in the letter he was able to proceed to Liverpool, where the means to return to Salt Lake City were provided. As he walked up the path to his home on the corner of First South and First West, sixteen-year-old Elizabeth was waiting in the doorway with Nancy and the children.

My mother said that Elizabeth had deeply luminous brown eyes and rich dark hair. Secretly she felt that God had told her Edward—then thirty-five years old—would become her husband. Six weeks later, on October 28, he married her in the Endowment House. She lived with Nancy for many years, until he built her a two-story home on the same corner. In 1869 Nancy obtained a temple divorce, saying Elizabeth had come between her and Edward. But in a letter to Brigham Young, Edward denied the charge. He listed facts of time, attention, and money that he had spent on Nancy—besides, he had taken a third wife in April 1857.[12]

Elizabeth accepted her as she later received the fourth wife. But apparently Nancy found no spiritual comfort great enough to dispel her emotional problems, unless perhaps it was her work in the Logan Temple during her last years. She had married in polygamy Edward's brother-in-law. But she finally went to the temple to serve as a "priestess." Her beauty lost nothing to the white clothing she wore. A picture seems to symbolize the spiritual purification she must have gained.

When Elizabeth was thirty-eight years old she jotted down some notes which reveal her ardent nature and her high-spirited pleasure.[13]

> April 19, 1876. Brother Jensen's folks all came after the afternoon meeting took Supper with us and staid the evening. We had a pleasant time. Monday wash day in the evening went to a surprise on Sister M T Gibbs had a lovely time, tuesday worked all morning then went to a Surprise on Sis Marth Cannon at the Farm—had a grand time & a banquet. Wensday went to the Temple Came home ironed then at night went to hear F Carpenter—at the Theatre. thursday to the Temple went through for one, home ironed. friday went to . . . meeting attended to my duty and home backed a bach of bread half a dozen pies prepared Supper—went to a two o'clock weding diner at the Temple in honor of Brother W. Woodruff being married to a Swedish woman. I wated on her in the morning seems a nice woman had the grandest kind of a time President Snow was so jovial & so were all the rest leaving the Temple at 20 minutes to four we went right up to Dr. E. R. Shipps by invitation . . . that I was delighted to see her lovely home does not half express it we again had a lovely time. [Here time passes. The next entry is:] 8 October. went over to the kindergarden party with my husband danced with the Bishop had a grand time. Saturday got my husband off on the 7 train [for a mission to former Church centers: Kirtland, Independence, Richmond, Missouri, etc.].

Elizabeth had that March lost a baby the day he was born; still her enjoyment in her activities is plain. It seems that she offset her intense sorrow over the deaths of five of the seven children she had borne through the sublimation of her faith and her husband's influence. With my mother—"the first fruit of polygamy" in this family—I found the tiny white marble headstones nestled against the grass of the city cemetery. They were carved with the names: Mary, James, George, Samuel, and Brigham—who had died the day he was born— mute reminders of human heartbreak and pioneer tragedy. For the mystery behind the deaths of her children Elizabeth apparently did not probe.

In Richmond, during the intense excitement of his visit, Edward hastily jotted down some notes which he later used in his memoirs and which seem to have provided some of the source material encountered in connection with the story of the fate of the golden plates after they left Joseph's hands. I here offer some excerpts verbatim, which, like Elizabeth's notes, are to be savored with the eye as well as the ear:

W. B. Hudgins Hotel
Richmond   Ray, Mo.

1877 Dec 22nd—Sat . . . After breakfast we [Edward and his companion] took a walk to see David Whitmer Who will be 73 in Jan next, he had a Son David I. born in Liberty Clay Co Mo. in 1833, was invited to take breakfast and [was] treated very courteous & was Shown the origenal Manuscript of the Book of Mormon Written By Martin Harris oliver Cowdry, Emma Smith & Christian Whitmer—it is foolscap & about 2 or 2 1/2 inches thick, as Sister Z. D. Young [Aunt Zina] wished me to ask David about one of the Nephites [David related:] Oliver Cowdry & myself was driveing along   Joseph the Pro.[phet] was rideing Behind. An Elderly Gentleman about 4 feet 10 in. [tall] Stout-built, with an old armey knapsack Straps over the shoulder & Seemed to have A Square box was going [ahead] over to the hill Cumorah. They [David and Oliver] soon looked around [about] and Could See no one. Which caused them to feel very Strange and they asked the Lord & Received that it was one of the Nephites & [he] had the Plates & [the Lord] Said that Joseph was Writer. it was said that Person was very Pleasant and Kind on arriveing at home uncle david said that it was made manifest to him that this Same Person was under the Shead [shed] & Joseph Enquired & it was So & in the morning Davids mother Saw him and he Showed her the plates and turned them over & She felt them & [said] that a Portion that held together & would not open were fastned on Rings like this . . . . So that in opening them they would Pass from the Square around . . . .[14]

Edward drew a picture of the book with the rings.

A man of his persuasion could do no less than to rely upon the Lord to comfort his wife in her bereavements. Yet when the Manifesto was pronounced and Edward had to choose an official wife, he selected Emily, the third wife, who was capable of bearing more children and who had already given him several sons who needed their father's companionship and guidance.

In addition to my mother, two of Elizabeth's children grew to maturity.

But, indeed, upon the death of her last born the high-spirited light left her eyes. Moroni Charles died at the age of twenty years, soon after his return from his mission to Germany. Appendicitis took him, and with his death she entered a world of sorrow, but she remained on the General Board and active in her other church work. During her seeming widowhood I occasionally stayed overnight with her. I remember sitting in the lamplight of her sitting room almost without conversation. Occasionally she would look up from her reading and I would hear a sigh as from the depths of the earth, reflecting her suffering—her lostness. Yet she was always kind to me. After we had knelt together in prayer, she would take me upstairs, tuck me into a high bed with a feather mattress and kiss me good night; then to comfort me in my aloneness she would place a kerosene lamp at the head of the long straight stairway.

As I look back, it seems that though a kind of mystical sorrow took the place of the joy she had once known, she stayed true to the light that had led her from Jersey to Utah, that had helped her to remain in the valley of hope, and that had named her husband; it had lessened her toil and suffering. And for her, as for the women of the valley as a whole, the spirit of their faith became a paean to God's holy presence in their lives. Through it the women found the strength to meet disaster and overcome sorrow. That mourning at times had its way should not surprise us. Nor that shock occasionally became dominant.

In my darkened room the flames of Mary Remon Du Fresne's candles illumine both the lament and the strength. And down the valleys of the Great Basin, the voices of the pioneer women still echo the holy conjoining of their sufferings and their triumphs.

NOTES

1. Typescript, "Autobiography of Augusta Dorius Stevens (Record assembled by my nephew R. E. Dorius) [as compiled to June 16, 1922]" p. 5; courtesy Mrs. La Verne J. Stallings, Mrs. Dorius' niece, Salt Lake City, Utah.

2. Ibid., pp. 10, 11.

3. Mrs. Inez (Frank Merrill) Allen, Salt Lake City, as reported in an interview February 1944 for Claire Noall, "Superstitions, Customs, and Prescriptions of Mormon Midwives," *California Folklore Quarterly* 3, no. 2 (April 1944).

4. Ibid.

5. Interview with Dr. T. A. Clawson, Jr., Salt Lake City physician, 1964.

6. Helaman, 6:18; 4 Nephi, 1:42, 46.

7. See James E. Talmage, *House of the Lord* (Salt Lake City, Utah, 1912), as reported in the *Deseret News*, 1912, p. 232.

8. John H. L'Amy, *Jersey Folklore* (first published 1927, J. T. Bigwood, State's Printer, 13 Broad Street, Jersey), Introduction, pp. 13, 14.

9. Edited and published by Joseph Grant Stevenson, *Stevenson Family History*, vol. 1, 2d ed. (Provo, Utah), 1955, pp. 26, 16; cf. Edward Stevenson, "Incidents of My Early Days in the Church," *Juvenile Instructor* 29 (September 1, 1894): 551-52.

10. Ibid., p. 29.

11. Nancy's original letters are in the Claire Noall historical collection.

12. *Stevenson Family History*, pp. 232-33.

13. She used a strip from the brown cover of a ledger and two sheets from the same book, cut to match the strip, some 4 1/2 inches wide. Later she kept a more regular journal, but at this time she was teacher, traveler, temple worker, member of the General Board of the Relief Society, besides being a meticulous housekeeper. These notes are in the Claire Noall collection. I have quoted her verbatim, spacing to indicate inferred punctuation.

14. Notebook, Claire Noall collection.

Rosabel Ashton

A Strange Gift

When I was four years old, my parents noticed that I possessed an unusual gift. If anything of importance occurred in our family life, I dreamed of it in advance. Before people who were known to Father and Mother, but strange to me, came to our home, I would have previously seen them so distinctly in a dream that my parents would recognize them from my description and prepare for their coming. People learned to heed my warnings when Indians were on the warpath. I would dream of seeing them and hear their whoops as plainly as if I had been awake. One summer morning, early, I awakened from one of those frightful dreams and sprang from bed and ran out of the house screaming, "Papa, the Indians are coming. They are right here with their bows and their arrows!"

A neighbor heard my cries and ran over to our home to learn what was the matter. He found me on the ditch bank, going upstream in search of Father, who had gone to turn the water down to irrigate his garden. I told this man why I was crying, and he picked me up in his arms and ran up the ditch bank to find Father. Before we had gone far, we could look across the valley and see the Indians on the march toward our small village.

In a dream, I saw Chauncey West on his big white horse, and told my parents how he was dressed in full military uniform, and how his horse reared and pranced. About eleven o'clock of the same day he came to organize the men into a battalion. The Indians were giving so much trouble it was decided that every man would have to train and serve in the militia. Father had been an officer under General West in the Echo Canyon campaign and his services were required.

One morning Mother overheard me telling Father about an old peddler woman she had known in Ogden, Utah. I had seen her in a dream, coming up the hill below our home. The old lady drove a span of mares, one with a white face, and a colt was tied to each harness. In the round opening of the covered wagon sat the little old Quaker lady in her sunbonnet, smoking her corncob pipe. Before noon she came, just as I had seen her in my dream. She drove straight to our home and called. Mother went out and was very happy to see her; Father followed and was just as pleased. I had never before seen oranges, and I had told them she would have yellow apples.

I well remember when I was called by an unknown voice for the first time. I was out in the hills picking sego lilies, and I kept going farther and farther from home. The first call sounded like Mother's voice, the next more anxious than the first. The third call was sharp and stern: it caused me to drop my apronful of lilies and turn back and run for home as if a wild animal were pursuing me. It was dark when I reached the house. I asked Mother if she had called me, and she answered, "No, child, but I wondered where you were."

I replied that I had heard someone call my name, and that it sounded like her voice. Then I began to cry. Father looked up and called me to him, then lifted me on his lap, and wiped away my tears. I said, "Papa, I heard someone call me, *three* times."

He asked me to tell him what had happened. Then he said, "Dear little Daughter, don't feel bad; Papa has heard voices, too. Let me tell you a true story. When I was a soldier in the army, fighting for the land where our home now stands, which then belonged to Mexico, I was in great danger of being shot. I heard a voice tell me to drop to the ground; and by doing so, I saved myself from being pierced through the heart with a bullet. It cut through the roll of blankets folded over my left shoulder. On another occasion a voice warned me to fall to the ground. This time I was saved from having my head cut off with a sword. As I dropped, the swordpoint struck my collar bone and made a gash in my shoulder."

My father impressed the fact on my mind so thoroughly that he and others of my ancestors had heard voices that I tried not to be worried after that time.

Then he told me what he believed was the reason for the voice's calling me. The hollow that I had started to cross was infested by wolves and other vicious animals. On the other side the Indians were camped. I was not in the habit of going in that direction to play, and my parents might have searched the hollow too late if I had been lost.

Very early in life I could find lost articles and was called "the little peep-stone girl." I found missing silver thimbles, located animals that had strayed, and told people where to dig for wells. I would go into a dark place, usually a cellar, and sit down and meditate. At first I didn't get a marker, but later I learned to look for a tree or some familiar object to identify the place where the lost article could be found.

I saw my husband in a dream six months before I met him and remembered every detail of his clothing, even to his necktie, and the color and material of his suit.

These experiences have continued all through my life. Doctor Wilder, a cousin of my husband, had corresponded with him, and my husband had often related my unusual experiences to him. He said he had been looking for just such a person. Finally he visited our home and asked if I would make a test with him. I replied that I would but he would need to give me time to prepare for it. We agreed on a date, a month from that time. I knew this was an important piece of work since he was an educator and a scientist. I left off meat and all heavy foods, and put myself in condition to "tune in." He had returned to his home in New Jersey; I lived in Logan, Utah. The day and hour were set, my husband and I retired to our library, and I sat with my head on my arm and concentrated on my task. A half-hour passed, and then a picture came into my mind just as distinctly as if I had stepped through a door. I saw his living room with a big fireplace in it such as I had never seen before. He was seated in a ladder back chair before a table, facing east, while the sun shone in from the south. He sat with pencil and paper as if he expected to write something. He was a man with white hair and beard. The thing that impressed me most was the magazines and papers, which were stacked waist-high and continued along the east wall to a large bookcase full of books. There was a big pile of magazines and books on the floor beside each chair that he used. The carpet was rose and blue, badly worn. Above the mantel hung a picture of Lincoln, and there were old pipes and an hourglass on the shelf.

As I gave this description, my husband wrote it down, then he made a copy and sent it to Doctor Wilder. He wrote back and said the description could not have been more accurate if I had visited him.

I depended greatly upon my husband, who had always recorded these experiences for me. After his death I asked that this gift be taken from me; but I was told that as long as I lived a worthy life, truths would continue to unfold, and I would have dreams of great worth that would be faith promoting for the human family.

Not long after this I visited a planet in a dream. This planet has been inhabited longer than the earth, and conditions there are in advance of those here. I was told that a permanent peace had been established and that all men shared alike.

I did not start to write at first. It seemed too great a task for an old lady to undertake, especially one without education who is not able to spell simple words correctly.

Sleep was taken from me for about two weeks while I failed to do as I was instructed. I would lie awake all night; then toward morning I would doze; the story would be given, and as soon as it was finished, I would awaken. I began to be afraid to go so long without sleep, for its lack was telling on me. But still I failed to record those glorious experiences. I am unable to use a pen because of a stiff hand; but I finally turned to my husband's typewriter and set down, as best I could, the information I received each morning. After my first day's writing, I went to sleep and slept soundly all night. When I awakened, I felt refreshed and like a new woman.

The story of Uranus is read to me from a book of history, in a foreign tongue, and then translated. As the account is given, the scene usually passes before my vision. The language is beautiful, but most of it is lost; I can only give it in my imperfect way. When I rise immediately, the story is vivid in my mind and I am able to record the main events, as well as many of the details. After I have written it in a rough way, I send it to my co-worker to organize and prepare for print. There is material on hand for a number of books.

4

Of Polygamy, Wine-making, and Murder

hree articles are presented in this section, each on a phase of Utah's history. Social experiments, discontinued vocations, homicide and suicide will always interest a wide variety of readers.

Recorded in Mormon history are facts regarding the practice of plural marriage, and its frequency of occurrence. Mormon theology defends it as a good principle in those days when it was advocated and condoned by the church; and the church has never said that it was not right prior to the "Manifesto of 1890" which announced discontinuance of the practice.

Because the custom of a man having many wives has been considered a retreat to barbarism by many modern people, because the social pattern of equality between men and women can not exist with it, and because people have thought of it as a yielding to lust rather than to a divinely inspired sacrament, polygamy has given the church a bad name. Having been an incessant thorn-prick in the side of the Mormon Church even after it was officially discontinued, polygamy has been avoided as a subject for investigation and publication; church historians have written but little to dispel misconceptions or misinterpretations, and that which has been written is too often colored with attempts to present the ideal.

The multitudinous problems of living in polygamy, the family stories, remain the property of the folk; children of polygamous fathers still live in whose memories stories remain. Journals, diaries, family histories contain ample polygamy lore. Here William Mulder presents an account of one such source he has unearthed.

Wine-making as a big industry in Southern Utah has long since been discontinued. Its evils outdistanced its values according to church leaders who saw drunkenness increasing. Joseph Smith had long before presented to the Saints a revelation which condemned strong drink as not good, and proper conduct of church people demanded complete abstinence from imbibing alcoholic beverages. The cluster of stories presented herein from the grapevine (a folk source) have lived in the heart of the writer long enough to ferment—now they burst into print.

"Ditties of Death in Deseret" is the only article in this book treating folk song exclusively. It contains sufficient blood and thunder from Orrin Porter Rockwell, "the Mormon triggerite," and Saturday night liquor-trigger "Shoot-'em-ups" to leave a gory vision in any eye. And these stories are real events interpreted by folk poets.

T.E.C.

William Mulder

Prisoners for Conscience' Sake

When N. P. Madsen came home from prison, Mt. Pleasant turned out the brass band to welcome him. A bishop and polygamist, he had been convicted on a federal charge of "unlawful cohabitation" and sentenced to serve 108 days in the Utah Penitentiary. That was in 1888, when federal marshals, armed with punitive legislation and crusading zeal, swarmed Utah territory to hunt "cohabs." Mt. Pleasant, a stronghold of Scandinavian Mormons, saw many of its cohabs go underground. But spotters, generally apostates, were busy and the arrests were becoming more numerous. Speaking of the general situation, Isaac Sorensen of Mendon noted in 1886 that "so many had went to prison that it seemed as if it had become more popular, and there was not so much excitement when a person was arrested." "A man," he said, "would rather suffer than have his family brought before these courts to testify and often asked indecent questions. To the praise of the Heroes, they stood it in nearly all cases bravely, a few recanted, but their numbers were small." To people of Mt. Pleasant, Madsen was a hero; he had stood his prison test.

The cohabs were "Prisoners for Conscience' Sake." The phrase runs like a refrain through their letters, journals, and memoirs. The Dane Andrew Jensen, himself one of those prisoners for a time, used it for the title of his manuscript list of names of those who had been imprisoned in the Utah, Yuma, and Detroit penitentiaries from 1884 to 1892. Compiled from prison files and private journals, the list of 883 names includes 216, nearly one fourth, that are recognizably Scandinavian, and memorializes the charge, the judge, the fine, and the prison sentence—withal a most curious Book of Martyrs. Ten years ago I was given a furtive look at it in the L.D.S. Church Historian's Office, long enough to make the count and note some names.

One of these "Prisoners for Conscience' Sake" was Mads Christensen, Danish carpenter, who in 1857, at 32 years of age, had joined the Mormons and with his wife Maren Johanne Jensen, crossed the Atlantic that year in the *Westmoreland* and the plains in Christian Christiansen's handcart company. He fled Johnston's Army in the "Move South," then worked his way back from American Fork to Salt Lake City and thence to Farmington; in 1864 he drove a "church team" to the Missouri River for poor emigrants; and from 1883 to 1885 he answered a church call to colonize Arizona. In 1881, at 56, he had "yielded obedience to the higher law of marriage," as his pious biographer puts it, and married Hanna M. Christiansen as his plural wife. Seven years later, in February 1888, he was arrested and convicted of unlawful cohabitation, entering the Utah Penitentiary within a few days after Bishop Madsen had left it so triumphantly, and served seven months. Mads Christensen moved to Idaho in the 1890's to Robin Creek, Marsh Valley, in Bannock County. He became a Patriarch, and died June 14, 1914, at Robin, full of years and honor, and justified of his polygamous marriage: a son of that union, born the year Mads was in prison, was Parley A. Christensen, the beloved "P. A.," the late Professor of English emeritus at Brigham Young University, who acquainted several generations of students with Shakespeare, Milton, and Matthew Arnold, and whose books *All in a Teacher's Day* and *Of a Number of Things* everyone with a stake in the humanities owes it to himself to read.

It was from P. A. that I learned that Mads Christensen, like so many of his fellows, kept an autograph album during his term in prison, a mirror of the sentiments which brought him there and sustained him during his weary months. He began it on February 12, 1888:

> Go litle book thy distined cours pursue,
> Colect memorials of the just and true,
> And call on evry frend, far of, or near,
> For a token of remambrans dear

There are 87 "memorials of the just and true" addressed to Mads by his fellow prisoners, a pretty complete roll call of the Mormon inmates. Transcribed, the entries run to thirteen typescript pages, single spaced, too many to reproduce here. But they afford a rich sampling of humor and irony, of Mormon doctrine and sentiment, of history and biography, and even a kind of poetry. The spelling is frequently charmingly phonetic, for these Mormon farmers and artisans were men of little learning. Many of them were immigrants, who as adults had to learn English, a language dear to them, for it was the language of the restored gospel, perhaps even the Adamic tongue—certainly good enough for the Book of Mormon—and they had begun to learn it in the old country as a religious exercise. But the album's inscriptions are as quaint as the colonial records of New England townships kept by clerks who wrote as they pronounced.

"You are confined for doing the works of Abraham," wrote William Willie of Mendon, "whom God by himself sware Saying, Surely blessing I will bless you, and multiplying I will multiply thee." The figure, "the works of Abraham," is unerring. It states the rationale of polygamy succinctly and colorfully, in Old Testament imagery. Plural marriage was "celestial marriage," ordained of heaven, practiced by the old patriarch Abraham. As doctrine, polygamy assured the Mormons they were providing earthly homes among the righteous for preexistent spirits who otherwise were condemned to be born into ungodly environments. A man's family here would be his in the world to come. If he desired eternal increase, a progeny as numerous as Abraham's with which, like God, he would one day people an earth of his own, he could make a realistic beginning in polygamy. The parable of the talents, said some Mormon preachers, meant "plurality of wives." "Increase will mark your way," Brother W. L. Muir, writing with a firm hand, promised Mads, "the god of Heaven will give you all your heart desires in righteousness   your wives and sons & daughters will enjoy the same blessings   your enimies will serve & obey you, the fat of the hills, and the flowr of the valley will all minister to you   Horses & Cattle together with the riches of Heaven & earth with your brethern & sisters with Eternal life honor & glory above all all are yours." These blessings seemed as tangible and attainable to Mads Christensen as they were to the rejuvenated Job. It seemed incredible to the cohabs, in view of their celestial obligation, that they should be punished for following the biblical injunction to multiply and replenish the earth. Their autographs underscore the irony. Over and over they echo John L. Anderson's resentment: "in three monts I am here fore I leved viht my own wifes." Charles Burgess, originally of Wiltshire, England, was equally specific and indignant: "sentenced to Six Month in the Penitentiary on Oct 11 and to pay a fine of 25.00 Dollars and costs for living with my wives and acknowliging my children." And in rhymes surely unique in American autograph albums they celebrated their loves and loyalties:

> We Love Our Wives & Children
> As Long as wev got Breath
> Wel Keep the Covernants
> We have Maid
> & Claim them after Deth

And again:

> You and I, our children and wives,
> Make Eternal increase and endless lives,
> While spite and prison life cannot last,
> And Edmunds Tucker law will be past.

And:

> Sweeter then Honey is the bread of life
> Dearer than life are the ties to our wives

Implicit in these defensive barbs and lyrics is an indictment of gentile prostitution, which dishonored women. Aaron Hardy of Moroni looked to the day

> When honest men can own their wives
> And wives can love the men
> Who'er not afraid to honor them
> By going to the "Pen."

And David Chidester sounds Cromwellian in his declaration: "I thank God that I am Worthy of the charge." Who does not hear an echo here of the English Reformation? Imprisonment for these high moral reasons was not a stigma but an honor, and the autographs emphasize the victory in temporary defeat, the better days ahead sweetened by the remembrance of the fortitude with which trials were being borne now. They called themselves "sufferers for Christ's sake," a "band of brethren" confined "within these mud walls for obeying the laws of God and being true and faithful to those who are dearer than life itself." A man like Dr. F. G. Higgins was proud to note that he was "the first man arrested for 'Cohabitation' in St. George, Washington County," and that he was sentenced "all the law would allow." There are echoes of the long-suffering Nephi in the Book of Mormon in the admonitions to Mads and his fellows to bear their imprisonment "without murmuring." The benefits would be "everlasting," for the Lord would take note of their sufferings. In the Father's house were many mansions, Apostle Orson Hyde had once bluntly reminded the Scandinavians in Sanpete: there was the parlor, the kitchen, the back kitchen, and then again the outhouse. If they wanted the highest glory, they had better obey *all* the commandments, from ceasing to curse their teams in the canyons to taking more wives that "those Spirits that were never in the flesh might be tried to find out if they were worthy of an inheritance among the sons and daughters of God." Mads Christensen and his religious martyrs, if the autographs are any indication, were counting on the parlor.

Apart from the celestial glory—though that was the theological heart of the matter which infused these conscientious objectors with a martyr spirit—polygamy worked some immediate and practical results, and its prosaic practicality is also implicit in the arguments of the autographs. They reflect Mormon sociology: polygamy sought to eliminate prostitution and adultery and to ensure every woman a worthy husband. Salvation was a slim hope for an old maid or a woman married to a gentile. Better to have part of one good man than none at all, or than all of a bad one. Providing for the widow or spinster immigrant was a community obligation. It was a good bishop who saw that no woman went without a husband. One of Christensen's signatories was Charles A. Anderson from Hyrum, where the Swedish bishop sent Caroline Swensen, newly arrived immigrant, to Norwegian stonemason Gustave Anderson's to make her home, and she became his fourth wife. Hans Jensen Hals took his late neighbor's widow as his plural wife to give her a home, and to raise up seed to the departed, a Mosaic custom. It was not unusual for the fruitful wife of a polygamous household to give one of her children at birth to a barren wife of her husband. In May 1866 shoemaker Peder Nielsen recorded that his wife Hulda had given birth to another son; in September he noted with satisfaction that "Hulda gave him to my wife Marie that she might have him as her son, as if she herself had given birth to him. . . . This made Marie rejoice very much; may the Lord bless this act and all my family and everything under my care." The term "aunt," by which the children in polygamous households knew the "other mothers," had special significance in Mormon communities.

With the divine purpose and the practical point of view eliminating romantic love, no situation proved too awkward to handle: Goudy Hogan courted one of Knud Nelson's girls when the family arrived in Bountiful in 1853. He had his eye on Bergetta, the younger, but when they got ready to go to the Endowment House, Christiana, the eldest sister, persuaded Goudy to take her along as chaperone, and once there persuaded him to make her his wife too—and as the eldest she became the "first wife." Hans Christian Hansen, about to leave on a mission to Scandinavia, by chance encountered a new arrival at a friend's home in Salt Lake. The spirit whispered that Mary Jensen was to be his plural wife. How was he to get word to Hedvig, the first wife, miles away in Plain City? The spirit had told her too, and she had been prompted to come to Salt Lake, where she herself attended the ceremony and escorted the new wife back home while Hans went off on his mission. The plural wife, strong and capable, proved a godsend in the farm work.

This piety, this practicality, this mystique, a folk faith in action, united the whole society with patriarchal bonds. It is the spirit in which the entries in Christensen's album have to be read, for the Mormon community was a state of mind framed by the Old Testament, with daily affairs constantly seen in the light of eternity.

So the album is something of a testament: to the believer, a faith-promoting memorial; to the outsider, a sort of *Grace Abounding*, though closer to Sanpete than Bedfordshire in literary attainments. There is a good deal of cant and cliché, not a few insipid inscriptions, and much incredibly bad verse. But the jingles are refreshingly different from the "Roses are red, violets are blue" variety.

> Dear Brother, be faithfull
> And Keep all of God's laws
> You now are engaged
> In heaven's good cause

Another advises:

> Dream not of helm and harness
> The sign of valor true
> Peace hath higher tests of manhood
> Than battle ever knew

And occasionally humor breaks the solemnity, as in Bent Larsen's description of the penitentiary as "the grand US Hotel" where the prisoners are boarding with "Oncle Sam." Lorenzo Waldram of North Ogden played on the imagery of stars and stripes: they were wearing the stripes and the stars were dimly seen, but were surely shining resplendent "in the realms above."

The album is historical too. Mads renewed old friendships, encountering some of his original fellow emigrants and former missionary companions, like C. H. Monson, now of Richmond, and C. C. N. Dorius of Ephraim, who recalled the event in verse:

> Thirty years in Utah spent
> Since you and I with handcart went
> Together puled acros the plains
> Two hundred, remember not their names.
> The gospel cleansed us free from stain
> Obedience bro't us to this pen.

Frederick Petersen was proud to recall that "I with 27 more Arived in Utah the 16 of Ogtober 1852 being the first Emigration from Denmark." A

Copenhagen potter, Petersen had given hospitality to Erastus Snow in 1850 when Snow arrived to open the Scandinavian mission. The prisoners formed a goodly fellowship, a spiritual elite, signing themselves "Yours in the Covenant." The covenant was the "new and everlasting covenant" God had made with his chosen in this, the last, dispensation. They were able later to write an absorbing chapter into their memoirs, even becoming the subjects of stories stranger than fiction, like Hans Sorensen of Sevier, whose disguises to elude the "federals" were so complete with pipe and beard and miner's togs that only the family dog recognized him.

My illustrations have been largely Scandinavian, since Mads was Scandinavian, and I have probably given the impression that all Scandinavian Mormons were polygamists. Seventeen of the album's eighty-seven inscribers were Scandinavian, or about twenty percent. Of 462 convicted for polygamy in the Territory of Utah in the 1880's, eighty-three, or eighteen percent, were Scandinavian. Of 219 cohabs in the Utah Penitentiary in 1888, the year Mads Christensen served his term, sixty-one, or twenty-eight percent were Scandinavian. The percentages reflect the general situation. Polygamy, of course, was a minority practice among the Mormons generally, as it was among Scandinavian Mormons—not limited to the two or three percent usually quoted, but closer to twenty percent of marriageable males, as a study by Stanley Ivins has shown. "All do not strive for heavenly glory," President John Taylor told a Swedish journalist in 1883. Hans Zobell's wife certainly did not. When Hans broached the subject to her, she put two potted geraniums on the table for dinner one day, one plant young and full of swelling buds, the other nearly bloomed out which had been about the house a long time. "Which of these will you keep?" she wanted to know. "Study them, take your time, then tell me what you decide." Hans understood and no second wife ever crossed the threshold. And young Knud Svendsen, just arrived in Zion in 1857, far from contemplating polygamy, would take not even one wife until he heard from Matte Pedersen, the sweetheart he had left behind in Denmark, though he found his friends marrying all around him, urging him to follow suit, and insistent Ellen Kartrine even lent him a copy of *Celestiale Aegteskab*, a Danish translation of Orson Pratt's persuasive defense of "celestial marriage."

On the other hand, Jens Hansen's blessings outran those the Lord gave Father Jacob: his family numbered thirty-seven, but his house was a house of order. In 1877 a Danish editor found him at dinner time sitting at the head of the table, his eldest wife at his left followed by seven others in order of marriage. At his right sat his eldest son, other sons descending by age like steps to the youngest. The daughters sat at the foot of the table. "The enemies of polygamy," commented the editor, "have said that this system weakens the race," but Patriarch Hansen seemed to refute the notion. Congress ought to do something to encourage others to follow the patriarch's example, he thought: give a man forty acres of land for every woman he married and ten acres for every child; and every man who reached his twenty-fifth birthday and was still unmarried ought to pay the government $250 and thereafter $100 annually as long as he remained single. Patriarch Hansen, one of Mormonism's earliest converts in Denmark, wearer of the Cross of Dannebrog for bravery in the war with Germany, increased his wives to fourteen before his death, an unchallenged distinction among his countrymen. He had lost his first wife in 1854 in crossing the plains. When his brother died in the same emigrant company, Jens had married the widow, honoring once again the Mosaic law that one should raise up seed to his brother.

I would like to believe that this is the Jens Hansen to be found in Mads Christensen's autograph book, who wished "joiful meeting on the other side," but one hails from Spanish Fork, the other from Brigham City. And there were about as many Jens Hansens among the Scandinavians as Peter Petersens.

Most of the Scandinavian polygamists contented themselves with two wives. The census taker had his problems: he would usually describe the first wife's occupation as "Keeping House," and say of other women in the household "Assists in House."

One or two Scandinavians became the center of momentous polygamy trials. In September 1888, the month Mads Christensen was released from prison, Hans Nielson was tried and convicted on two counts on the same day for the same offense—one indictment under the Edmunds Act for unlawful cohabitation and one under the Edmunds-Tucker Act for adultery with his alleged plural wife. After serving his sentence for the first charge he was denied his petition of habeas corpus at his arrest on the second, and his case was taken to the Supreme Court of the United States, which understood it to be a test case and advanced it upon the calendar, arguing it within a month after Nielson's arrest. The Supreme Court ruled that multiplication of punishments was not the policy of the law. To proceed upon the principle of "segregation," which held a polygamist guilty of a new offense every time he stepped into his plural wife's house, would require centuries of time to discharge. Nielson's release freed several others convicted in like fashion.

Hans Jesperson of Goshen, arrested a year later on the testimony of his second wife, who confessed under oath that she had come to Utah the previous November and married Jesperson in the Manti Temple and later at the Endowment House in Salt Lake City, gave the Mormon Church some embarrassment because President Wilford Woodruff had stated that the church was refusing to give recommendations for plural marriages. It was "incredible," he said, and he was looking into the matter. It was prelude to his Manifesto of 1890 which called on the church to obey the law of the land.

Plural marriages, of course, had never been promiscuous. They had to be contracted with permission of the first wife and approved by the president of the church, the ceremony performed by the priesthood in the Endowment House, forerunner of the Salt Lake Temple. "Dear Brother," Brigham Young wrote Bishop Seeley of Mt. Pleasant, "You are at liberty to baptize James Christensen, and if you can recommend him as a good man, he can have Anna Christine Jensen sealed to him." Away on missions, husbands might find converts they wished to marry, but the ceremony could not take place until they returned, though sometimes in their impatience they made promises, and it proved a trial to the wife at home to discover that the husband had already made his selection. Anders Nielsen, who had left two wives at home, on his return to Sanpete after his mission stopped in the Endowment House to marry two more, both converts he had brought back with him; but one of his wives in Manti went out the back door as he came in, taking her children with her, not to return. One of those children became the father of Lowry Nelson, distinguished sociologist, from whom I have this story. Peter Hansen of Hyrum noted with sorrow that against his will he had been brought to give his third wife, Stine Marie, a divorce, leaving him but two wives and sixteen children. For those who took their role as Abraham seriously it was a distinct loss.

I have gone beyond Mads Christensen's autograph album to illustrate the spirit and significance of its inscriptions. The album is a unique piece of western Americana. I wish that with every inscription like the one beginning "Cell No. 32 North 'Cohab' Row" I had a face, that I could see the mouth working as fingers more used to an irrigation shovel than a pen wrote out deliberately "Six months and costs for honoring my own." I should like to see the whole assembly of Mads' well-wishers as Frans Hals or Rembrandt might have painted them in chiaroscuro—not a "Night Watch," but beleaguered defenders of their faith, Zion's burghers, strong-faced, smoldering, resigned but impenitent, self-righteous and dedicated—every one a Gray Champion. It would be an ancestral portrait worthy of Hawthorne. And as for the album as social document: will the draft resisters and social revolutionaries now crowding jails, today's prisoners for conscience' sake, leave some such testament? Folklorists would not want to overlook it. Mads Christensen's autograph album reminds us what folklore adds to history, to sociology, and, if I may use the term loosely, to literature.

Olive W. Burt

Wine-making in Utah's Dixie

In the scores of books that have been written about Utah, one subject has been strangely neglected—the wine-making that once was a major operation in "Dixie." I have, of course, found a few references to this activity. Juanita Brooks gives two pages to the subject, and Mabel Jarvis, whose grandfather was the official Church wine-maker in St. George, gives it one page.[1] Both of these authors must have had a wealth of stories concerning wine-making, typically a family project whose lore and reminiscences were not always shared with the public.

My mother had no such restraints. According to her yarns, wine-making in Dixie was a happy business with a wealth of anecdote and superstition, of which I have found no published account. It is only through study of available journals and through oral tradition that I have been able to garner a small portion of this delightful harvest.

Some years ago the *New Yorker* published a bit of "Incidental Intelligence." The writer had seen a sign above a tavern, WINE LIKE GRAND-MOTHER USED TO MAKE. He thought it worthy of public attention. I thought so too, because the tales my mother told about the potency of Dixie wine made such a claim a true recommendation. I began to collect, haphazardly, I'll admit, some of the yarns about the wine our grandparents used to make. I found some material in published journals, recorded some of my mother's anecdotes, and tried to dig some out of the oldsters who lived in Southern Utah during that period. Oddly enough, no one but my mother knew any stories. One friend, in his eighties, even swore that he could not remember any wine ever being made in Toquerville.

John D. Lee, for whose published diaries we are indebted to Mrs. Brooks, was not, it seems, too interested in wine: whiskey and beer were more to his liking, to judge by more than a score of references to these beverages.[2] With unconscious humor he relates a few anecdotes that bear retelling.

There was the time in 1858 when Lee returned from a trip to Salt Lake City and discovered that the bishop had "broke open my door and took out ten gallons of whisky."[3] Angered at this betrayal of trust, Lee made the bishop apologize. And at the Twenty-fourth of July (Pioneer Day) celebration in 1866, beer was given as prizes for foot races. But the juvenile crowd gathered around the beer barrel like "pigs around a swill tub."[4] One of the men stood by with a stick with which to rap away the youngsters, but in his zeal he struck one boy in the face, causing the blood to flow. The angry father started a fight and a general melee nearly wrecked the celebration.

Lee did make several references to wine. On the Twenty-fourth of July, two years after the above incident, he was at Toquerville where "many treated me to all the wine I could drink." "Tokerville is a wine District," he added succinctly.[5] Lee had one wife in Toquerville who, in spite of the cheering effects of the town's most famous product, seemed always in a cross mood when her husband visited her. But when Lee was ill in that settlement, Mrs. Haight nursed him with "sweet wine, grapes, etc."[6]

It was in Toquerville, the wine District, that my mother was born and reared. And her yarns, while I cannot vouch for their accuracy, are often confirmed by other sources. There are her tales, for example, about sacramental wine. Mother often related that in her day a large mug of wine was passed from hand to hand, each person expected to take one sip. But the older men would not stop with a swallow, and would empty the mug. A boy with a pitcher of wine followed along down the aisle, refilling the mug each time it was emptied.

Juanita Brooks tells the same story about the brethren in St. George, and John D. Lee gives contemporaneous confirmation. In his diary entry for May 1, 1869, he tells of Brigham Young's sermon in the basement of the new Tabernacle in St. George. Before the sacrament was passed, the Church President warned the worshipers that older men who got drunk should be cut off from the Church; that wine should be an article of export, and not drunk here save for the sacrament, and then only one swallow should be taken. Some would take a pint if the tumbler held that much. But there was a remedy—he would have tumblers made that would hold only one swallow and no more. This might well be taken as a prophecy, for today's sacrament service uses just such tiny "tumblers," though filled with clear water.[7]

I know of my own experience that this imbibing of the sacramental wine did take place, and that in Toquerville, at least, wine was used in the ritual for some time after the order went out in 1900 to discontinue the practice and to substitute water for the more symbolic wine of earlier days.

When I was a small girl, my parents sent me for several summers to Dixie to stay with relatives, on the theory that the air, the food, and the climate were more conducive to physical growth than was my Salt Lake City environment. The summer I was ten I was visiting my mother's youngest brother, Uncle Ben Forsyth. Of course I went to Sunday School, and was delightfully shocked to get a mouthful of sweet wine instead of the tasteless water I was accustomed to in the Salt Lake City religious services. I looked forward to the next Sunday's treat, and was in my place in good time. But alas! a bearded "old" man took his place on the aisle end of my bench. And when the sacrament was passed, I watched with dismay as he drained the glass. There was no boy with a pitcher, and we little girls simply made a futile gesture of touching the empty glass to our lips. The incident made a great impression on me, because I feared damnation for this deception in the holy act of communion. But when I worriedly told Uncle Ben about it, he just chuckled and assured me that I need have no fear: if that meant damnation, half of Toquerville would go to hell because it was often necessary to practice this act of deceit, the goblet being empty a good deal of the time—God understood perfectly.

Toquerville wine had an enviable reputation for potency. Lee relates how, in Salt Lake City, President Young produced a decanter of wine "of his own make" and treated his guest with the boast that it was as fine an article as could be bought in Dixie.[8] Mother claimed that drummers coming to the town could drink any amount of the wine without getting drunk—till the next day. When they drank water enough to dilute the wine "so it could enter their blood-stream," they became really inebriated.

My mother had an anecdote that illustrated this point. Her mother was an expert glove maker—in fact, family tradition says that before she joined the Mormons and came to Utah, Grandma made gloves for Queen Victoria. A rich Spaniard from Pioche, Nevada, was marrying one of the "girls" from Silver Reef. He ordered from Grandma twenty-six pairs of gloves. For his bride and himself the buckskin was to be bleached as white as snow. For the twelve bridesmaids, it was to be dyed pink, and for the twelve groomsmen, blue. All were to have gauntlets that reached almost to the elbow, embroidered in gay flowers. And for the wedding celebration at Silver Reef he ordered several kegs of Toquerville wine.

The party was a great success, but the spigots were too slow for the thirsty celebrants, so they poured the wine out of the kegs into a huge wooden tub, from which it could be more rapidly dispensed.

The next morning the bride and groom with their twenty-four attendants mounted their horses to ride to Pioche. They were a gallant sight, holding the reins in their elegantly gloved hands, arms akimbo, ladies sitting sidesaddle with their plumed hats nodding as the horses pranced down the street. But something was wrong. The two leading horses were not behaving with proper decorum. They side-stepped and danced and wove from side to side. Their eyes sparkled and their lips were lifted as if in ribald grins. No one could explain their actions until it came to light that the boy who tended the horses had watered these two from that very same wooden tub that had held the wine the night before. The dregs left in the bottom—and you may be sure there were not many—diluted with the water put there for the horses had sufficed to intoxicate the animals.

I suppose every family in Toquerville made wine, though it is difficult today to get their descendants to admit it. It is a well established fact that John Naegle built a large, two-story, sandstone structure as a winery. The building still stands on the right-hand side of the street as you travel south through the town. Of course today it is put to less joyous use. The cellar was entered by means of a wide ramp down which a team could draw a heavy wagon, loaded with grapes. Naegle made a trip to California for late-model presses and stills, and for some years produced both wine and brandy. Mother always claimed that the drummers believed that Toquerville girls had the whitest feet and legs in the Territory, due to tromping out the grape juice with their feet. I think this was an exaggeration, for Naegle had good roller presses that did an efficient job. He was assisted by his half brother, Conrad Kleinman, and their wine, known as Nail's Best, was deservedly famous. Many a 50-gallon keg stood in that cellar, and many a 40-gallon keg was shipped by wagon to Salt Lake City.

But the Toquerites themselves did not rely on this rather commercial undertaking. As a rule each family made its own wine from its own grape patch in true European style. Many of these settlers, like Kleinman, had learned the art in Germany or Switzerland; but if they hadn't been so fortunate, they caught on easily and soon rivaled the experts. In fact, most Toquerites became so adept that they didn't have to rely on grapes alone for wine. As a youngster my mother learned to make "scrap wine," an art she practiced to her dying day in 1953. A large vessel was kept handy during the summer when fruit was being "put up." In later days Mother used a great, gray crockery churn, made, so impressed letters on the surface affirm, by M. Woodruff in Cartland (I use this as an umbrella stand in my front hall—nothing could be a more poignant footnote on how the joy in living has departed our times!). As the women prepared fruit for canning, into the waiting vessel would go peach, apricot and cherry pits, apple peelings and cores, somewhat overripe currants and berries—any bit of fruit substance they did not want to use in their canning. And from these scraps, by means of Toquerville necromancy, they would produce a most potent, sparkling red wine. I saw my mother carry out this ritual year after year, but to my everlasting sorrow, I paid scant attention, and now I do not know how she performed her magic. Did she add sugar or yeast or water? I think not, but I do not know. I do recall such terms as "pummies" (pomace), "rack off," "clarify," and so on, but that is as far as my memory goes.

The people of Dixie were not apologetic or furtive in their wine-making, and it seems too bad that their descendants are not as proud of their ancestors' skill as were the pioneers. I do not doubt that their wine helped them over many a difficult time, and of course it was sometimes used as medicine. To carry juice as wine was an excellent way to transport it on the way west. "Dr." Priddy Meeks mentions that when they stopped in the upper "edge" of the Missouri, at the Bluffs six miles from the river, they found large amounts of elderberries, just right for making wine. "We turned in and made 80 gallons of wine . . . and it proved the means of making a fit-out in the spring."[9]

In St. George the Church appointed George Jarvis as official wine-maker. It had been common practice to pay tithing in wine—an indication of how prevalent the business was—but the product brought in was of such uneven quality that the Church found it difficult to dispose of it. They accordingly advised members to bring in the grapes and let them turn it into wine. Brother Jarvis was a British sailor who had, in his travels, visited Málaga, Spain—and this, naturally, qualified him for the job of vintner.

Various types of homemade presses were used in home wine-making. There was generally some sort of hand grinder into which the grapes were fed to be mashed. This mash was fed into a press. A common type of press in Dixie was made of a barrel with the staves fastened together by hoops but not tightly grooved. This left cracks through which the juice could run into the pan or tub set to catch it. A metal plate in the top of the barrel was arranged so that it could be wound down by use of a hand screw. As the plate descended, the juice was pressed out. The Naegles of Toquerville, as previously mentioned, had roller presses from California. And perhaps in some cases the girls *did* tromp out the juice, or how could such a rumor have ever been started?

The pomace—called pummies in Dixie—was fed to the chickens or cattle, or "snuck" by watching youngsters. The wine was strained through a coarse cloth into the ripening barrels, where it was left to take its own good time to ferment, assisted only by the hot rays of the Dixie sun. Then it was stored in 50-gallon kegs and left to age. Brother Jarvis stored his kegs in the basement of the Opera House; at one time there was as much as 6,000 gallons stacked away down there—a fact which may account for the poignancy of some of the dramas produced on the stage by the amateur dramatic company.

Mother liked to tell about what happened to one ripening barrel in Toquerville. It was in the 1880's when U.S. government agents—deps, for deputies—were hunting men living in polygamy—cohabs. One of the most active deps was a fellow named McGeary. One night he came with an assistant named Armstrong to Toquerville to catch a cohab (Mother always used the names of all the folks she told about. It gave authenticity to her yarns—but I refrain). McGeary told his aide to go around to the back to watch while he stayed in front: they'd sure catch the miscreant that way.

The second dep went around to the back of the small house. There he saw a barrel, with a canvas cover held tight with a hoop. He thought he'd step up onto this canvas to get a look in at the tiny window. But his weight dislodged the canvas, and down he went, kerplunk! into the barrel. For only the briefest moment did he imagine he had fallen into the rain barrel. The fragrance of the ripening wine soon informed him. He climbed out, licked his chops, and then, using his cupped hands as a dipper, he went to work.

Some time later McGeary became curious about the stillness at the rear of the cottage. He tiptoed around, saw his companion stretched out on the ground fast asleep, took in the situation—and using his cupped hands as a dipper, went to work. The cohab and his plural spouse had an undisturbed night—and in the morning two red-faced deputies hurriedly left town.

Mother had a number of firm beliefs about wine-making and drinking:

Only Isabella, or California mission grapes, were suitable for Dixie wine.

Only Oregon redwood was perfect for the bung; but any kind of cork or stopper would do in an emergency.

No pregnant woman should be permitted to assist in the wine-making or her baby would be a drunkard.

A wine glass should never be turned upside down: it would bring bad luck.

Some beliefs were expressed in proverbs:

"Spill your wine before one swallow and bad luck will surely follow!" This bad luck could be averted by dipping the middle finger of the right hand into the spilled wine and rubbing it on your ear.

"Know the vintner, know the wine!"

Toquerville was jealous of its reputation as a "wine district," but other communities were not willing to grant the small settlement precedence. St. George, Washington, Virgin, Rockville, Leeds, all worked hard to be as favorably known as was Toquerville. During the Silver Reef boom Leeds wine was popular in the saloons of the mining town. It was not until the end of the nineteenth century that the product deteriorated. Then the urge to make a fast dollar overcame the producers and the Dixie product lost its good name. About that time farmers began resorting to quick "ripeners"; they became careless of the grapes they used and sold off the wine before it was properly aged. Even so, my family never passed a winter until well into this century without obtaining several five-gallon kegs of Dixie wine. Each one of my older brothers in turn sneaked samples of the wine until "caught out" by my watchful mother.

By 1900 the people had been counseled to stop making wine, even for sacramental use, and to tear up those Isabella vines and to replant the vineyards with seedless grapes to be converted into healthful raisins. I suppose it was hoped that Dixie wine would perish from the earth– and according to many folks, it did. Yet in 1916 I was again visiting in Toquerville. A group of us young people were sitting on the lawn in front of one of the homes one very warm evening. I began to tease my companions about their conformity to counsel at the cost of their most famous product. One young man asked, "Do you really want to taste some Toquerville wine?" I assured him that I really would like to sample it to see whether my mother's yarns were exaggerated. He reached behind him into a bush and drew out a bottle of wine. Another fellow extracted a bottle from the long grass along the fence. A third found one snuggled beneath the porch. And from actual experience I can vouch for the truth of Mother's stories of the superiority of Toquerville wine and also testify that a fine skill does not die at the word of counsel, authoritative though it may be.

NOTES

1. Juanita Brooks, "The Cotton Mission," *Utah Historical Quarterly* 29 (1961): 216-17; Mabel Jarvis, "Manufacture of Wine," Kate B. Carter, ed., *Heart Throbs of the West* (Salt Lake City: Daughters of Utah Pioneers, 1941), 3:234-35.

2. Robert G. Clelland and Juanita Brooks, eds., *A Mormon Chronicle: The Diaries of John D. Lee* (San Marino, Calif.: Huntington Library, 1955), vols. 1 and 2.

3. Ibid., 1: 148-50.

4. Ibid., 2: 24.

5. Ibid., 2: 109.

6. Ibid., 2: 141.

7. Brooks, "The Cotton Mission," p. 217.

8. Clelland and Brooks, *Diaries of John D. Lee*, 2: 72.

9. Priddy Meeks, "Journal of Priddy Meeks," *Utah Historical Quarterly* 10 (1942): 159.

Olive W. Burt

Ditties of Death in Deseret

When I was preparing for publication my book, *American Murder Ballads and Their Stories*, one of the publisher's staff suggested that it would be interesting to confine the work to the ballads of the West.[1] Although I had collected a good many unpublished, or seldom-published, western items, I did not feel I had enough for a whole volume without using many too-well-known songs, such as those about Jesse James or Billy the Kid. So I stuck to my original plan and used ballads from all parts of the country.

However, in the years since the book was published, so many murder ballads have been sent to me, particularly from this western region, that I think it worthwhile to get some of these into print so that others may enjoy them. I am quite sure that most of these have never been published save in documents which are not generally accessible. I shall deal here with ballads and other verse about murders of particular interest in Deseret—chiefly in Utah.

The Mormons, as has often been noted, have always been a singing people. It is not surprising that they put into song the stories of violence that marked their early days. Some of these songs attained the stature of hymns and were sung in Church services. They served to bolster the spirits of the harassed people, to fan their determination to survive in spite of hardship and persecution, to glorify martyrdom. Many of these early, defiant hymns have now disappeared from the sanctioned songbooks, yet the stirring, "Hail to the Man!" still lifts the heart as thousands of Semiannual Conference visitors sing it.

One of the most poignant songs written about the assassination of Joseph Smith, of which there are many, has been removed from the Church hymn books and is little known among the Saints today. Both words and melody were composed by David Smith, a son of the martyred prophet. It was inspired by the circumstances surrounding the secret burial of the murdered Joseph and Hyrum to prevent desecration of their bodies by the uncontrolled mob. The haunting melody may be found in older hymn books and is well worth learning.

THE UNKNOWN GRAVE

There's an unknown grave in a lonely spot
But the form that it covers will ne'er be forgot;
There the heaven-tree spreads and the tall locusts wave
Their snow-white flowers o'er the unknown grave.
    Over the unknown grave.

And near by its side does the wild rabbit tread,
And over its bosom the white thistles spread,
As if placed there in kindness to guard and save
From intruding footsteps the unknown grave.
    Guarding the unknown grave.

And there reposes the Prophet just;
The Lord was his guide and in Him was his trust;
He restored the gospel our souls to save,
But he now lies low in an unknown grave.
    Low in an unknown grave.

God grant that we may watch and pray,
And keep our feet in the narrow way;
Our spirits and bodies in purity save,
To see him arise from his unknown grave!
    God bless the unknown grave![2]

As a direct result of the troubles that culminated in the assassination of Joseph and Hyrum Smith, the Saints moved west and settled in the Great Basin. They called the region variously Zion, Deseret, Our Mountain Home, and so on. A hymn which both commemorates the assassination and links it with the name *Deseret*—and hints at violent reprisal if their peace here is disturbed—was popular in pioneer days. It stirred up the Saints at the first meeting of the "Reformation" at Kaysville, Utah, in 1856.

HOPE OF ISRAEL

Fear not, ye Saints of latter days, our Father's at the helm;
In patience walk in wisdom's ways, no foe can overwhelm.
We hear their threats, but heed them not, they envy us our happy lot.
In Deseret we're free to act and magnify our calling.

The wicked nations' cup doth fill with deeds of darkness rife,
Which doth the Prophet's words fulfill, for deadly is the strife.
Sweet peace is banished from their land, they've lost the power to command;
But Deseret knows all the Saints will nobly do their duty.

Our Prophet they have basely slain and drove the Saints away;
And now their blood boils hot again the same foul game to play.
But plains and mountains intervene, which makes the Saints feel all serene,
And Deseret is sure that they will nobly do their duty.

Our trust is in the living God, no arm of flesh we fear;
He'll smite the wicked with His rod when they in wrath draw near.
But let not boasting fill our hearts, nor envy hurl her fiery darts,
For Deseret expects that all the Saints will do their duty.

Here peace and plenty crown our days through all these valleys fair,
And joyful sounds the song of praise, and deep the fervent prayer
That we may be preserved and blest, that mobs may never us molest—
For Deseret is sure that all the Saints will do their duty![3]

One of the most prolific composers of hymns about the violence suffered by the Saints was Parley P. Pratt, who ironically became the victim of an assassin. The story is well known: Pratt had converted Mrs. Elenore McLean and, so it was claimed, had taken her as his twelfth wife. Mrs. McLean's three children by her former husband had been sent to New Orleans by their father to get them far away from contact with Mormons. When Apostle Pratt assisted the mother in regaining her children, the irate father caught up with the party, and near Van Buren, Arkansas, shot and killed Pratt. I have found no Utah verses concerning this event, but have received from an Arkansas correspondent a fragment believed to refer to it.

Just let this be a warning to wife-stealers—Stay away!
    You cannot come to Arkansas and steal another's wife.
And if you dare to try it you will surely have to pay,
    Yes! You must pay most dearly with your life![4]

Parley Pratt had composed some verses which he wished to have inscribed upon his tombstone. They seem vaguely to foreshadow his unhappy death.

Thou art gone to thy rest in the mansions of glory,
    Thy toils and temptations and trials are o'er;
And joined with the father who entered before thee
    The road of the tyrant shall reach thee no more.

Thou art gone to thy rest, but we will not deplore thee,
    Though the circle bereft are so dreary and lone.

There are souls thou hast loved that have gone there before thee,
  And they welcome thy spirit, returned to its own.

Thou art gone to thy rest, and thy loved ones, forsaken,
  Must tarry a moment in sadness below;
Till the living are changed, and thy dust shall awaken,
  And the circle completed no sorrow shall know.[5]

The murder of Apostle Pratt did not cause a great ripple in Deseret. It was the spring of 1857 and United States troops were on their way to Utah. The Saints had plenty to worry them. General W. S. Harney, who at first was in command of the expedition, had boasted that he would winter in "Utah or hell." He got as far as Kansas, where he spent the winter of 1856-57. This interruption caused many derisive jokes among the Saints. But as the troops moved forward that spring the Saints, instead of singing about the assassination of Parley Pratt, were passing around a small yellow penny sheet broadside and singing the song thereon. I have one of these decorated items.

OLD HARNEY
(Tune, "Kate Kearney")

Did you ever hear of Old Harney?
He's the greatest old rip in the army!
    The upholder of laws,
    And the killer of squaws,
Och! a wonderful hero is Harney.

He has gathered his laurels so gory;
His fame smells of powder and glory;
    Though bright his renown,
    There's smoke in the frown
Of the brave and the gallant Old Harney.

But of him we will gently be speaking,
And his favors we ought to be seeking,
    For the papers all say
    He is coming this way,
Then won't we be gracious with Harney.

Don't you feel to be inwardly caving,
And about blood and thunder be raving?
    For do what we may
    There will be hell to pay,
When he gets here—the gentle Old Harney.

Old Zack is in Tophet before him,
When *he* goes, we will not deplore him;

And soon they will meet,
In that shady retreat,
Then at *home* will be gallant Old Harney![6]

In '57 the command of the expedition was taken over by Col. Albert Sidney Johnston, and the troops came on toward Deseret. But before they reached their destination, a tragic event took place in the southern part of the Territory. In early September, a band of emigrants from Missouri and Arkansas was ambushed and slaughtered at the Mountain Meadows, southwest of Cedar City. The terrible event had in it all the elements necessary for a folk ballad, and such a ballad was composed. It was sung only clandestinely for many, many years. Today it has been published a number of times. I have collected four variants, but the differences are only minor and indicate that the one version was widely known, changed only because of the vagaries of hearing, memory, and reproduction. One melody was published in my *American Murder Ballads*. Dr. Lester Hubbard gives another in his *Ballads and Songs from Utah*.[7]

THE MOUNTAIN MEADOWS MASSACRE

Come, all you sons of liberty,
And to my rhyme give ear –
'Tis of a bloody massacre
You presently shall hear.

In splendor on the mountains
Some thirty wagons came.
They were awaited by a wicked band –
Oh, Utah! Where's thy shame?

On a crisp October morning
At the Mountain Meadows green,
By the light of bright campfires,
Lee's Mormon bullets screamed.

In Indian garb and colors
Those bloody hounds were seen
To attack the little train
All on the meadows green.

They were attacked in the morning,
As they were on their way,
And forthwith corralled their wagons,
And fought in blood array.

When Lee, the leader of their band,
His word to them did give,
That if their arms they would give up
He'd surely let them live.

When once their arms they had give up
    And started for Cedar City,
They rushed on them in Indian style,
    Oh, what a human pity!

They melted down with one accord
    Like wax before the flame;
Both men and women, young and old,
    Oh, Utah! Where's thy shame?

Both men and women, young and old,
    A-rolling in their gore.
And such an awful sight and scene
    Was ne'er beheld before!

Their property was divided
    Among this bloody crew,
And Uncle Sam is bound to see
    This bloody matter through.

The soldiers will be stationed
    Throughout this Utah land,
All for to find these murderers out
    And bring them to his hand.

By order of their president
    This awful deed was done.
He was leader of the Mormon church,
    His name was Brigham Young.[8]

The crime went unavenged for twenty years, but on March 23, 1877, John D. Lee, one of the participants, was executed on the very site of the atrocity. Although it had been a band of whites and Paiutes who attacked the emigrants, Lee was the only person convicted and punished. His execution gave rise to a little-known ballad, a simple parody on the ballad of James Bird, executed by court-martial after the battle of Lake Erie in the War of 1812. I have only a fragment:

See Lee kneel upon his coffin,
    Sure his death will do no good;
Oh, see! they've shot him!
    See his bosom stream with blood!

Farewell, Lee, farewell forever,
    By loved ones you'll no more be seen,
For your mangled form lies buried
    On the Mountain Meadows green.[9]

That the Saints were bitterly resentful of the coming of the troops and were ready to oppose them, even at the cost of violence, was evident in songs of that period. At the mass meeting held in Salt Lake City in January of 1858—the purpose of which was to formulate resolutions to be sent to the government detailing the actual conditions in Deseret—the people sang:

THE KINGDOM OF GOD OR NOTHING
(Tune, "The Rising of the Lark")

Rejoice, ye chosen Saints,
God hears all your complaints
   And glorious days are now at hand.
The nations far and near,
Begin to quake with fear
That God will by His people stand.
     Then be ready,
     Watching steady,
With your armor always on.
     Warm in praying,
     Cool in slaying,
Till the victory is won.
Till Saints in God are one,
And sinners wasted from the land.

Long driven and oppressed,
We've hardly found a rest
   Ere mobs rush to this far off land.
Then Liberty or death!
We'll shout while we have breath,
Whatever comes, we'll nobly stand.
     God's great Lion
     Watches Zion;
Tyrant's blood shall stain each sword.
     Rights we'll cherish
     Though we perish,
For "the Kingdom of our Lord
Or nothing!" is the word
That greets the foe on every hand![10]

Four years later a group of dissidents had turned a fervid Mormon hymn into a song of hate against the parent church. A simple Welsh convert named Joseph Morris began having revelations of his own—his published book contains more than three hundred songs. They were often contrary to the teachings of the established Church, and Morris and his handful of followers were excommunicated. They went north and established a tiny settlement on the Weber River above Ogden. They consecrated all personal belongings to their community and began to farm and make a communal life of their own. But Morris, following the example of his former leaders, objected strongly to apostasy from his teachings. When two young men wished to leave the community there was trouble over what they could take away. The two were arrested and put into a makeshift jail. They appealed to Brigham Young, who sent Colonel Robert P. Burton, Salt Lake county sheriff, with troops to rescue the imprisoned men.

On the morning of June 13, 1860, Burton, with a hundred men, appeared on the bluffs above the miserable little colony. They ordered Morris to release his prisoners, but Morris went into his tent to ask divine counsel. Emerging a few moments later with a written revelation, he promised his flock that if they held firm, not one of his people would be harmed. At once a cannon roared and two women, robed in white and marching behind their prophet, fell dead. The Morrisites dashed to their cellars and their ramshackle houses, and for three days valiantly defended their camp. It was an unequal battle, and at last they had to surrender. The troops then had a holiday, looting the miserable community of its sparse possessions. The dead were brought to Salt Lake City and Morris's body, in the white robes and crown he had affected, was displayed to the scorn and edification of the Saints.

I have received a copy of a Morrisite hymn—a parody of the Mormon hymn "The Royal Family"—from Lillian Metcalfe Benedict. I tried for years to obtain the music for these verses, knowing the hymn had once been popular. One writer in the *Deseret News* had asked, "Where is that hymn, 'The Royal Family,' that we used to sing with such gusto?" I never did find it, but Dr. Hubbard includes it in his comprehensive book of Utah ballads and songs. Here is the Morrisite text:

> We'll see Morris, Banks, and others,
> Joseph, Hyrum with the Martyrs,
> On Mount Zion in great glory
> With the Savior and His army.
>
>> Oh! how glorious they'll be,
>> Oh, how glorious they'll be,
>> Dressed in white and crowned with glory
>> 'Mid the Royal Family.
>
> On the banks of Weber river,
> Joseph Morris died a martyr,

Slain by Burton, cruel Mormon,
Legal servant of the dragon.

> Their day is nigh at hand,
> Their day is nigh at hand,
> Every murderer now shall suffer,
> Sons of Israel will command.

Blood of children, men and women,
Cry aloud to God for vengeance,
From the grounds of Weber Valley;
Woe to murderous Salt Lake City!

> Their day is now at hand, etc.

Woe the wicked Jews and Romans,
Woe the States and cruel Mormons
That have shed the blood of martyrs,
Now the Saints have got the power.

> Their day is now at hand, etc.

Now the faithful Sons of Israel
Sit in judgment with Prince Michael;
God hath given the third kingdom,
Now begins the resurrection.

> Oh, how glorious it will be, etc.[11]

In April of 1959, *Western Folklore* published an article of mine, "Murder Ballads of Mormondom." Soon thereafter I received a letter from a man in Seattle, Washington, whose great uncle, he advised me, had been one of five men arrested in 1871 for the murder, five years earlier, of Dr. J. King Robinson in Salt Lake City. My correspondent said he had some old family papers including a handwritten account of the trial, a list of questions propounded by Governor John B. Weller and flippant answers thereto, a few old letters, and finally some verses he thought I would like to have. When I read them I immediately wrote to tell my friend how happy I was to have the verses, as they were the first I had found on this particular crime.

Dr. Robinson had been surgeon general at Camp Douglas until he was mustered out in 1864. He stayed on in Salt Lake City, married a Mormon girl, and built up quite a medical practice among the Gentiles of the city. He envisaged a profitable venture in establishing a health resort at the warm springs northwest of town and immediately filed claim on the property. Then his troubles began. His bowling hall was wrecked. A shanty he built on the warm springs ground was burned. Then on the night of October 22, 1866, he was called from his home on the urgent plea that a man had broken his leg and was in need of immediate attention. A few feet from his front door, the doctor was set upon by a number of men (witnesses accounted for seven), and he was beaten and shot to death. Non-Mormons believed the attack had been ordered by Church authorities, and a great furor arose. However, no one was arrested until five years later, and then the accused men were acquitted. No one was ever punished for this crime.

The verses sent me were obviously written by someone in sympathy with the attackers, possibly one of the men involved. (It is not as brilliant as another parody on the "Du Dah" song made popular when the U.S. troops were coming toward Salt Lake Valley.)

A NEW DU DAH SONG

Seven men they say went out one night,
   Du dah!
To give a Gentile a terrible fright—
   Du dah! Du dah day!
Now let them catch us if they can,
   Du dah!
For no one at all saw any a man—
   Du dah! Du dah day!

     Then let us be on hand,
     For our firm rights to stand,
     And if our enemies appear
     They'll be swept from the land.

They called up a grand jury,
   Du dah!
To search out in their fury
   Du dah! Du dah day!
The loyal servants who, they tell,
   Du dah!
Sent a dirty Gentile straight to hell—
   Du dah! Du dah day![12]

For many of the murders committed in Deseret the people had an automatic suspect—Orrin Porter Rockwell. The stern-visaged bodyguard of Joseph Smith and Brigham Young, "Old Port," was suspected and often accused of having a hand in the death of every Gentile or apostate who succumbed in Deseret. With a ballad about Rockwell, I felt smugly unique, but now I have learned that Dr. Hubbard has an entirely different ballad about the "Terror of the Plains," and Harold Schindler has a third.[13]

The exclamation, "Wheat!" was the man's war cry.

"OLD PORT"

Old Port Rockwell has work to do,
    So he saddles his sorrel and rides away;
And those who are watching wonder who
    Will be a widow at break of day.
The waiting wife in the candlelight,
    Starts up as she hears a wild hoof-beat,
Then shrinks in terror as down the night
    Comes the wailing of Port's dread war-cry, "Wheat!"

Wheat! She looks at her babes and tries to pray,
For she knows she's a widow and orphans are they.

Old Port Rockwell looks like a man,
    With a beard on his face and his hair in a braid,
But there's none in the West, save Brigham, who can
    Look in his eyes and not be afraid.
For Port is a devil in human shape,
    Though he calls himself "Angel"—says vengeance is sweet;
But he's black, bitter Death, and there's no escape
    When he wails through the night his dread war cry "Wheat!"

Wheat! Somewhere a wife with her babes kneels to pray,
For she knows she's a widow and orphans are they.[14]

In the 1880's as the federal government stepped up its campaign against polygamy, the Mormon missionaries sent out over the country ran into bitter opposition. Particularly in the South were they subjected to many indignities, often beaten, and sometimes murdered. J. A. McCuiston, on a mission in Tennessee, sent home a bit of doggerel that was being sung by the people in the region where he was laboring. It hints at the violence the missionaries from Deseret might expect if they continued to preach their gospel. It was sung to the tune of "Up on Old Smoky."

MORMON POETRY

A string of fool women,
    All in a row,
The Mormons can find them
    Wherever they go.

They will preach their false doctrine,
    So pure and so fine;
They will gull them fool women
    And leave them behind.

We will hunt up these Mormons
    Before it is day,
Give them a lecture
    And drive them away.

We will take up John Linton
    And his friend, Elder Bean,
Make them acquainted
    With Forrest and Freen.

We will take out them Mormons,
    So rosy and red,
Give them a shearing
    And feather their head.

If the Mormons don't like it,
    The less they can say,
Is wind up their business,
    And all get away.

If the brick pond company
    Get them in tow,
They'll hang up them Mormons,
    Or straighten their row.

W. A. Watkins,
    The merry old coon,
Thinks that the Mormons
    Will rattle out soon. [15]

The missionaries paid scant heed to the warnings. Obsessed from childhood with the idea of martyrdom as a tribute to God and the Church, they went on preaching. In July of 1879 young Joseph Standing had been killed near Varnell Station in Whitfield County, Georgia. The desultory investigation brought forth the odious comment, "There's no law in Georgia for Mormons." And in August of 1884 the warning in the ditty above was made tragically real. A mob, fired by a local preacher's wild talk, collected at the home of James Condor in Tennessee, where a missionary meeting was being held, and started a riot. In the melee, William S. Berry and James H. Gibbs, Mormon elders, and Mrs. Condor's two sons were all killed. Feeling in Utah ran high. The columns of the *Deseret Evening News* were filled with editorials, letters and poems condemning the crime. I published one, "The Cane Creek Massacre," in *American Murder Ballads*. Here is another, more appropriate for singing, composed by Emily H. Woodmansee, a pioneer poet.

IN MEMORY OF THE MARTYRS

A little household band,
 Convened to praise and pray,
Seeking to understand
 Truth's simple, perfect way.
The land was free, why should there be
 One soul to say them nay?

Hark to the tramp of men [?]
 Of fiends in human guise.
Not tigers in their den,
 Glare with such baneful eyes.
Blood! Blood they seek. Ere one can speak
 Behold the sacrifice!

Ah, not in vain they fell,
 And not in vain they bled—
All with the just is well;
 Hail, ye illustrious dead!
But as for thee, sweet liberty,
 Oh, whither hast thou fled?

Embalm the forms so bruised,
 For all who loved them dear;
Love's right is not refused
 To weep around their bier.
To hearts that show such depths of woe
 God send the Comforter.

Think not ye weep alone,
 All Israel keenly smarts—
Your grief is Zion's own.
 Thousands of faithful hearts
For you indeed now intercede
 To Him, who peace imparts.

"How long, Oh Lord, Most High,
 Must human rights be crushed?"
"How long," the martyrs cry,
 E'en from the bloodstained dust.
Lord, why delay the reck'ning day,
 For come it surely must.[16]

After Utah had won statehood by clearing up its difficulties with the federal government and abandoning the practice of polygamy, people began to commit murder for more mundane reasons—jealousy, greed, drunkenness, conflict over rights and possessions. I have ballads illustrating all of these motives, and more. Even before statehood such earthy crimes were known. On Pioneer Day, 1891, at Moab, the celebration was interrupted by a disturbance that ended in the death of two people. The accustomed dance was going merrily along when one of the cowboys, Tom Roach, entered the hall. He was very drunk, and waved a loaded pistol threateningly. The merry-makers scattered, all but one. Roach's friend, Joe McCord, thinking the fellow was joking, stepped forward to remonstrate. Roach shot McCord dead. Now Mrs. Jane Walton, one of the first settlers of the town and a highly respected woman, went to the murderer to beg him to throw down his pistol. They talked quietly for a few breathless moments, during which Frank Adams slipped out and got a rifle. As Adams came back into the hall, he saw Roach and Mrs. Walton standing close together, and, fearing for the woman's life, raised the gun and fired. At that moment Roach moved aside, and the bullet from Adams' gun struck and killed Mrs. Walton. In the confusion following the double slaying, Roach escaped. A posse went after him, but he was never apprehended. Albert R. Lyman, a long-time resident of the San Juan country, provided many details of this story. The verses of the following song recounting the story (to be sung to the tune of "The Blind Child") were written by Otho Murphy of Moab.

THE DOUBLE TRAGEDY

Bright lights were shining in the hall,
    Everyone seemed happy and gay;
Making merry, one and all,
    As by the music they did sway.

Tripping feet of dainty maid,
    Scuffing feet of booted men,
Laughing remarks to pardners made,
    Rang out o'er mountain glen.

When quickly out upon the floor
    In anger strode Tom Roach,
His gun was glistening in his hand,
    There was no one to reproach.

At the bark of gun the startled crowd
    Whirled 'round toward the door.
The smoke was billowing as a shroud
    About the gunman on the floor.

"Out! File out! Everybody out!
    Speed up all," cried he.
He knew not what he was about,
    He was filled with raw whiskey.

Men and women, gasping dread,
    Fled out upon the street,
When with a shout and flying lead
    He cut off their retreat.

Now there are some that may return,
    But others out must stay;
With planted feet and countenance stern
    He forced them to obey.

Then walked up in confidence,
    Smiling, came McCord.
He said to Tom, "You'll let me in,
    For I've always been your pard."

But with a flick of gun Tom barred his way,
    "Not another step," he said.
McCord advanced that fatal step,
    And Roach's gun belched lead.

A look of surprise flashed in his eyes,
    "Roach, you've killed me," he said.
And with a last heartbreaking sigh,
    At Roach's feet fell dead.

The music swelled in sweet refrain,
    The floorman gave his call.
"Swing your pardners to the set!
    Let's on, boys, with the ball!"

Mrs. Walton standing by,
    With gentle voice did plead,
And Tom, with ever calming eye
    Her quieting voice did heed.

When suddenly within the door
    Frank Adams sprang.
In his hand a Winchester bore;
    His voice loudly rang.

"Roach!" Roach swayed aside,
    As the trigger was pressed,
And Mrs. Walton, falling, died
    With a bullet in her breast.

The confusion of the moment
    Of this last tragedy
Was the cover by which Roach
    In silent haste did flee.

The fatal shot that Adams fired,
    When in anger driven,
By Mrs. Walton's friends and kin
    Was in deep sorrow forgiven.[17]

Eight years later another Pioneer Day celebration was saddened by violent death—a murder and suicide, which took place July 23, 1899, in Kanab, Utah. A feud over water was behind it: William Roundy thought that Dan Seegmiller was "stealing" the irrigation water which it was his turn to have. On this hot summer morning, Roundy mounted his horse and rode up to Seegmiller's cabin. He called the owner outside. Seegmiller came, carrying his baby, and was shot down at his very door. Roundy then rode home, told his wife what he had done, shook hands with her and his son and went out into the yard and shot himself.

The crime shocked all Southern Utah. Both men were well-known, well-liked and respected citizens. Both were friends of my family. My great uncle preached the funeral sermon for each. The ballad concerning the case was found among my mother's papers after her death.

THE KANAB TRAGEDY

In Kanab they will always remember
   This Twenty-Fourth of July—
For this year there's no celebration,
   No band plays and no pennants fly.

The speeches they give in the church house
   Do not boast of our brave Pioneers;
There's no shouting, no dancing, no picnic;
   But there's sorrow and mourning and tears.

For two of the town's best men are lying
   In their coffins awaiting the earth;
[Line illegible where paper was folded]
   There's no room in our hearts now for mirth.

It happened because of hot anger—
   A quarrel about their water right,
William Roundy accused Dan Seegmiller
   Of stealing his turn in the night.

So Roundy jumped up on his pony,
   Rode right down to Seegmiller's door;
He shouted, "Come out and I'll show you,
   You'll not steal my turn any more!"

And Dan, little thinking of trouble,
   Came out with his babe in his arm;
His wife Emma stood there beside him,
   Neither yet felt the faintest alarm.

Then Roundy quick lifted his shotgun—
   Aimed it straight at Dan Seegmiller's heart;

Emma screamed and ran forward to stop him,
   [Another illegible line]

Dan fell to the ground with his boy.
   Weeping, poor Emma knelt down,
Not knowing if both husband and baby
   Were dead beside her on the ground.

Roundy turned then and rode to his own house,
   Where he kissed his wife fondly goodbye;
Then out into the yard he staggered,
   By his own cruel hand there to die.

So today there is no celebration,
   Kanab has no thought for Pioneers;
Two fine men now lie in their coffins—
   No wonder the town's bathed in tears! [18]

Whether the atmosphere of Southern Utah was more conducive to violence than the climate of other areas, or whether it was only that more versifiers lived in that region, I do not know, but I have more murder ballads from Utah's "Dixie" than from any other part of the state. Perhaps it is because my people came from there and I have had a better opportunity for collecting them there.

Utah's most noted crime in the classic tradition of a young man murdering his sweetheart to avoid marriage also took place in Southern Utah. It happened in Orderville, not far from Kanab, in the spring of 1908. Mary Steavens, 18, disappeared one day shortly before she was to graduate from the eighth grade. Lack of teachers, buildings, and books reduced the length of the school year so that scholars were a bit older when they finished elementary school than they are today. The long, anonymous ballad tells the story completely. It is sung to the tune of "The Fatal Wedding."

THE ORDERVILLE MURDER

Mary Steavens she had disappeared
   And nobody knew where.
Her mother was so worried,
   Her face was lined with care.
The neighbors said, "We'll go and look
   Up Gordon Hollow way."
For Mary was seen walking there
   Upon that April day.

They went to Gordon Hollow
   And there the searchers found
A pool of blood that had seeped up
   From underneath the ground.

It had been covered over
　　With a layer of red sand,
But it had seeped up through this
　　Like an avenging hand.

They looked about more carefully
　　And where some boulders sat
They saw the bright blue ribbon
　　Of Mary Steavens' hat.
They pulled away the boulders,
　　And underneath the stack
They found poor Mary's body
　　With four bullets in the back.

Now all the town was worried.
　　Who could have done this deed?
They looked about for other clues
　　And found one they could read.
It was some deep-made footprints
　　That made a wandering track—
Two sets to Gordon Hollow,
　　But just one coming back.

They got the shoes of every man
　　That lived in Orderville
To see if any fit those tracks—
　　Alvin Heaton's filled the bill.
The folks would not believe it;
　　Alvin was a favorite.
They shook their heads and muttered—
　　That clue was not read right.

But Alvin was arrested,
　　Placed in Kane County jail;
He listened to the charges;
　　His courage did not fail.
Justice Ford he kept a-questioning,
　　The whole county was distressed.
Then when no one was expecting it,
　　Alvin Heaton he confessed.

He said he'd been friends with Mary,
　　And had promised to be true;
She wanted him to marry her,
　　For a wedding was her due.
He begged her not to press him,
　　Some excuses must be found;
For she was not attractive;
　　She weighed two hundred pounds.

w would force him
child his name;
uldn't change her mind
well-planned game.
iotgun with him,
l slow in the track,
well behind her
he back.

he stream bed,
· with rocks.
ipon the ground;
a shock.
rith sand,
ed home,
ie stable
ɔw that he had roamed.

isaying
rang true.

ould do.
in,
done,
ity
n.[19]

'n portion of the state is a ballad concerning the mur-
… old man named Phipps. Phipps and a companion named Bowington—no first names given—settled down as neighbor hermits in a canyon above
Escalante. They were so isolated that the townsfolk never knew much about
them, nor were the details of the crime ever discovered. All that is known is that
Phipps was shot and Bowington confessed that he had done the deed.

THE MURDER OF POOR PHIPPS
(To be sung to the tune of "Birmingham Jail")

Remote in a canyon with walls of gray stone,
Two men had wandered, each to make his own home.
A handbreadth of farmland they divided and then
Each built his own shelter, for their journey must end.
The old man made a dugout, with a fireplace bright;
The young man a cabin, with logs that seemed right.
They lived there as neighbors and friends we suppose,
What were their past secrets,—there is no one who knows.

A cowboy found them, while looking for range;
Why they should live there seemed just a bit strange.
He reached for a handshake. "My name's Lay," he said.
"I'm Bowington, Mister." Then Phipps raised his head.
The cowboy came often, brought them food as of old,
Thought them army deserters because they had gold.
He sold Phipps a horse, and likewise his friend
Bought a horse and some cattle, then bartering did end.

Atop a small mesa, Phipps found a spot
He called it his pasture for the horse he had bought.
A short trail he made, while humming a tune,
Not knowing that here he would soon meet his doom.
These two men we thought friends—had they quarreled? We don't know.
Bowington wanted Phipps dead and plotted it so.

At the foot of the trail, perfect ambush he found,
Soon a bullet he fired; poor Phipps hit the ground.
In panic he fled, writhed in anguish all night,
Returned to the spot in the dawn's early light.
No comfort he found in the wail of coyote,
In circles the buzzards o'er the scene seemed to gloat.
Why had he lost reason and brought to an end
The life of an old man who had been his friend.

The corpse must be buried. He recoiled at the thought
Of touching his victim, the man he had shot.
He went in all haste to the residence of Lay—
Gave himself up; for his crime he must pay.
Brief was the story, not much written down;
In Phipps' little pasture grass waves o'er a mound.
'Tis the murdered whose soul sleeps in calm delight,
The murderer in anguish rolls in misery all night.[20]

In spite of the next to the last line, my informer assures me that the townsfolk believe that old Phipps's ghost wanders about the meadow. She has offered to take me to the site, but as yet I have been unable to accept the offer, much as I would enjoy obtaining a picture of this little-known grave.

There have been, of course, scores of murders in all parts of the state, and I do not mean to cast an invidious slur upon any one portion. I simply do not have many ballads from other areas. If these sections wish to be represented in the "Ditties of Death," their civic-minded people should see that I receive the ballads composed about their local tragedies.

NOTES

1. New York: Oxford University Press, 1958.
2. Hymn Book (Salt Lake City: Church of Jesus Christ of Latter-day Saints, n.d.), song no. 8.
3. *Deseret Evening News*, September 24, 1856, p. 2.
4. Collected from Francis Williamson, Little Rock, Arkansas, January 14, 1959.
5. Reva Stanley, *The Archer of Paradise* (Caldwell, Idaho: Caxton Printers, 1937), p. 333.
6. From my mother's scrapbook.
7. Salt Lake City, Utah: University of Utah Press, 1961, p. 445.
8. Collected from a friend in Virgin, Utah, who asked not to be identified, June 18, 1955.
9. Collected from Park Woolley, South Pasadena, California, date not noted.
10. John S. Davis, *Deseret Evening News* (Salt Lake City), February 17, 1858.
11. Collected from Lillian Metcalf Benedict, November 17, 1958.
12. Collected from Sylvester Greenhouse, Seattle, Washington, July 1959.
13. Hubbard, *Ballads and Songs from Utah*, p. 426; Harold Schindler, *Orrin Porter Rockwell—Man of God, Son of Thunder* (Salt Lake City: University of Utah Press, 1966), p. 359.
14. From my mother's scrapbook.
15. *Deseret Evening News*, August 28, 1884.
16. *Deseret Evening News*, August 23, 1884, p. 2.
17. Collected from Austin E. Fife, Logan, Utah, about 1956.
18. From my mother's papers.
19. Ibid.
20. Collected from Mable Baker Haycock, Escalante, Utah, March 1954.

5

Of Culture Heroes

Folklore has its gallery of culture heroes, historical or pseudohistorical personalities, who come to represent in caricature or in a hyperbolic way the basic character patterns of certain types of people. In Mormon society Joseph Smith, Brigham Young and others have gained some ascendancy in folklore; J. Golden Kimball has been elevated to the unique place of an heroic-comic character without equal. Others are emerging, two of the most prominent of whom are Samuel Brannan and Orrin Porter Rockwell, the subjects of these two essays.

The stuff of which folk heroes are made is voluminous and disparate. First of all, to attract interest and become a subject for oral and written lore a person must be an adventurer, an individual who distinguishes himself by being a nonconformist, a shocker, an enigma. He can belong to any profession, but he cannot be humdrum. He may be a wit and a swearing church official as was J. Golden Kimball, or he may be a reputed killer with a charmed life as was Orrin Porter Rockwell, the modern Samson and "destroying angel." He may also be a man of undaunted courage, strength, endurance, bravado, showmanship and duplicity, as was Samuel Brannan.

One special trait J. Golden Kimball, Samuel Brannan, and Porter Rockwell had in common, and that has led people to write and tell stories about them, is their paradoxical mixture of righteousness and perversity. Although saintliness was possessed in varying degrees by all three, each shows certain mundane traits which strip him of piety and make of him a follower of the primrose path. In such a role every man sees himself, for he thinks he is good despite his yielding to folly. Hence in a kind of self-justification he identifies with such personages and repeats and exaggerates their stories.

Nearly every dyed-in-the-wool Mormon who hears the name of Porter Rockwell immediately imagines a daring man with long braided hair and shaggy beard, a fearless, courageous, hard-drinking, devil-may-care gunman who loyally stood by Joseph Smith and Brigham Young, the prophets he believed in and loved. The name of Sam Brannan in like manner presents an image—the handsome dandy, the Rhett Butler of the California gold rush, the Midas for whom everything turned to gold, the positive, trigger-quick thinker, the saint and Elder who lost sight of God in his thirst for power. These are the images the folk have, and since they are property of the masses and since stories about these men are repeated to support the images, the men may be placed in the gallery of emerging Mormon culture heroes.

Mormon hero stories are derived from many sources, from local and family stories, from journals, church lesson manuals, and historical accounts.

Those presented herein would fail to qualify as genuine products of oral lore, a fact which in the eyes of some folklorists might disqualify them for inclusion in a book on folklore. On the other hand, Davy Crockett, John Henry, and Casey Jones emerged more through publicity than through oral lore, as Orrin Porter Rockwell and Sam Brannan are emerging. In these days when nearly all the folk write and when paper, not the memory, preserves records of the past, oral lore yields to paper. But their stories and legends are nevertheless the property of the folk.

T.E.C.

Gustive O. Larson

Orrin Porter Rockwell --The Modern Samson

Have you heard of Porter Rockwell?
He's a Mormon triggerite.
They say he hunts for horse thieves
When the moon is shining bright.
So if you rustle cattle
I'll tell you what to do;
Get the drop on Porter Rockwell
Or he'll get the drop on you.

They say that Porter Rockwell
Is a scout for Brigham Young—
He's hunting up the suspects
That haven't yet been hung.
So if you steal a Mormon girl
I'll tell you what to do;
Get the drop on Porter Rockwell
Or he'll get the drop on you![1]

That the Mormon "Danite" organization of Missouri days was continued in Utah has never been admitted by the Mormons nor ever doubted by certain non-Mormons. But the existence of a rugged, protective fringe of the society, made up of frontier stalwarts, has been recognized by everyone—admired and loved by the Saints or hated and feared by their enemies. The struggle to fix their image continues today as Utah's writers either glorify them on the one hand or vilify them on the other. These intrepid men were saints, patriots, martyrs, visionaries, fanatics, rogues, or murderers depending on their interpreters. Out of this controversial fringe emerges Orrin Porter Rockwell, one of the most colorful of Mormon scouts, Indian fighters, frontier lawmen, and "avengers of the Lord's people."[2]

Porter Rockwell stood apart from his associates in that he was invulnerable to enemy bullets due to a prophetic shield thrown about him; that is, he was protected if he met the conditions of the prophecy.

This modern Samson story began when Porter Rockwell, long-haired and bedraggled after several months in a Missouri prison, stumbled unexpected into a Christmas party given by Joseph Smith at the Mansion House in Nauvoo, Illinois. He had fled the Mormon society shortly after he and the Mormon prophet were sought as suspects in the attempted murder of Governor Boggs of Missouri. Lonely in Philadelphia and longing for some word of confidence from his prophet leader, Porter contacted Joseph by letter through a mutual friend. The letter began:

> Dear Brother Joseph Smith—
>
> I am requested by our friend Orrin Porter to drop a few lines informing you that he is in this place. His health is good, but his spirits are depressed . . . . He is most anxious to hear from you, and wishes you to see his mother and the children and write all the particulars, how matters and things are, and what the prospects are. I pity him from the bottom of my heart. His lot in life seems marked with sorrow, bitterness and care. He is a noble, generous friend. But you know his worth; any comments from me would be superfluous. He will wait in this place until he hears from you. . . .[3]

Rockwell soon ventured westward only to be captured in St. Louis and imprisoned to await trial. However, it was assumed that Porter was only the gunman for Joseph Smith in the attack on Boggs, and it was the latter the Missourians wanted brought to trial. During the days of imprisonment, deprivation, and suffering, Porter was repeatedly offered his freedom in return for betrayal of Joseph Smith into legal custody.

"You only deliver Joe Smith into our hands," said Sheriff Reynolds, "and name your pile."

"I will see you all damned first and then I won't," replied the friend of the prophet.

In the hope that it would entice the Mormon prophet into Missouri, Porter was held prisoner in Independence and Liberty for nearly ten months. He was never indicted for murder, but after an unsuccessful attempt to escape he went on trial on that charge.[4] He was acquitted and reluctantly released only to be hunted out of Missouri by those who knew only the law of revenge. With vengeance in his own heart and a natural endowment for survival, "Old Port" was already in the making when he presented himself so unceremoniously at the Mansion House party on December 25, 1843. The prophet was overjoyed upon penetrating his friend's disguise and pronounced a blessing upon him, adding a prophecy which Port related in later years as follows:

> Many years ago, the prophet Joseph Smith gave me a blessing and prophesied that as long as I let my hair grow, no bullet could ever touch me. He told me I'd be strong like Samson against the enemies of the church and never fall into their hands. It is a true prophecy and no bullet has ever touched me yet and none ever will, either. Yes sir, Joseph Smith was a true prophet.[5]

This conviction of invulnerability, strengthening a natural resourcefulness, brought Porter Rockwell into a leading role in the building of the Mormon kingdom. He was included by Joseph Smith in the select "Council of the Kingdom of God"; he not only assumed the role of bodyguard for his beloved prophet, but his guns began to speak against lawless attackers of outlying Mormon settlements. Soon the Illinois newspapers were referring to him as "the notorious Porter Rockwell," and it required all his cunning to elude his enemies. On one occasion, dressed as a woman in black, he passed in and out of the Mansion House where the pursuing officers sat at dinner.

When Joseph Smith decided upon escape to the West following the *Nauvoo Expositor* incident it was Rockwell who rowed him across the river, and he also who rowed him back again when his leader gave himself up and "went like a lamb to the slaughter." It was Rockwell also to whom Sheriff Backenstos, fleeing from an anti-Mormon mob, appealed for help and who then, as deputized officer, shot and killed Frank Morrell, one of the men who had played a leading role in the prophet's murder.

The prophet's death presented Rockwell with a test of allegiance. He managed to transfer his loyalty to Brigham Young not only because Joseph wanted it so, but because he found in Brigham another compelling personality to whom he could pledge his all. The exodus from Nauvoo and the journey to the Great Basin brought Porter's name repeatedly into many diaries, witnessing manifold activity including hazardous messenger service between Winter Quarters and Nauvoo, scouting the trails and supplying the exiles with buffalo meat. Finally he did liaison service between Brigham Young and Orson Pratt's advanced company of pioneers as it entered Salt Lake Valley, two days ahead of the Mormon leader. Then, before the year was out, Porter was on his way to California together with Jefferson Hunt to secure livestock, seeds, and other provisions for the infant colony. Upon his return, he brought one of the first reports of gold discovery and, together with most of the Saints, resisted the temptation to abandon Salt Lake Valley for the promise of California wealth.

The Mormons spread out rapidly to occupy the western slopes of the Wasatch, and Porter selected an isolated corner of southern Skull Valley for a livestock ranch. Horses being his first love, he traded shrewdly with the California migrants, and soon the brand O P became known to Mormons and Gentiles alike as representing the best in horse breeding. Later, when the Overland Stage road passed close by, he added and maintained two stations on that important route—one at Faust in Rush Valley and one at the Point of the Mountain at the south end of Salt Lake Valley.

As the gold rush emigration surged through the infant settlements and Gentiles began to infiltrate the Mormon kingdom as federal appointees, merchants, prospectors, and soldiers, the old conflicts of Missouri and Illinois were renewed in the Great Basin. It was inevitable that cattle rustling, horse thieving, and highway robbery would bring Porter into action. He was appointed deputy marshal in 1849 and continued in that capacity most of his lifetime. As a deputy he earned the appellation of "avenging angel of the Lord." In the eyes of the Gentiles he was chief of the Danites as reactivated in a Utah setting with a double responsibility of "taking care of" both offending Gentiles and straying Saints. This he did at the bidding of his ecclesiastical masters to save the errant souls who wandered too close to the brink of hell. Incidentally, he also provided eager Gentile writers with many bloody pages of unhistoric print.

"There is no record," wrote Kelley and Birney, "of a single killing of which Porter Rockwell was guilty during the 1850's, but he was known as a bloody-handed assassin from the Platt River to Cajon Pass. His name was synonymous with terror along the trails. . . . Porter and his fellows were everywhere regarded as murderers. It is certain that the reputation was earned, yet it is impossible for the historian to state that at such a place a certain man was killed by Porter Rockwell . . . ."[6]

Upon this premise the author presumes to lay bare, and even allow a certain benevolence in the motives behind the "holy murders" of the avenging angel. "Porter Rockwell murdered friends and foe alike at the order of his superiors, for the glory of God; keeping not one penny of the spoils for himself but turning everything into the treasury of Zion."[7] Thus while engaged in the duties of a frontier deputy marshal, he crept into the pages of Gentile literature as "killer for the Saints."

Indians too came to know "Old Port" as Brigham's lawman and found him closer to their own way of life than were most of the white settlers. When the war chief, Walkara, returned to the Mormon settlements following his flight from war on the Saints in 1853, Brigham Young sent Porter Rockwell and George W. Bean to meet him with a wagonload of trading goods. They were instructed to "keep Walkara in hand for a year even if it takes $10,000 to do it."[8] A peace conference was arranged to be held at Chicken Creek when Young would arrive there on his spring tour of the settlements. When that distinguished company arrived at Salt Creek (Nephi), Port and George W. were sent ahead to announce the president's arrival. They found the chief's lodge on Chicken Creek surrounded by eighty Indians and many chiefs present. The two were well received, especially when Port handed the chief a bottle of whiskey. Walkara knew it did not come from Brigham Young, so he gulped part of it down and hid the bottle under his blanket. Later, when an interpreter appeared announcing that the governor would receive the chief in his carriage, the Ute growled, "Tell Brigham if he wants to talk, he come here. I not leave tepee." The president, with some comment about "the mountain going to Mohamet," entered the tepee.[9]

An expert horseman, Porter was readily identifiable as he rode with long, black, gray-streaked hair flowing across his shoulders. Usually he wore it in braids which hung down his back Indian style or coiled in a tight bob at the nape of his neck. However, it often hung loose and his long beard hugged his chest as he sped into the breeze. He was of medium height with broad shoulders and a "chest round as a barrel." Skillful hands managed the reins lightly while huge spurs protruded from behind his stirruped feet above which leather leggings reached to his buckskin shirt. Revolver handles showed conspicuously on either side of his blouse. Port usually sawed his gun barrels to two inches so that they could fit handily into his blouse or pockets. His steel blue eyes searched out from below shaggy eyebrows in a somewhat high forehead. Characteristic too was his high, squeaky voice which rose to a shriek as he galloped across the hills and valleys with pistols firing or a lasso twirling above his head.

If Porter contributed to rumors reaching Washington that the Mormons were a law unto themselves, he was prepared to lend reality to rumor as the United States Army approached Utah in 1857. He and A. O. Smoot "hitched up two spans of our best animals [at Fort Bridger] to a small spring wagon," and setting out on July 18, he drove 513 miles in five days, reaching Salt Lake City on the twenty-third.[10] As the Nauvoo Legion went into defensive action, his own command, following Lieutenant General Daniel H. Wells's orders, harassed the invading troops by stampeding their animals, burning the grass before them, blockading their approaches, keeping them from sleeping at night, and driving off hundreds of their beeves to be delivered into the Mormon tithing yards. Then, after the U.S. Army had been pinned down for the winter in the Green River country, it was he who interrupted the official peace conference in Salt Lake City with news of its renewed advance.

The president's peace commissioners and Governor Cumming were seated on the rostrum with Brigham Young and his counselors. The new governor was addressing the Saints when Porter burst into the hall and marched up the aisle to President Young. Porter talked with Brigham in whispers for a moment, then stepped to the side of the platform and stood with his hands on the butts of his pistols. Brigham arose, took in every member of the official delegation with a sweeping glance, and said, "Sirs, are you aware that the federal troops are now on the march to this city?" And while the delegates looked at one another inquiringly, Brigham shouted, "Brother Dunbar, lead the assembly in Zion."[11] The whole assembly arose and with a fervor never before put into those lines they sang:

> In thy mountain retreat God will strengthen thy feet;
>   On the necks of thy foes thou shalt tread;
> And their silver and gold as the prophets foretold,
>   Shall be brought to adorn thy fair head.
>
> Oh Zion, Dear Zion! home of the free;
>   In thy temples we'll bend, all thy rights we'll defend
> And our home shall be ever with thee.
>
> Here our voices we'll raise, and we'll sing to thy praise,
>   Sacred home of the prophets of God;
> Thy deliv'rance is nigh, thy oppressors shall die,
>   And the Gentiles shall bow 'neath thy rod.

Old Port had no sympathy for the fleeing Governor John W. Dawson, who was beaten and robbed by some young ruffians on New Year's Eve of 1861. But the attack on federally appointed officers put the Mormons in a bad light and the hoodlums had to be punished. Three of them, headed by Lot Huntington, stole a highly prized mare and headed for California. The owner of the mare, Sam Bennion, appealed to Porter for help in recovering the animal, and soon a mounted posse was in pursuit. With unsurpassed skill in sign tracking, the long-haired scout soon singled out the horse's hoof prints from the many others, followed them in circles which were made to confuse pursuers, and then headed south through Jordan Narrows and on to Camp Floyd. It was clear the three fugitives were taking turns riding as they followed the Overland Stage road. At daybreak of the third day they overtook the thieves at the Faust Station. Old Port sent word for them to come out of the cabin and give themselves up. Two of them did so, but Huntington ran to the stable and led the mare out while carefully keeping her between himself and Rockwell. But one of the bars of the corral gate struck the mare in the flank and she plunged away from it, exposing Huntington momentarily. In that moment he fell dead from Porter's gun.[12] The other two were returned to Salt Lake where, it was reported, police officers shot them down as they attempted escape.

The next governor, Stephen B. Harding, gave a speech upon his arrival in which he announced that one of the first things he wanted to do was "to rid the country of that cutthroat, Porter Rockwell." Surrounded as he was by Gentile friends as well as Mormons, he paused for an expected demonstration of approval of his bold statement. But instead came Porter's high-pitched voice declaring, "Now Governor, you know damn well I never killed anybody who didn't deserve it."

However, Porter apparently thought quite a few did deserve it, and outlaws, robbers, and horse thieves stayed out of his way. They may not have believed it, but they were familiar with the rumor that somehow this Mormon two-gunman had a charmed life. Nor did Port forget the promise given him by his prophet friend and therefore allowed no scissors or razor to touch his hair or beard. Some said that he wore his hair so long that he could conceal a revolver in it.[13] Others told of how this redoubtable son of Dan had his hair singed by bullets, his hat and clothes pierced, and once he took off his coat and shook the slugs out upon the floor after an affray "but the word of the prophet held good. His hide was never so much as broken by a bullet."[14]

Merchants, cattle dealers, Wells Fargo Company and later the Union Pacific Company found use for his services. Each had stories to tell how the deputy marshal always got his man but that he didn't always bring him back alive. There was the time in 1861 when he helped Frank Kerrick recover eight mules and a horse which had disappeared from his outfit. The young freighter had just delivered a load of telegraph wire to Salt Lake City from Sacramento and appealed to Brigham Young for help in recovering his stolen animals. The president said, "I can't tell you that Porter will go, but if he does go with you, you'll get your mules back!" Porter went and four days later they overtook the thieves in spite of every trick used to throw the pursuers off the track. They had removed the shoes of the animals and dragged sagebrush to cover their tracks, but there was no escaping Old Port. Upon recovery of the animals Porter sent Kerrick ahead with them on the return journey. When Rockwell overtook him later that night, the grateful owner never inquired about the fate of the thieves nor did his benefactor mention them. When Kerrick later sent him a $500 saddle and a gallon of the best whiskey from Los Angeles, the old scout was especially pleased.[15]

Added to his skill in sign tracking was Rockwell's patience when in pursuit of criminals. Wells Fargo Company hired him to track down a clever highwayman who had stopped a stagecoach by playing dead in the desert. He received the strongbox at gunpoint and after shooting off the lock escaped with the gold. Porter trailed him to Cherry Creek and from the surrounding hills watched his movements for two weeks. His patience was rewarded one day when the robber dug up the gold by a cedar tree and put it into his saddlebags. Porter moved in, made the arrest, and transferred the gold to his own saddlebags. On the way back to Salt Lake City he stopped with his prisoner at his brother's ranch. While he slept, his charge slipped away and Port trailed him to Vernon and Fairfield before giving up the chase. Later the bandit made the mistake of sending a message to Wells Fargo Company from Fort Bridger accusing Porter Rockwell of stealing the gold. This time old Port got his man, but he had to track him to Butte, Montana, to do it.[16]

There were those who doubted Porter's invulnerability and for the prestige involved were willing to take a chance on disproving it. One such was Dave Dibble, recognized generally as a good shot. Porter was drinking in a Murray saloon. When he drank, he insisted that everyone drink with him or leave the place. But Dibble chose not to drink and pulled his six-shooter on Porter, emptying the gun with intent to kill. Rockwell was unscratched and Dibble was so unnerved that he ran from the place. Later he warned his friends not to try killing Rockwell because he couldn't be hit.[17]

Another who sought fame through exploding the myth of Porter's invulnerability came all the way from California. Porter was approaching his way station at the Point of the Mountain in his buckboard when he was accosted by a horseman who asked: "Are you Porter Rockwell?" Eyeing the stranger carefully, Port admitted he was. At that moment he caught sight of a pistol pointing at him from the saddle horn.

"I hear you can't be killed because of your hair," continued the stranger. "Well, I've come a long ways to kill you. This is your last minute on earth."

Port eyed him coldly and in his high-pitched voice mocked, "You can't kill a man without a cap on your gun." The horseman glanced down involuntarily at his cocked pistol, and in that instant Port's gun blazed away to close the episode.[18]

Notables who visited Utah in her early days included Porter Rockwell among those who must be contacted to make their stay complete. One at least placed Old Port second only to Brigham Young as the most interesting man in Utah.[19] Several left vivid impressions of the man. While most of them carried preconceptions of him as Brigham's "destroying angel," or "avenging angel of the Lord," they found him, on personal contact, friendly disposed and, as Sir Richard F. Burton reported, "He had a manner of a jovial, reckless, devil-may-care English ruffian." The old scout insisted that Burton's party join him in a "squar drink," which meant spirits without water. "Porter raised his glass with cocked little finger to his lips and with a twinkle of the eye ejaculated 'wheat,' that is to say 'good' and drained the tumbler to the bottom."[20]

Fitz Hugh Ludlow found the shaggy scout a "friendly entertainer" but couldn't forget that he could easily become an executioner. He reflected that Porter was "a terrible instrument to be handled by fanaticism having a powerful physical nature welded to a mind of narrow perspective, intense convictions and tenacity."[21] Remy and Brenchley also referred to his fanaticism, adding that Port was "incapable of doing wrong except under impression that he was doing right. . . . A lion in a lamb's skin, but a brave generous lion . . . ." He was "capable of the grandest devotion, ready to sacrifice himself in behalf of anyone who gained his esteem without regard to sect or person . . . ."[22] His hobnobbing and cooperation with Gentiles like Colonel E. J. Steptoe and General Patrick E. Connor was a source of no little concern to Brigham Young and other church leaders.

One witness caught Old Port in a playful mood. W. L. Morgan, quoted by Kelly and Birney, remembered "seeing Porter drunk as a lord, driving a bobsled loaded with boys and girls up and down Main street shouting his famous war cry as he lashed the horses at top speed. The hard packed snow was thrown in every direction by the flying hoofs, the children squealed with delight, and no one seemed to be having more fun than Porter—Old Port, chief of the Danites."[23]

Kelly and Birney continue with another pen picture of Porter gathered from Josiah F. Gibbs who stopped overnight at the Rockwell station on the stage line. "Porter Rockwell had loosened the braids of his long hair and was playing with his young grandchildren. He bounced them on his knee then got down on all fours and 'played horse'—the little ones straddling his back and driving him around the room with his long hair as reins."[24]

Never forgetting the prophet's promise about his hair, and not unmindful of a certain distinction it gave him, he grew proud of his long braids. George W.

Bean, who was assigned by Brigham Young to work with Rockwell among the Indians, referred to him as "a diamond in the rough." "He was always well armed," he said, "since his Nauvoo experiences, even though the Prophet Joseph had told him to wear his hair long and he would never be killed by an enemy. He believed in that promise. On many occasions when he stayed over night with me, my wife Elizabeth would plait or braid his hair, and Porter would comb it into a flare next morning, which emphasized his high forehead and his aristocratic air."[25] But usually it was his oldest daughter, Mary, who combed and did up his hair. She said:

> He couldn't comb it himself, and I have done it up hundreds of times. It was often in bad shape after a trip, and I enjoyed washing it out and doing it up again. Father used to fall asleep while having his hair combed, it was so pleasing and soothing to him. Once in Southern Utah a woman friend combing his hair undertook while he slept to snip off the tips to even it up. He was startled awake by the click of the shears as if it had been the click of a gun. We always made two great braids, one back of each ear and folded them four times across the back, and tied them . . . no woman ever had more beautiful hair than father's, and we were all proud of it, believing with him that it served in some manner to protect him.[26]

But there came a time when Old Port was forced to make a choice between what he regarded as personal safety and a good deed for another. On one of his visits to California he met the widow of the prophet's brother, Don Carlos, who had become bald through a fever. Without hesitation he sacrificed enough of his hair to make her a wig. It was the least he could do, he said, for one so near to the man he loved.[27] It was said that he complained in later years that he had difficulty in controlling his drinking habits after his hair was cut.

"Men of sixty-five or over in Utah today," wrote John Henry Evans in 1933, "remember Orrin Porter Rockwell riding wildly up and down main street in Salt Lake City, his long hair streaming in the wind, yelling like a Comanche and lassoing the signs hanging out from the store fronts; or standing half drunk, on a tree stump in front of a saloon and letting out one of his long hoots, a compound of all Indian yells, with something of his own added, which threw such a scare into the stranger as to make him take to his heels; or reeling into a saloon in one of the mining camps feigning intoxication and then all of a sudden whipping out his two guns, lining everybody up against the bar and taking out his man."[28]

Porter ran a delivery stable in Salt Lake City where he sold some of his thoroughbred horses. After attending a show at the Salt Lake Theatre on the night of June 8, 1878, he went to the stable to spend the night as was his habit.

He was found dead the following morning. Doctors pronounced the cause heart failure. Long after his body had been laid to rest in the Salt Lake Cemetery, a Grantsville citizen by the name of Richard Rydalch reported an unusual experience. According to Kelly and Birney he said,

> You know he used to be always yellin' at his horses, especially when he had a little liquor in him. When he was real lit up, you could hear him comin' a mile away. Well, anyway I was asleep one night when along about midnight something woke me up. I listened for a minute, and then I heard Old Port goin' by the house yellin' at his horses. Yes sir, just as plain as I'm talking to you now. It was him all right. I'd never mistake that voice. He was just tearin' down the road, and I could hear him hollerin' way down the valley. I never could quite figure it out. I wasn't dreamin', I was awake, the yellin' woke me up. I says to myself, 'Here comes Old Port, drunk again': Then I remembered that Port had been dead a long time.[29]

NOTES

1. Anonymous, quoted in Nicholas Van Alfen, *Porter Rockwell, The Mormon Frontier Marshal* (Salt Lake City, 1964), p. 157.
2. Most recent among efforts to interpret Rockwell is Harold Schindler's *Orrin Porter Rockwell—Man of God, Son of Thunder* (Salt Lake City: University of Utah Press, 1966). From an extensive research Schindler has presented Rockwell in a historical pattern without always discriminating between fact and legend. His interesting "history" contains a good deal of folklore.
3. *Millennial Star* 20: 215.
4. Monte B. McLaws, "The Attempted Assassination of Missouri's Ex-Governor, Lilburn W. Boggs," *Missouri Historical Review*, October 1965, pp. 50-56, probably represents the best research on this phase of the subject to date.
5. Kelly and Birny, *Holy Murder* (New York, 1934), quoting Don McQuire, p. 259.
6. Ibid., p. 114.
7. Ibid.
8. George W. Bean, *Autobiography* (Salt Lake City, 1945), p. 94.
9. Ibid.
10. Edward Tullidge, *History of Salt Lake City* (Salt Lake City, 1886), p. 157.
11. Austin and Alta Fife, *Saints of Sage and Saddle* (Bloomington, 1956), p. 88.
12. This story is well told in Van Alfen, *Porter Rockwell*, pp. 101-8.
13. Ray B. West, Jr., *Kingdom of the Saints* (New York, 1957), p. 132.
14. Wallace Stegner, *Mormon Country* (New York, 1942), p. 153.
15. Van Alfen, *Porter Rockwell*, pp. 140-49.
16. Ibid., pp. 116-21.
17. Ibid., p. 95.
18. Ibid., pp. 113-15.
19. Fitz Hugh Ludlow quoted by Kelly and Birney, *Holy Murder*, p. 223.
20. Richard F. Burton, *The City of the Saints*, p. 545.
21. Fitz Hugh Ludlow, quoted by Van Alfen, *Porter Rockwell* p. 134.

22. Remy and Brenchly quoted by Van Alfen, *Porter Rockwell*, p. 139.
23. Kelly and Birney, *Holy Murder*, p. 249.
24. Ibid., p. 249.
25. Bean, *Autobiography*, p. 175.
26. Kelly and Birney, *Holy Murder*, pp. 255-56.
27. John Henry Smith, *Joseph Smith, An American Prophet* (Salt Lake City), pp. 268-69.
28. Ibid.
29. Ibid., pp. 263-64.

Thomas E. Cheney

Samuel Brannan -- A Double Exposure

Rich legend generates in the fertile soil of folk imagination around the name of an unusual man. Folk of every society love to retell exciting tales, and in the retelling the folk hero emerges.

"Dreamer . . . Leader . . . Empire Builder" are the words written on the tombstone of Samuel Brannan in San Diego, California, heralding the deeds of this colorful western adventurer. A dreamer, leader, and empire builder is sure to catch fire in the imagination of the folk. And Samuel Brannan did. Records of adventure in early California supply a great variety of stories of Sam Brannan: Sam Brannan and His Ship of Mormons, Sam Brannan and the Gold Rush, Sam Brannan and the *California Star*, Sam Brannan and the Vigilantes, Sam Brannan—the Builder, Sam Brannan—the Multi-millionaire, Sam Brannan—the Drunkard.

Articles and books about him have been entitled *The First Forty-Niner and the Story of the Golden Tea Caddy, Samuel Brannan and the Golden Fleece*, "Herald of the Gold Rush—Sam Brannan," *Sam Brannan, Builder of San Francisco*, "Immortal Sam Brannan on His Way to Empire," "Sam Brannan, Great Man of History," and *The Gay Saint*. The enterprising, adventurous, daring, courageous individual that Brannan was put him in the limelight.

Brannan at the age of seventeen had served apprenticeship as a printer and had become a traveling journalist. His wanderings brought him into contact with the newly organized Mormon Church, which he joined and for which he became publisher and editor of the newspaper *The Prophet*, and its successor, *The Messenger*, in New York.

A study of the man's life from this point reveals an ambivalence rarely encountered. Although anyone studying printed accounts of him and his activities would be cognizant of his change, of his being a developing character, few would be able to determine what countenance the man really wore. For that reason I shall present two portraits, piece together various accounts, and thereby show startlingly different faces. The reader may prefer the conservative portrait or he may favor the crimson-colored approach to this remarkable man.

SAMUEL BRANNAN – A PASSPORT PORTRAIT

In 1844, when Brannan was twenty-five years old, he was publisher of the Mormon paper *The Prophet*. On June 29, 1844, he published a song which began:

> The God that others worship is not the God for me,
> He has no parts or body, and cannot hear and see
> But I've a God that lives above
> A God of power and love,
> A God of revelation, O, that's the God for me.[1]

An Elder in the church, he was an active leader and defender. During part of the time that he published *The Prophet* and *The Messenger*, he worked under the editorship of the Prophet Joseph Smith's brother, William Smith, and later under Elder Parley P. Pratt. The January 25, 1845, issue, however, appeared with Brannan's name as both publisher and editor.

In 1845 Elder Orson Pratt of the council of apostles of the Mormon Church was presiding in the eastern states. Joseph Smith and his brother Hyrum had been killed by a mob, and the Mormons who were being harassed in Illinois were now contemplating moving beyond the borders of the United States. On November 8, Elder Pratt issued a message to the Saints of the eastern and middle states, calling upon them to join in the exodus of the church from Nauvoo, Illinois, to the West, and to do it by the ensuing spring. (Original spelling and punctuation have been preserved in this and the following quotations.)

> "We do not want one saint to be left in the United States after that time," said the message. "Let every branch," he continued, "in the east, west, north and south be determined to flee out of 'Babylon,' either by land or sea, as soon as then." "If all want to go," said he, "charter half a dozen or a dozen vessels and fill each with passengers, and the fare among so many will be but a trifle" . . . President Pratt announced in his message that Elder Samuel Brannan was appointed to take charge of the company that would go by sea. And all who might go with him were admonished "to give strict heed to his instruction and counsel."[2]

A conference was convened in New York on November 12, "Elder Samuel

Brannan laid before the conference his instructions from the authorities of the church, directing him to go by water to California; and he called upon those who desired to go with him to give in their names."[3]

Brannan set sail on the ship *Brooklyn* with 238 Mormons aboard on February 4, 1846, and arrived at Yerba Buena—San Francisco Bay—on July 29, 1846, five months and twenty-seven days later.

En route Brannan had stopped at Honolulu to deliver cargo and take on provisions. The war with Mexico had attracted the attention of the adventurous Mormon Elder. Ralph B. Jordan tells the following story:

> "I'm going to California," Sam boasted to Stockton, "and take a place on San Francisco Bay called Yerba Buena from the Mexicans. There I'm going to build a city for my people and the United States. I've got a battalion of well-drilled men but I need guns."
>
> When the *Brooklyn* resumed her weary way, one hundred fifty rifles were stacked beneath her billowing canvas.[4]

Brannan and his group arrived in California; Jordan's story continues:

> His eyes alight with the fires of conquest and adventure, Brannan stared eagerly at the tiny hamlet of Yerba Buena—the San Francisco to be—as it clung miserably to the steep sandhills.
>
> "Not over fifty or sixty people in the town," Brannan murmured, letting his eyes run over the three hundred, including the crew, who lined the rails of the *Brooklyn*. "There should be no real resistance."
>
> And then his fiery gaze fell on the flagstaff of the Mexican customshouse, the "Old Adobe," in the center of the sandblown Plaza. He gulped in astonishment. For snapping in the breeze was not the flag of Mexico, but the Stars and Stripes. Captain John B. Montgomery on the United States sloop *Portsmouth* had beaten Sam to Yerba Buena by three weeks.
>
> "I swore at that American flag," Brannan said years later. "I could have torn it down. That's how badly I wanted to take the town myself."[5]

On January 9, 1847, a half year after arrival of the *Brooklyn* in San Francisco Bay, Brannan published California's first paper, *The California Star.* He had brought along two young printers who had worked with him before, E. P. Jones and Ed Kemble. The paper was royal sheet size, about twelve by fourteen inches, and written in three columns. In content, make-up, and mechanical perfection it was superior to much of the journalism of the day. This publication reflects the character, ambitions, interests, and attitudes of the publisher. In the first issue the following item appeared and was repeated in several subsequent issues:

Prospectus of "The California Star"

The undersigned in common with the rest of the citizens of the United States, having experienced the good effects of the press in diffusing early and accurate information on all important subjects, in advocating and defending the rights of every class of people, in detecting, exposing, and opposing tyranny and oppression and being anxious to secure himself and the citizens of his adopted country, the benefits of a free, fearless and untrammelled Newspaper—purchased and brought with him to California a press and all the materials necessary to effect this desirable object.

We shall at all times speak truth of men and measures. We will endeavor to render the "STAR" pleasing and acceptable to all classes of readers by collecting and publishing the latest news from all parts of the world.

. . . and will eschew with the greatest caution every thing that tends to propagation of sectarian dogmas.

The *Star* will be an independent paper uninfluenced by those in power or the fear or abuse of power, or of patronage or favor.

Samuel Brannan[6]

Brannan kept his promises in this prospectus. He did not limit the newspaper (as his previous publication, *The Prophet*, had been limited) to explication and promotion of the Mormon sect.

Brannan's becoming and being an empire builder is explicit and implicit in the tone of *The California Star*. On March 14, 1847, the following appeared under the title, "Our Town and its Prospectus":

. . . the most thriving town or city on the American continent.

300 to 500 houses will probably go up this year.

The town of Yerba Buena is destined to be the Liverpool or New York of the Pacific Ocean![7]

In the March 20 issue appeared the following: "Our readers will perceive that in our present number we have conformed to the change recently made in the name of our town by placing at the head of our paper San Francisco instead of Yerba Buena. The change has now been made legal and we acquiesce in it, though we prefer the old name."[8]

Within its first year of publication *The California Star* listed the total population of San Francisco as 449, of whom 34 were Indians, 40 South Islanders, 10 Negroes. It further breaks the population down into 138 females, 331 males and specifies that 89 could not read or write. It concludes the statistical report with the prediction: "San Francisco is destined to become the great commercial emporium of the North Pacific coast."[9]

To promote building of the empire, Brannan had earlier made plans for a school. He said: "We have no children, but we feel a deep interest in the proper education and moral training of the children in the country—We will give one half of a lot of fifty varos square in a suitable part of the Town, and fifty dollars in money."[10]

In the third issue of his paper, January 23, 1847, Brannan refers with derision to a competitor, *The Californian*. Of his own paper he says, "We have the only office in all California, in which a decent looking paper can be printed."[11] It appears that *The Californian* retaliated, for on September 4, 1847, the *Star* carried the following item:

> "The Mormon Press"—This is a ridiculous appellation applied to this establishment owned by Mr. Samuel Brannan, by Messrs. Buckdew & Co. of the newspaper "Californian". . . .
>
> How contemptuously weak and unprincipled: To attempt the coupling of a sect with an independent *press* of acknowledged neutrality.[12]

This is a justifiable expression of indignity since Brannan's paper had assiduously avoided sectarianism.

The tone of the paper is serious and humanitarian, showing a Christian spirit of service. For example, periodic news of the suffering of the Donner party is printed, solicitations made for their welfare, and a report given of Yerba Buena having raised $1500 for relief "of these unfortunate people."[13]

The *Star* also carried philosophical and ethical editorials; following is an example.

> Have the courage to discharge a debt while you have the money in your pocket. Have the courage to do without that which you do not need, however much you admire it. Have the courage to speak your mind when it is necessary that you should do so; and to hold your tongue when it is better that you should be silent. Have the courage to speak to a friend in a "seedy" coat, even in the street, and when a rich one is nigh; the effort is less than many people think it to be, and the act is worthy a king. . . . Have the courage to pass your host's lacky at the door, without giving him a shilling, when you know you cannot afford it—and what is more, that the man has not earned it. . . .
>
> Have the courage to tell a man why you will not lend him your money; he will respect you more than if you tell him you can't.
>
> Anonymus[14]

On April 26, 1847, Samuel Brannan left Yerba Buena going overland toward the east to meet Brigham Young and the Mormon emigrants. In the September 18 issue of *The California Star* appeared a report as follows: "Mr. S. Brannan, publisher of the paper after an absence of nearly six months arrived at this place on Friday morning last, 28 days from Fort Hall."[15]

The article reports further that they may expect no more than ninety wagons to arrive that year in California. Of the Mormon emigration it says that up to August 7, 480 souls, mostly men, had arrived in the Great Salt Lake Basin. "They have laid off there and commenced a town, planting large crops which are flourishing and have in supplies eighteen months provisions and general health is good." Then the article continues, "They contemplate opening an entire new road through to this country, in connection with the present rendezvous, and when completed, they move *en masse* to the valleys of California."[16]

Following is an account of Brannan's experience with Brigham Young as recorded in 1881:

> Members of the Mormon Battalion who met Sam Brannan returning from his trip to meet the Saints in September 1847 report this account of him: "We learned from him that the Pioneers had reached Salt Lake Valley in safety, but his description of the valley and its facilities was anything but encouraging. Among other things, Brother Brannan said the Saints could not possibly subsist in the Great Salt Lake Valley, as, according to the testimony of mountaineers, it froze there every month in the year, and the ground was too dry to sprout seeds without irrigation, and if irrigated with the cold mountain streams, the seeds planted would be chilled and prevented from growing, or, if they did grow, they would be sickly and fail to mature. He considered it no place for an agricultural people, and expressed considerable confidence that the Saints would emigrate to California the next spring. On being asked if he had given his views to President Brigham Young, he answered that he had. On further inquiry as to how his views were received, he said, in substance, that the President laughed and made some rather insignificant remark, "but," said Brannan, "when he has fairly tried it, he will find that I was right and he was wrong, and will come to California."[17]

The complete story covering the letters, documents, and a multitude of available material on Brannan's dealings with Brigham Young between the time of Brannan's rise to leadership in the church and the time of his being disfellowshiped in 1851 could be a book in itself. It shows persistence of Brannan in attempt after attempt to attract the main body of the church to California and a stubborn resistance by Brigham Young. It reveals a continuing decline in Brannan's religious interests and a growing interest in power and wealth and empire building.

> It is related in the diary of William Clayton that Brannan reached Brigham Young on the Green River, June 30, 1847 . . . . The triumphant Brannan painted a glowing picture of the West Coast. He assured Brigham Young he had found the haven for the Saints. He described San Francisco, New Hope, and the vast resources of the Pacific Coast awaiting the touch of Anglo-Saxon genius. With high enthusiasm he urged Brigham Young to press on to California. However, the great leader had been instructed—

whether by inspiration or revelation—that the Valley of the Great Salt Lake was to be the abode of the Mormon people and the source of their economic and spiritual vitality. While Brannan persisted, Brigham Young stood adamant . . . . He [Brannan] could not understand Brigham. It seemed to him sheer nonsense. He was dismayed and discouraged for his opportunity for influence and leadership in the Church had vanished. Brannan stayed only a few days in the Salt Lake Valley and these were days of discouragement, deflation, and to him disillusionment. His faith in the Prophet of the Lord was "shell-shocked." From that moment forward he began to cast his lot with the adventurers and wealth seekers of California. He was moving out of the company of the builders of the new Zion in the Valley of the Mountains.[18]

As we follow the story of Brannan we cannot help but see his great love for California. Paul Bailey says, "Few mortals have loved California more fervently than did Samuel Brannan. In his belief that the Saints eventually would go to the Pacific Coast he labored stubbornly and long. He could not conceive that eventually history was to back up Brigham's choice, or give proof to [his] contention that California was poor nurture-ground for Mormonism."[19]

En route home from Great Salt Lake Basin, Brannan stopped briefly at Sutter's Fort and projected a mercantile business there, an extension of his San Francisco store, with Charles Smith as partner. This carried him onto the road of riches, for gold was soon to be found in the region in surprising abundance.

Brannan was a man with astute vision (when free enterprise looked golden) and an adventurer and gambler who often made the wheel of fortune turn exclusively for himself.

Henry W. Bigler, one of the Mormon men, tells of the discovery and mining of gold as follows:

[We found] 7 of them [Mormon Battalion men] at work and had taken out that day two hundred and fifty dollars. This was the spot where the few particles were found at the time Willis and Hudson were returning from the sawmill in March . . . . It was about this time that one or both of the Willises had business that called them away from the digings and went to the 'Yerba Buena' (as it was then called, now San Francisco) where they met with Sam Brannan and reveals to him the gold discovery. Brannan tells them he could secure their gold mine as church property and advised that all the Battalion boys go to work diging gold and pay to him [Brannan] one tenth as their tithing and he would see that it was turned over to the Church with the understanding that he was to come in with the Brother Willis and Hudson as one of the share holders in the claim until it was secured to the Church. Brannan published the discovery in his paper, "called the *California Star*," that gold was found in rich abundance by the Mormon boys on the south fork of the American River and in a verry short time all of California and I may say all the world was on the move for the land of gold, seeking their fortunes.[20]

Of gold discovery the *California Historical Society Quarterly* says,

> When Sam was ready for the news to be *known* and ready for the rush on his stores for equipment, he roused the lethargy in San Francisco in a most dramatic way. Rushing to San Francisco's plaza, he doffed his broad-brimmed black hat, and holding it aloft a bottle of glittering particles in his left hand he bellowed in his great bull voice:
> "Gold! Gold! Gold! From the American River."
> The Gold Rush was born that instant. Uncertainty passed from the minds of his listeners, for Sam Brannan was well-liked and regarded as the foremost of business leaders. Almost over night the town was deserted and the stampede was on.[21]

Opportunist that Brannan was, he soon had his finger in every pie. His three mercantile houses during the restless peak months of the gold rush did a business of $150,000 a month. Fantastic stories of his worship of riches and his free giving and spending are almost sure to leave a glitter in the eyes of any reader, regardless of the rung of the ladder of personal acquisition on which he rests. One writer summarizes as follows:

> By the early '50's, Brannan owned one-fourth of Sacramento, one-fifth of San Francisco, including all of Market Street, 160,000 acres in Los Angeles county, tracts in Honolulu and a fleet of ships, in addition to his newspaper and the huge Sacramento business. He was one of the richest men in the world, fifteen times a millionaire. One time, to celebrate the opening of a new Sacramento hotel, he entertained the entire city. He floated the huge bond issue with California gold with which Mexico threw off the yoke of Maximilian and personally paid the bills of the Mexican Foreign Legion, known during the period as Brannan's Contingent.[22]

Muir lists other accomplishments as follows:

He founded Yuba City.
Established lucrative ship trade with China, Hawaii, and the East Coast.
Organized the first vigilantes committee to combat crime.
Opened City Hall in Sacramento.
Founded and was first president of the Society of California Pioneers.
Founded the San Francisco Fire Association.
Founded two railroads.[23]

Concerning his dealings with the Mormon colony, the Bancroft notes quote the "Annals of San Francisco" of 1846 as saying that Brannan "dealt perfectly with the emigrants he brought to California on the *Brooklyn* although his enemies have asserted that he converted the property of the company to his own use."[24]

Many of Brannan's letters show a spirit of religious orientation, as for example the following written April 26, 1847, telling of his experience crossing the pass where the Donner party had met its terrible fate. Brannan had crossed in twenty-six hours on ice-crusted snow.

> We traveled on foot and drove our animals before us, the snow was from twenty to one hundred feet deep. When we arrived through, not one of us could stand on our feet. The people of California told us we could not cross under two months, there being more snow on the mountains than had ever been known before; but God knows best, and was kind enough to prepare the way before us.[25]

The following incident told by Amelia D. Everett in an article entitled "The Ship *Brooklyn*" published in the *California Historical Society Quarterly* appears to reveal the spiritual character and humility of Brannan:

> . . . [A] few days after leaving New York, she [the *Brooklyn*] encountered a great storm. . . . On the passenger deck, all manner of household furnishings were crashing into each other. "Sister Laura Goodwin was thrown from a ladder and lay critically injured. Old Brother Ensign and his daughter Eliza were dead. It was only by realizing that the Lord holds the waters in His hand that we could have faith to be delivered from our perilous condition."
>
> As they neared the treacherous coast of the Cape Verde Islands, Samuel Brannan adjured them to "Sing! Sing all!" And, with "The Spirit of God Like a Fire is Burning," and "We Are Going to California," the Saints sang down the howl of the winds and the roar of the waves. Captain Richardson, having given up hope went below to prepare his passengers for the worst. He was astonished to find them singing, singing all, in the face of a watery grave. Suddenly the wind died to a sailing breeze; the sun came out, and, in thanks for their deliverance, the voyagers knelt in prayer.[26]

Amelia Everett also makes the following generalization regarding his religious activities in California: "Elder Brannan is said to have officiated at the town's first American wedding—Lizzie Winner to Basil Hall. He continued to urge his flock to hold strictly to the regulation for meetings, and not let themselves be led astray by the ways of the Gentiles. For a time he was the only preacher in the community; . . ."[27]

Many writers, as they study Brannan and attempt to determine his true religious attitudes, quote Sergeant William Coray's diary. Of it Eugene Campbell says:

> There has been some conjecture as to whether he [Brannan] was a sincere convert to the Mormon Church. Sergeant William Coray, a member of the Mormon Battalion who knew Brannan in San Francisco, recorded in his journal that Brannan "would play billiards and drink grog with the greatest blacklegs in the place, saying that it was policy to do so. He said to me one time when he was intoxicated, 'every act of my life

is through policy.' " If this is true, there may be some basis for a question as to the sincerity of his espousal of the Mormon cause.[28]

It is true that Brannan's sincerity may be questioned. However, Coray's experience with Brannan came after Brannan had been excommunicated, when he was deteriorating from drink and gambling and when he might himself have been questioning his own motives.

Coray also wrote the following in his journal which might reveal more of the true spirit of the man than does the above statement made when he was drinking: "However, Brannan seems to have taken 'his position as a Mormon leader seriously,' at least up to the time the saints were established in California. He demanded that the saints keep the Sabbath and conduct themselves honestly and morally. He lectured regularly on board the ship and in Honolulu, and also in California after the saints' arrival there."[29]

Brannan is often said to have been arrogant and proud, one who chose never to stoop. Yet an incident in his early experience shows at least one time when he bowed to authority. It occurred in 1845 when he was publishing *The Prophet* for the church in New York under the direction of Apostle William Smith. Joseph Smith and his brother Hyrum had been murdered in Carthage. William Smith did not support the decision of the Council of Twelve in their choosing to allow the mantle of the Prophet Joseph to fall on Brigham Young. In fact, he was setting himself up as a claimant to the office. He vociferously denounced Brigham Young for usurping authority. Brannan followed Smith. When Wilford Woodruff, one of the Council, reprimanded Smith and Brannan for seditious and inflammatory doctrine and informed them that the Council at Nauvoo had disfellowshiped them from the church, William Smith was in a rage and continued to rail against the "Brighamites" for breaking the Patriarchal order in taking the church from the Smiths. As a result, William immediately went to Nauvoo to put them right. Parley P. Pratt, a capable and tactful member of the Council, was on his way to New York to preside over the church in that area. Finding Brannan still loyal to the restored gospel, Pratt advised him to go to Nauvoo and plead for reinstatement. Brannan said that he did not want to lose the earthly and heavenly benefits the church offered and that he could answer the charges. Accordingly, he went to Nauvoo, presented himself humbly before the Council of Twelve Apostles, said he was enormously stricken with the loss, and in complete repentance pledged allegiance to the established leadership.

His plea was accepted, he was reinstated in full fellowship, and within a year had been chosen by the Council to manage the exodus from New York to the west coast by water.[30]

This meeting in Nauvoo was Brannan's first personal encounter with Brigham Young. When the *Brooklyn* was in preparation for sailing, Young refused to sign a contract for the church which Brannan had asked him to sign. But the blow which finally nailed Brannan to the floor was Brigham Young's refusal to bring the body of the Latter-day Saints to California.

Then, at Sutter's Fort, Sam Brannan, with gold dust in his eyes and glittering opportunities pounding at the door inviting him to fame, power, and riches, dedicated himself to the service of his own vaulting ambition.

Whether he collected tithes from the California Mormons—both those brought around the Cape and the soldier boys of the Mormon Battalion who had joined in the diggings—for personal gain or not is difficult to determine. At the time the gold rush began, Brannan may still have had hopes of bringing the main body of the church to California, and he may have said and meant what Reva Scott says he did: "We ought to build a church out here on the coast, and maybe later a temple. I think I'll collect more than ten per cent of your wages. The church needs money now, and if you boys can have gold just for the picking it up you ought to be willing to give more to the Church."[31]

Records, however, show clearly that none of the money was turned over to the central church. Brigham Young wrote to Brannan asking for the tithing to be sent to headquarters and added to it a bold request for extra funds for himself and counselors. Sam was in a rage, but before Young let the matter drop, he sent Apostle Amasa Lyman accompanied by Apostle Charles C. Rich and the long-haired scout, Porter Rockwell, to collect. Confrontation between Lyman and Brannan reportedly resulted in the Apostle's demanding authoritatively "the Lord's money." Sam answered, "I'll give it to Him when you bring me a receipt signed by the Lord."[32]

When Apostle Parley P. Pratt visited San Francisco in 1851, he knew it was useless to ask again for the tithing money. Sam Brannan was invited to come to church, but declined, being too deeply hurt. Accordingly, "Fellowship was withdrawn from Brannan by a unanimous vote for a general course of unchristianlike conduct, neglect of duty, and for combining with lawless assemblies to commit murder and other crimes."[33] The concluding statement refers no doubt to Brannan's leadership in the Vigilance Committee in which he was active at the time of his being disfellowshiped from the church.

The Gold Rush had brought to California a lawless element, many of whom were former Australian convicts who could not be controlled by the ineffective and poorly organized law. These ex-convicts and ruffians called the "Hounds" held San Francisco in a reign of terror. Sam Brannan stepped into one of his finer roles in restoring law and order to the harassed city. It was the spring of '49 when he first took action. The Hounds in an organized group attacked the Chilean section of the city in an appalling, hellish orgy of arson, theft, rapine, and murder. The handful of police were deaf to the horrified cries of San Francisco's residents to put a stop to the bloody, burning, screaming madness. But Sam Brannan was not afraid. He passionately aroused a committee of men and set out to punish the Hounds. But immediate help for the people of "Little Chili" came first. He put a gold piece in his hat, passed it around, and shortly handed a hat full of gold to Banker Adams. "Put that in your safe," he said, "and come back. We'll be getting a posse together."[34]

And Brannan did just that. The posse, organized under the name of The Committee of Vigilance, began immediate action. Offenders were brought to trial, convicted, and hanged. In revenge the rascals again set fire to the city.

> ... But this proved to be the last of the Six Great Fires: Sam's Vigilantes saw to that. By the end of the month they numbered between five and six hundred members, and a decrease in crimes of all kinds ensued.
>
> Sam led in the work of incessant re-building, and each time he saw the city grow stronger. Makeshift storehouses ... were succeeded by large fireproof warehouses, Sam actually importing dressed granite for that purpose from China. Other fireproof materials included lava from Honolulu, and bricks from Australia, New York, and even London.[35]
>
> President of the ever memorable Vigilance Committee of '51, he placed himself in a position of danger few would be willing to accept; and then his friends were in constant fear for his life. But he never for an instant quailed, nor faltered in the discharge of what he conceived to be and was a righteous duty. As to his generosity, he has been a public benefactor.[36]

In 1859 when Sam was forty years of age his fortune changed. Four factors contributed to his rapid disposal of his plentiful lands and gold: first, he was generous to a fault, a reckless spender, a careless philanthropist; second, his wife appeared to be bent on dissipating his fortune, a true helpmate in casting money to the winds; third, his gambling both at the card table and in wildcat ventures increased; fourth, he began drinking. Typical of his reckless spending is an incident revealed in the following: "In 1853, he was elected state senator, but resigned at once, because of 'important business engagements in New York.' The honor, however, he treasured. It was the time of his greatest affluence and his greatest power; the time when the way to advertise a product in California was to announce on huge signs: 'Sam Brannan Buys It!' When the exotic Lola Montez appeared at the American Theater in May, 1853, Sam Brannan, who had met her on the ship coming back from one of his New York trips, paid five hundred dollars for a box at her opening night."[37]

Of his philanthropies, the incident told below is most exciting. He became known as an "easy touch" and not without reason. About 1868, when France was supporting Maximilian as "Emperor" in Mexico, the former President of Mexico, Juarez, hoping to restore Mexican rule, sought to sell bonds at 12½ cents on the dollar to raise money for a Mexican revolt. New York bankers would give him nothing. "One of them half in jest, said to the man, 'Why don't you see Sam Brannan, the California millionaire? He'll buy *any*thing they tell me.' "[38] He loaned Juarez the money, an investment which saved Brannan from disaster in later years.

The following reveals something of his wife Eliza's extravagant living: She had left California with their children in 1854. They lived in Europe, where the children attended the best schools; the girls studied music with the best artists. Eliza had been generously supplied with finances before she left, and she could get more for the asking. She returned to San Francisco in 1860 to set herself up to live more lavishly than a queen. Then she divorced her adventurous husband and made the best of obtaining both what the law allowed and what Sam's natural generosity would permit. Reva Scott pictures the outcome as follows: "Sam had to turn over in cash, to Ann Liza, one half of the value of their community property." After Sam went over the books with his bookkeeper, he "knew that he had come to the end of his resources unless he found some new way to make money."[39]

Always an adventurer, Brannan was willing to gamble. Joe Bruce, Brannan's employee, who claimed to know something of Sam's complex finances, said that in his years of decline he gambled on everything from Hawaiian sugar plantations to three-card monte. Bruce had seen him lose $80,000 at the Eldorado Saloon in a single night's play.[40]

Another of his gambles was the huge Calistoga project. In 1859 Sam bought a square mile of geysers and springs in Napa Valley. He bought more and more land until the estate exceeded two thousand acres. On it he laid out plans to build a mammoth resort hotel, a distillery, race tracks, cottages, and sulphur baths. He named it "Calistoga." His brother John begged him to forget his lavish plans:

"Do you realize that it will take the best part of a million dollars to do all the things you want to do? And do you realize that you can never hope to take out in revenues what you'll sink in your original investment?"

"I don't care," Sam said heatedly. "What good is money if you can't do the things you want with it?" . . . "It's my money, and I can have what I want."[41]

After Calistoga was completed, Sam built the Napa Valley Railroad from Napa to Vallejo at a cost of $10,000 a mile. Then he advanced several hundred thousand dollars to have the track extended to Calistoga. In Napa Valley Sam planted huge grape vineyards and built distilleries. The wine and liquors he produced were known for quality in both the East and West. But this project became a debit to him, for he was now addicted to his own product, an addiction which contributed to his failure and toppled him from his eminence of wealth and power. He became an alcoholic, his wealth melted away, and he made a skid to penury.

In the Bancroft notes is a statement copied from Rychman MS, "Vigilante Committee," as follows: "He is a rather unfortunate fellow because he drinks all the time. . . . He was rather an off-hand, flippant fellow."[42] Another penciled note in the Bancroft collections says of Brannan: "Cold and coarse, cold except when in his cups and then hot and coarse, brutal in his instincts and cruel."[43] *The San Francisco Alta* of August 1, 1876, reported a celebration "yesterday afternoon at the Hall of Pioneers" in honor of the thirtieth anniversary of the arrival of Hon. Samuel Brannan, sponsored by the San Francisco Musical Fund Society.

> Judge Hall spoke, "We have met to do honor to a distinguished citizen,—to one whose character and to whose disinterested benevolence every member of the Music Fund Society will be pleased to pay dutiful homage"—his liberality toward you necessitates no details. In every public and in every private enterprise he had a primary and public connection. He was benevolent and generous to an extravagant degree. "This is a social meeting. Let us drink heartily to the future success and prosperity of the Society and let us raise a rousing cheer for our honored guest."

Brannan, now fifty-seven years old, dissipated and financially ruined, responded with some of his old spirit. "He declared that even the semblance of ingratitude would be improper to the occasion." Then he told of the gold rush days and the growth of San Francisco. In conclusion "he ventured a hope that all before him would 'die in good health at a green old age.' "[44]

But in his descent to poverty he still had courage. Defending his rights at one time he took eight bullets in his body without flinching. However he became half paralyzed. Fortunately, in 1861 he was granted an enormous acreage of land in Mexico in partial payment for his bonds. Then came reformation and partial restoration of health. He courageously overcame his alcoholism and his paralysis. He married a Mexican beauty, the thirty-five-year-old daughter of Sonora, and began to make grandiose plans to colonize his Mexican estate. Then, in response to a request, the Mexican government paid him $49,000 in interest on his huge loan. He took the money, returned to San Francisco, and with some of the old sparkle paid every debt he owed and again became a pauper. He returned to the Mexican desert country where he lived like a peon until his death on May 14, 1889.

SAMUEL BRANNAN—EMERGING FOLK HERO

This account is one in which the folk process can be observed. It could be designated "tales of Sam Brannan which serve to cast light on the character of the man." For in the many-sided interpretations of a many-sided man, truth can emerge. To the world a man exists only as he emerges in the consciousness of others who build his character according to their own interpretations of him. It may therefore be accurate to say that Brannan is everything we present here. Yet he is not everything we present here to every man. It remains for each reader to see the true Samuel Brannan as he appears somewhere beyond or behind the legends and tales which characterize him. Some of the writers quoted here consciously fictionalized Brannan's story. To assist the reader to see continuity in these stories, they are presented as nearly as possible in chronological order.

In the library of the University of California in Berkeley in the H. H. Bancroft collection of notes is a newspaper clipping of 1882 entitled "Hon. Samuel Brannan, a Biographical Sketch." A statement from it follows:

> At 23 he had considerable wealth. He started the *New York Messenger* [Really called *The Prophet* at first, the organ of the Mormon church in New York]. This made more money than he anticipated so that in 1846 he conceived the idea of visiting, with the avowed purpose of remaining, the Pacific Coast. He fitted a vessel at his own expense of 370 tons and called it the *Brooklyn*. On February 4 with 236 passengers, of whom 60 were women and forty children, an improved printing press and a flour mill. Having money he purchased 174 stands of arms.

A verse from a song is preserved which is identifed as "an affectionate exhortation of the departing saints to some female disciple to join him [Brannan]" in western migration:

> Sister see yon evening star
> Shining o'er the hills afar
> Shines it not for you and me,
> Over the California sea
> Rejoice, rejoice the wilderness shall blossom.[45]

The Sacramento Daily News of September 11, 1866, carried an article under the heading "Twenty Years Ago" entitled "The *Brooklyn* Mormons in California." Of Sam Brannan and his coming into prominence in the Mormon Church it says: ". . . he was not long in making his mark among the brethren. A sallow, cadaverous, hard featured man, debilitated by a long attack of Western fever,—he was nevertheless, a power among the dull, pliant minds about him . . . preaching on Sundays and carrying captive his hearers with his nervous, impassioned declarations."[46]

The competitor of Brannan's *California Star*, *The Californian*, made the following fragmentary statement in the July 23, 1847, issue: "Samuel Brannan, the leader of the Mormons, who was brought up by Joe Smith himself, and is consequently well qualified to unfold and impress the tenets of his sect."

Brannan's leadership on the ship *Brooklyn* has been interpreted by many people as supremely authoritarian. Ralph B. Jordan gives a vivid picture:

> The *Brooklyn* beat down the east coast of America day after day and week after week. On board bugles blared. "Attention!" barked Brannan at his men. "To your work," he cried to the women, who made up the cabins and cooked. The whole ship was on schedule hour by hour and even the winds seemed to heed it.
> A boy was born. "Name him Atlantic after the ocean of his birth," Brannan suggested. Atlantic it was. The *Brooklyn* rounded the Horn. A girl was born. "Call her Pacific," proposed the irrepressible Brannan. Pacific was her name.[47]

Amelia Everett in the *California Historical Society Quarterly* presents this picture: "Brannan never took his fellow voyagers into his full confidence; and they, on their part, liked neither his pomposity nor his forceful methods of ruling, but, with Mormon loyalty to leadership, they obeyed . . . ."[48]

Leo J. Muir, an active leader in the Mormon Church and one who studied the church records, has said, "Throughout the journey he ruled with a strong hand. His leadership did not inspire confidence, rather it commanded obedience, which was more important to his method of operation. He took staterooms for himself, his wife and one child, and probably his mother-in-law, near the quarters of Captain Richardson, disdaining to mingle with the families of the Saints."[49]

Reva Scott fictionalizes Brannan's words and the excommunications on the ship *Brooklyn* as follows:

> "In spite of the warning I gave you in Honolulu the Captain tells me you are carrying on something scandalous; that you are practicing polygamy among us." They looked at him, but none of them made reply. After a moment Sam continued, "My counselors and me have decided to cut you off from the Church. Take notice that you are now disfellowshipped." Pell arose quickly and spoke. "You mean that we are not going to get a hearing before the rest of the company, and a vote; that you think you can cut us off in this high-handed manner?" "Exactly. I hold full authority for such an act, and I am the only one who can baptize you into this company or throw you out. I will this day post a notice in the hall notifying the rest of the company of our action." "I won't be bound by any such action," Pell retorted. "You'll have to be. On this ship I am the law as far as our company goes. If I tell our folks to have no more to do with you, they'll have no more to do with you. You'll soon find that out."[50]

In the Stearns collection at Huntington Library, Pasadena, California, is a blank check of Tradesman's National Bank, date 187- [about 1878] on the back of which is recorded in minute handwriting an account of Brannan. Of his arrival in Yerba Buena it says: "Mr. Brannan at the sight of the U.S. flag flying on the place exclaimed, 'By God, There's that d(?) American flag.'" Miriam deFord also quotes Brannan on that occasion: "'There's that damned flag again,' cried the Mormon elder, flinging his hat on deck. Some report he said 'rag.'"[51]

Ralph E. Bieber questions the truthfulness of the story Bancroft told of Sam Brannan's shouting "Gold! Gold! Gold! From the American River" as he displayed a bottle of gold dust in San Francisco: "Evidence that this incident occurred consists principally of the reminiscences of Benjamin Hawkins, George M. Evans, and James Findla; but no evidence has been discovered thus far to substantiate the oft-quoted statement of Hubert H. Bancroft that Brannan shouted: "Gold! Gold! Gold from the American River!"[52]

The following quotation supplies an interesting origin of a meaningful cliché and shows something of Brannan's activity during the exciting times of the gold rush. Brannan too may have been able to come up with sizable amounts in a pinch:

> ... Beginning with Nov., '49, the monthly output trebled what it had been in the summer. And the miners, coming down from the mountains for supplies, told Sam what had happened. Driven by the rise of the river away from placers, or bars up into the ravines, or "dry diggings," for shelter, they found there seams and ribs and rich

pockets of gold exposed by the wash of the rains. From these dry diggings gold now poured down to San Francisco in a steadily increasing stream. . . . Gold dust had become the chief medium of exchange. The freehanded miners, when paying for drinks, would hold up their buckskin pouches and let the bartenders take out a pinch with their fingers, so as to save weighing. Saloon-keepers . . . soon learned that in this, as in all things, practice makes perfect; whence arose the test question addressed to their would-be assistants, ''How much can you raise in a pinch?''

All through this welter of gold-dust and mud and champagne rings the loud voice of Sam Brannan, moving back and forth restlessly between San Francisco and Sacramento City. His activities covered the whole range of the city's wild life, from gambling to banking.[53]

Hamilton Boner tells how a less enterprising man than Brannan, John Breuner, may have been envious of those who made more money than he during the gold rush days, particularly of Sam Brannan. "While Sam Brannan bought gold for six dollars per ounce from his Mormon workers, and made a handsome profit of ten dollars, John Breuner struggled along trying to get an honest dollar out of their six dollars that Sam paid 'em by making equipment that would help them extract more gold from the sands of the American River."[54]

A penciled record in Bancroft's notes copied from the *Alta Californian*, August 1866, under the title "Santiago's Reminiscences of Sutter's Fort" says the following about Brannan's store in Sutter's Fort: "Gold dust seemed a drug at his place and of no more value than Simon Pure 'dirt.' He was 29 full of life and activity elastic step never tired—'no penniless stranger, seeking provisions or goods ever left his store without being supplied.' "

Franklin A. Buck, writing from California in 1850, said, "There are some rich men here. Samuel Brannan, one of the proprietors of Sacramento City and who owns the city hotel there, has an income from his rents alone of $160,000 a year, besides a store here at the place. When mine amount to that I shall come home."[55]

The reader will note that the report of Sam Brannan's ambivalence in serving God and Mammon simultaneously and hypocritically as presented in the following citation is not in accord with some accounts herein presented. "The richest man in California was now Sam Brannan, who every Sunday preached a fine layman's sermon in San Francisco, who organized Sunday Schools and in every other way indulged in exemplary observance of the Lord's Day after each week's painstaking devotion to God Mammon."[56]

The following statement is particularly interesting because it is said to have been made by John August Sutter. Perhaps Brannan did plan on building a temple in California:

> Mr. Brannan made a kind of claim on Mormon Island, and put a tolerably heavy tax on "The Latter Day Saints." I believe it was 30 per cent, which they paid for some time, until they got tired of it, (some of them told me that it was for the purpose of building a temple for the honor and glory of the Lord.)
> So soon as the secret was out my laborers began to leave me, . . .The Mormons did not like to leave my mill unfinished, but they got the gold fever like everybody else. After they had made their piles they left for the Great Salt Lake. So long as these people have been employed by me they have behaved very well, and were industrious and faithful laborers, and when settling their accounts there was not one of them who was not contented and satisfied.[57]

Some of the Mormon men became disgruntled at paying tithing to Brannan. One is purported to have asked Governor Mason, "What right has our High Priest to collect tithes from us?" The governor answered, "Why he has a perfect right to collect as long as you Mormons are fools enough to pay." Bancroft's notes present the following quotations from "Bilden."

> Brannan extracted a tenth of their gold. Finally they told him they were not going to pay him any longer.
> "You have come to that conclusion, have you?" asked Brannan.
> "Yes," was the reply.
> "Well," said he, "All I can say is, You are damned fools to have paid it as long as you have."[58]

Bancroft's notes also provide the following from "Ayers Personal Adventures" in *California Pioneers*: "Paid tithe of 30% every Saturday at Samuel Brannan's store on Mormon Island weighed on bad weights. But on arrival of Ayers and his party a meeting was held and the tithe stopped.[59]

Brannan's collecting of tithing and refusal to give it to the church is a story interpreted in several ways. Brigham Young and Samuel Brannan, it appears, were not kindred spirits. The following stories, whether factual or not, may show development of animosity which resulted in Brannan's apostasy and disfellowshiping.

Anyone who digs into the history of Samuel Brannan encounters stories and references to the Kendall and Benson contracts. Before leaving New York, Brannan was made to believe, or pretended to believe, that the United States government would be opposed to the Mormons' emigrating beyond the bounds of the country. It appeared that they suspected the Mormons would join hands with Mexico (or Great Britain, with whom trouble was brewing) against the United States. Brannan signed a document with Kendall and Benson, influential politicians, to give them half of all the lands his Mormon group acquired and settled, and, in return, to be permitted to leave the United States unmolested. Brigham Young refused to sign the contract for the church. To him it appeared that Brannan was being victimized by political sharpies. Whether accurate or not, this account of a conversation between Brannan and Brigham Young at Green River reveals a growing clash of personalities.

> "By the way, Brother Brannan, what personal reasons did you have for sending me that Kendall contract and urging me to sign it?"
>
> "None," Sam said hotly, and rose to his feet.
>
> "None, you say, and yet you urged me to sign a 'covenant with the Devil,' as you put it, and the Lord was to deliver us from it. You look like an intelligent man, Brother Brannan, yet if you make covenants with the Devil expecting the Lord to deliver you, then you are a bigger fool than you look. I was angry with you for ever listening to their words and sending me such a villainous document. Nothing could have made me sign it, to deliver my loved ones into the hands of greedy politicians."
>
> "They told me that our signing that contract was the only way of delivering our people out of bondage; not only us in New York but all of you in Nauvoo."
>
> "They could have told you anything, and I suppose you would have believed them—?" Brigham shook his head; as he talked he slowly paced the ground inside his tent, his hands locked behind him. "Oh, no, Brannan, you didn't believe them. You only pretended to because you had something to gain by favoring their little scheme. I thought so from the first, and I still do. When you sailed from New York, you were not stopped by the Government, which is proof that they were only trying to use you." He turned and shook his finger at Sam. "The trouble with you, Brother Brannan, is that you are too ambitious. I am not blind to the reasons why you wanted me to sign that contract, nor to the reasons why you want the Saints to go on to the coast and settle where you are already an established leader. You want to further your own ends. You want to share authority with me, and maybe eventually to take my place. But it will never be so. You are too ambitious for your own good, and I think that before you leave us we will teach you something about humility."
>
> Sam clenched his fists involuntarily and found himself suddenly disliking the man. "I am ambitious," he retorted aggressively. "Any man worth his salt is. But I doubt that you or any other man can make me humble."
>
> "We shall see," Brigham said. Sam turned and strode from the tent.[60]

Brannan stories provide a few entrances and exits of "Destroying Angels," "Danites," or "Exterminators."

> In the American River, about two miles from Folsom, Brannan staked a claim on an island which he called Mormon Island. It was worked by members of the "Mormon Battalion," originally formed by Brigham Young; and as an elder of the church Bran-

nan collected tithes of their takings . . . Brigham Young, back in Utah, heard about this unauthorized tithe taking, and sent an apostle to demand the money for the church. It was the Lord's money, said the apostle, and must be given to Him. "You go back and tell Brigham," retorted Brannan, "that I'll give up the Lord's money when he sends me a receipt signed by the Lord." When Brigham Young got this message back, he excommunicated Brannan forthwith, on the grounds that "his course and habits were not consistent with the life of a Latter Day Saint." Over and over again, for several years, Young sent his "Destroying Angels," or "Danites," who might be described today as gunmen, to get the tithe money from Brannan, but Brannan always had the "Angels" met in the desert by his own bodyguards, whom he called "Exterminators"; and after five years of seeing his "Angels" regularly "exterminated," Young let the matter drop. But, as someone has remarked, Brannan's life wouldn't have been worth ten cents in Utah after that.[61]

Western frontiersmen are usually pictured as straightforward men who speak the naked truth and whose descriptive vocabulary consists chiefly of profane words. Did a fallen churchman speaking to the leading churchman roll out oaths like the following? He may have; westerners' language was pretty tangy:

> Sam rose quickly from his heels and stood, tall and straight, before Brigham. "I take orders from no man, Brigham Young, not even from you. I had full charge of bringing a shipload of Saints from New York to the coast, and I did a damned fine job of it if I do say so myself. I've proved my ability; and no man is going to make me eat crow to please his vanity. You may be the Lord High Mucky-Muck here, but you're only one man among hundreds to me. William Smith warned me that you were an ambitious man when his brother Joseph was killed, and said that Joseph never wanted you to take his place; that you would try to usurp power that did not belong to you, because you crave to be a dictator. I didn't believe him then. I do now. I'm leaving for the coast in the morning, and I'm riding with Charles Smith. If your god-damned company wants to follow me it can. But I'll take orders from no man in it."
>
> Brigham Young leaped to his feet, quivering with anger. "Take heed, Sam Brannan, take heed. Do not try my patience too far lest you be cut off from the Church."
>
> "You won't cut me off the Church because I'll quit first. You'll be in a hell of a fine fix trying to get these men to the coast if I refuse to show them the way. They might make it, but it would take them twice as long as it will me. And they might get caught in the snow like the Donner party did last year. It's getting late in the season, and the Snowy Mountains are treacherous. I think you won't cut me off the Church, not while you need me worse than I need the Church."
>
> Brigham stood looking at him for several moments, and then he relaxed. "Let us not part in bitterness," he said at last.
>
> "I don't give a goddamn how we part," Sam said, and turning, strode from the tent.[62]

The following story does not name destroying angels, but it makes use of

Porter Rockwell, the long-haired gunman who was said to be one of Brigham Young's destroying angels:

> "Brother Brigham sent us to fetch his money," Rockwell said coldly.
>
> "His money? What do you mean, his money?"
>
> "I mean all that tithing you collected from our Mormon miners. . . . That money belongs to the Church, all of it, and I want it.'
>
> "You don't say!" Sam said sarcastically.
>
> "Yes, I do say!" Rockwell shouted, and in a flash Sam found himself looking down the muzzle of a pistol. Sam smiled slowly, and maddeningly.
>
> "Put that gun away. It won't get you anything. I've looked down hundreds of them, but most of the men behind them are cowards like you." Sam arose slowly . . . [and] went on speaking in a cold, ominous tone. "What I've got is mine. I take what I can get, and when I get it, I keep it, just like Brigham does. Does he send me any tithing money? Does he give any of you a share of it? No . . . Who is the Church and who will keep all you bring to the Church. I'll tell you: Brigham Young!"
>
> Rockwell replied coldly, "That money belongs to the Lord, Sam Brannan, and I ain't leaving here till I get it.'
>
> "Have you got a receipt from the Lord?" Brannan taunted him.
>
> "No, I ain't. I ain't even got a receipt from Brigham Young, but I aim to collect just the same."
>
> "You'll play hell! I'll give you that money on the day you bring me a receipt from the Lord, marked 'Paid in full'; until then get out!"
>
> Sam strode to the door and threw it open.
>
> Rockwell put his gun back in the holster and moved deliberately out into the [store] room.[63]

This statement, purportedly taken from an old journal, not only characterizes Brannan but the whole Mormon society. In this, "angels" are particularly mobile. It sounds apocryphal rather than historical:

> Like most of the early Mormon leaders, he [Samuel Brannan] was of a coarse-fibered nature, with a rather forebidding, saturnine face, but singularly keen witted, resolute, and fearing neither man nor devil.
>
> The latter quality stood him in good stead. Brigham could not permit such a flagrant breach of church discipline to remain unpunished. Flock after flock of "destroying angels" took flight from Salt Lake City, duly commissioned to bring back Samuel's scalp or perish in the attempt. But their holy work was always a dismal failure. Brannan must have had some foreknowledge of their movement against the security of his person. Liking not to meet "angels" unawares of any kinds, he arranged to encounter the "destroyers" halfway out in the trackless dessert, or mountain fastnesses, with a competent group of exterminators he seemed to keep on hand for such occasions, and it was the "angels" who were always taken unawares. Some of them got back to Salt Lake City minus tail feathers and otherwise damaged, but the majority of them never returned at all. At last the disciplining of Brannan became so manifestly an extra-hazardous risk that it was finally abandoned. How he defied the whole power of

Mormonism and actually conducted a private and successful war against the Church was one of the old romances of the Pacific Coast.[64]

After Brannan had been disfellowshiped from the church, Elder Parley P. Pratt wrote the following in his autobiography:

> . . . He [Brannan] was a corrupt and wicked man, and had the Church and myself been less long suffering and merciful, it would have saved the Church much loss, and, perhaps, saved some souls which were corrupted in California, and led astray and plundered by him. I have always regretted having taken any measures to have him restored to fellowship after he was published in Nauvoo as cut off from the Church. However, if I erred, it was on the side of mercy.[65]

It is amazing to find a man who knew personally *all* the Mormon leaders, including Brannan. ". . . Blackburn, who knew personally all the Mormon leaders, said that Brannan was by far the most capable, and greatest of them all, with high sterling qualities, and a man of his word."[66]

The following picture of unique operation of the law and Brannan's part in it is notable:

> [A man named] Pickett opened a trading post at Sutter's Fort, ultimately killed a man in self-defense and became the defendant in the first trial conducted at the fort. One feature of this trial was the amount of brandy consumed by judge, jury, defendant and spectators. Another was Sam Brannan, who at one point stepped down from the bench he had been occupying as judge and proceeded to make an impassioned plea for the prosecution.
> "Wait a minute," protested Pickett. "You can't do this. You're the judge."
> "I know it," replied Brannan, "and I'm the prosecuting attorney too."
> After he had argued the case before himself, Brannan resumed the bench to consider the points he had made as prosecutor. In the end, the jury disagreed. Pickett was tried again, and acquitted.[67]

Robert Louis Stevenson visited Brannan's beautiful resort, Calistoga, in the 1870's. In *Stevenson at Silverado*, Issler, in a chapter on "Sam Brannan and the Springs Hotel," said:

> Calistoga was, in a sense true of few towns, the creation of one man. Even the name was Brannan's boasting that he would make this little health resort the Saratoga of California—at a supper party, according to Stevenson—he spliced the names of California and Saratoga, and created Calistoga. . .
> By the time the railroad was ready to bring him guests, his millionaire hotel had long been completed, and Brannan gave a reception for some three thousand people. Where did they come from? Everywhere! In those days reckless gold travelers were arriving in San Francisco from every part of the globe. . . . They had money to spend

and they spent it. During the early seventies there were sometimes as many as a thousand guests at Sam's hotel in a single month.[68]

Ralph B. Jordan gives a different legendary story of the origin of the name Calistoga: "Legend has it that Brannan intended to call it "Saratoga" but having imbibed too freely before the ceremonies, thickly stuttered something the clerk understood as "Calistoga." Being a good sport, Sam let it stand, and later showed some pride in the new word he had coined."[69]

Following are some details of interest regarding the disintegration of a massive fortune:

> Sam gave lavish presents to family and community. He bought San Francisco a fire engine which cost him $10,000.[70]
>
> And his wife Liza sported expensive clothes and jewels. One string of pearls Sam bought her cost as much as the fire engine.[71]
>
> Sam sent to Asia for plants and established a tea garden. He conducted extensive experiments with silkworms in a mulberry orchard and built a feeding room for worms. But he was too restless to carry all of his projects to successful conclusions. He abandoned many in the halfway stage. This, however, was not true of viticulture. The brandy from his distillery was declared equal to French cognac.[72]
>
> In 1863 Sam bought more land in Napa Valley. He made gifts of town lots to his nieces and nephews; on each he built a dwelling house of rococo, almost Byzantine design.[73]
>
> Bit by bit Sam's properties dwindled away. He still had a few rents from his San Francisco buildings. What remained of his property in Napa County was heavily encumbered.[74]

Be a lender, not a borrower, if you want to keep your friends. Polonius was wrong:

> When Sam turned borrower instead of lender, his former "friends" did not crowd about him on Market, Montgomery and Sansome Streets, or even on Kearney Street where Jack Asses used to mire deep in the mud till he paved it with planks.
>> "This street is impassable,
>> Not even jackassable."
>
> Former "Friends" flew from him when they caught sight of his stately contour on the horizon. One could now play marbles on their coat tails as they hastily departed from view.[75]

Jordan adds the following story of Brannan, a story of his reformation in his old age after overcoming alcoholism:

> And then—a miricle. Brannan redeemed himself. Loafing like a peon around the ranch

his thoughts traveled back across the years to the days of his youth when he was an Elder in the Church of Jesus Christ. . . . Brannan fell to his knees and prayed for the first time in forty years, out there under the burning sun and in the biting wind of the desert. He prayed for a chance at redemption on this earth and in the great beyond.

Then he arose and during the remaining ten years of his life he faithfully lived in accordance with the teachings of the Church he had deserted, never again touching liquor or even tobacco. His stooped shoulders straightened, his eyes cleared, his paralysis disappeared. He was once more a keen, handsome, and vigorous man.[76]

It is a matter of recorded fact that Apostle Parley P. Pratt was the officer in charge when Brannan was disfellowshiped from the church. He had concluded that no mortal man could lead this proud man back into the fold. He abandoned him to the buffetings of Satan with the prophesy that the rich and haughty apostate would someday want for money enough to buy a crust of bread.[77] One is almost led to believe as he examines Brannan's behavior and sees him prodigally casting his riches to every wind that he had determined to make that prophesy come true.

The following fiction is a delightful conclusion to the prophesy story: After a few years of poverty and drunkenness, Sam had received $49,000 from Mexico. "Sam wrote [to his nephew, his former bookkeeper and financial advisor], 'Alex, get out my books. Find all to whom I owe money. Put it down in black and white. I want to pay my debts, Alex.' Alex did as he was told."

The bills were paid, $500 was what was left of the $49,000, and Sam took it in gold. "He would be the old Sam once more—an hour, a day or a week—till the rest of the money was gone, flinging gold pieces about, emptying his pockets for anyone who made a demand on him."

A short time later Sam Brannan died of a stroke in a boardinghouse. In his last moments he was delirious—he held a twenty-dollar gold piece in his hand and said to the boardinghouse woman, "Parley Pratt, the Mormon elder, said I'd die without a dime. I fooled him. I've got gold in my hand and my good wife beside me."[78]

We have now come the full circle touching some high spots in the life of a true adventurer. Sam Brannan will live forever, glorified more than condemned in the eyes of hero-worshippers. Lovers of freedom and free enterprise worship at the feet of the man who through courage, wits, and sheer energy found and cornered the gold at the end of the rainbow. And his losing it and dying a pauper, though bizarre, does not topple him from his kingdom in the hearts of the folk. It only makes him their brother.

NOTES

1. *The Prophet*, June 29, 1844. The photographic copies in the Bancroft Library show no pagination.
2. Brigham H. Roberts, *Comprehensive History of the Church* (Salt Lake City, Utah: Deseret News Press, 1930), 3: 25.
3. Roberts, 3: 26.
4. Ralph B. Jordan, "The Story of Sam Brannan," *Improvement Era* 39, no. 7 (July 1936): 403.
5. Jordan, pp. 403-4.
6. *The California Star* (published in San Francisco by Sam Brannan beginning January 9, 1847. Photographic copies in Bancroft Library, University of California, Berkeley; no pagination) 1, no. 1.
7. *Star* 1, no. 10.
8. *Star* 1, no. 11.
9. *Star* 1, no. 34.
10. *Star* 1, no. 2.
11. *Star* 1, no. 3.
12. *Star* 1, no. 35.
13. *Star* 1, no. 2.
14. *Star* 1, no. 2, quoted from *The Friend*, Honolulu, Sandwich Islands.
15. *Star* 1, no. 37.
16. Ibid.
17. Daniel D. Tyler, *A Concise History of the Mormon Battalion in the Mexican War* (n.p., 1881), p. 315.
18. Leo J. Muir, *A Century of Mormon Activities in California* (Salt Lake City: Deseret News Press, 1951), 2: 57-58.
19. Paul Bailey, *Sam Brannan and the California Mormons* (Los Angeles: Westernlore Press, 1943), p. 111.
20. Diary of Henry W. Bigler, 1 (1846-1850): 90.
21. Douglas S. Watson, "Herald of the Gold Rush—Sam Brannan," *California Historical Society Quarterly* 10: 307.
22. Jordan, p. 407.
23. Muir, p. 60.
24. H. H. Bancroft notes, University of California, Bancroft Library.
25. Muir, p. 57.
26. Amelia D. Everett, "The Ship *Brooklyn*," *California Historical Society Quarterly* 37: 234.
27. Everett, pp. 235-36.
28. Eugene E. Campbell, "The Apostasy of Samuel Brannan," *Utah Historical Quarterly* 2: 158.
29. Bancroft notes, quoting from the *Journal of William Corcy*, pp. 159-60.
30. See Parley P. Pratt, *Autobiography* (New York: Published for Russell Brothers, 1874), pp. 374-75.

31. Reva Scott, *Samuel Brannan and the Golden Fleece* (New York: Macmillan, 1944), p. 211.

32. Jordan, p. 404.

33. Reva Holdaway et al., eds., "A Mormon Mission to California in 1851" (from the Diary of Parley P. Pratt) *California Historical Society Quarterly* 14: 176.

34. Louis J. Stillman, *Sam Brannan, Builder of San Francisco* (New York: Exposition Press, 1953), p. 108.

35. James A. B. Scherer, *The First Forty-Niner and the Story of the Golden Tea Caddy* (New York: Minton, Balch and Company, 1925), pp. 101-2.

36. Bancroft notes, a cutting from the San Jose *Mercury*, March 17, 1884.

37. Miriam Allen de Ford, *They Were San Franciscans* (Caldwell, Idaho: Caxton Printers, 1941), p. 92.

38. Stillman, p. 184.

39. Scott, p. 423.

40. Stillman, p. 129.

41. Scott, p. 382.

42. Bancroft notes.

43. Bancroft notes.

44. Bancroft notes.

45. Bancroft notes.

46. Bancroft notes.

47. Jordan, p. 403.

48. Everett, p. 235.

49. Muir, p. 57.

50. Scott, p. 124.

51. De Ford, p. 77.

52. Ralph P. Bieber, "California Gold Mania." A paper presented as the presidential address at the forty-first annual meeting of the Mississippi Valley Historical Association in Rock Island, Illinois, April 22, 1948. Copy in Bancroft Library.

53. Scherer, pp. 90-91.

54. Hamilton Boner, "The House of Breuner," *Pony Express Courier* 8, no. 5.

55. Bancroft notes, quoted from Kathryn A. White, *A Yankee Trader in the Gold Rush*, the letters of Franklyn A. Buck, p. 54.

56. James Peter Zollinger, *Sutter, The Man and His Empire* (New York and London: Oxford University Press, 1939), p. 300.

57. R. R. Olmsted, ed., "The Discovery of Gold in California," *Hutchings' California Magazine*, 1856-1861 (November 1857), p. 182.

58. Bilden, p. 70.

59. Bancroft notes, quoted from "Ayres' Personal Adventures" in *California Pioneers*, no. 26.

60. Scott, pp. 168-69.

61. De Ford, pp. 83-84.

62. Scott, p. 178.

63. Scott, pp. 247-48.

64. James H. Wilkins, ed., *The Great Diamond Hoax* (Norman, Oklahoma: University of Oklahoma Press, 1958), p. 120.

65. Pratt, p. 375.

66. "Immortal Sam Brannan on His Way to Empire," *Pony Express Courier* 10 (June 1943): 10.

67. Robert O'Brien, *This Is San Francisco* (New York: Whittlesey House, 1948), p. 236.

68. Anne R. Issler, *Stevenson in Silverado* (Caldwell, Idaho: Caxton Printers, 1939), p. 83.

69. Jordan, p. 404.

70. Stillman, p. 162.

71. Stillman, p. 148.

72. Stillman, p. 172.

73. Stillman, p. 174.

74. Stillman, p. 206.

75. Scherer, p. 88.

76. Jordan, p. 407.

77. Bailey, p. 192.

78. Stillman, p. 236.

6

Of Folkways, Superstition, and the Supernatural

T he roots of a culture are much deeper than is generally thought. The new and spectacular have such a way of engaging one's senses that a person may lose sight of elements of his environment which are so pervasive and so fundamental that they are taken for granted, or remain submerged in the unconscious.

With a total life extending into the past less than a century and a half, it might be presumed that the folkways of Mormonia are new and unique. Nothing could be further from the truth as the four studies comprising this section of *Lore of Faith and Folly* will reveal. The Mormon culture is not a closed system, but rather one of several parallel and interlocking streams of behavior which extend back through the Judeo-Christian and Greco-Roman nodules into prehistory. The theology of Joseph Smith (one remarkable man's accumulation of the myths and folkways of frontier Americans) and the Mormon pioneering experience give little more than a veneer of particularity to beliefs, customs, rituals, and practices that began centuries ago and whose half-life will extend centuries into the future. If man is but an ephemeral creation in the great scheme of things, his traditional ideas and values live on and on.

The first three studies ("The Cycle of Life among the Folk," "The Common Cold in Utah Folk Medicine," "Tales of the Supernatural") concern sayings, beliefs, customs, practices, and tales which many Mormons shared with other westerners during the first century of their sojourn in the Great American West. These are followed by an article ("Unsung Craftsmen") on the use first and second generation Utahns made of traditional skills and lore to solve the unique problems imposed by frontier living. This study of folkcrafts is among the first published in the area; more people have saved and displayed fancy quilts in museums than have written about them. Only a few have observed the small farmer's ingenuity in inventing corral gate latches and fewer still have photographed them or preserved accounts of them on paper. I have seen dried-up cubes of homemade laundry soap, but I have read but few accounts of how the poor pre-industrialized, rural, self-sustaining homemaker made it. This is indeed the area of unsung craftsmen.

A.E.F.

Austin E. and Alta S. Fife

The Cycle of Life among the Folk

If the folklore of a people is abundant in materials pertaining to man's relationship to the external world and to the life of the spirit, it is also abundant in materials concerning the human body, its essential functions, and relationships between the sexes. Folklore among the Mormons forms no exception to this rule and conforms in a large degree to the lore of other Anglo-Americans.[1]

By the characteristics of the body itself a great deal is supposed to be knowable concerning either personality or the future. Red-headed people have "high tempers," "Irish tempers," or "tempers like red pepper."[2] Men go bald-headed because they burn out the roots of their hair thinking so hard; "hair and brains don't go together." If women don't suffer the same affliction it is because their minds are inactive. "Do you know why women don't have whiskers? Because they talk too much." A man with lots of hair on his body or arms is strong, or has a strong character. A boy does not become a man until he has hair on his chest. If hair grows in the palms of the hands it means that the individual masturbates. A heavy head of hair is supposed to sap strength from a woman's body: "It just stands to reason, all that strength going into the hair. I've known a lot of women that had headaches constantly because they had a heavy head of hair and they've had to go and have it thinned." You shouldn't throw outside the combings from your hair: a bird will weave it into its nest and cause you to have headaches.[3] Some people used to carry locks of hair of a beloved individual or child in their wallets or lockets as a kind of memento.[4]

The eyes have their way of telling of personality too:

Blue-eyed beauty, do your mama's duty.
Brown-eye, pick-a-pie, run around and tell a lie.
Green-eyed greedy-gut, eat all the world up.

A sty is supposed to be caused by urinating in the middle of the road. Upon seeing a person with a sty the remark might be made, "Get out of the middle of the road next time you take a pee."

Various facial characteristics have their traditional meanings in the lore of the folk. A high forehead is a sign of intelligence.[5] "Dimple in the chin, devil within." A woman with a large mouth is supposed to have a large vagina. Large ears are a sign of a generous disposition; small ears, especially where the lobes are close to the head, indicate stinginess. A long, pointed nose is indicative of the gossip. A square jaw is a sign of stubbornness or dogged persistence. A small chin is a sign of weak character. A pug nose is the sign of a person who will "fight at the drop of a bucket."[6] Protruding teeth mean that one is of Irish descent. If your teeth are far apart you will receive money.[7] A bump on your tongue is supposed to be a "lie bump."

Long, tapering fingers are the sign of the future pianist, doctor, or stenographer; they also denote strength of character. Short, stubby fingers are the sign of the artist. Fat, thick hands are "lazy hands." An "M" in the lines of your hand means money. "Cold hands, warm heart." White spots on the fingernails indicate the number of lies you have told; sometimes they are called "lazy spots."[8] A fat person is good-natured.[9] Moles, especially on the face, are said to be "beauty marks." "Smoke follows beauty." It is lucky to have a mole on the right side of your body. "Mole on the neck, money by the peck." A mole in the middle of your back indicates riches.

Itching means somewhat more than a mildly unpleasant irritation of the skin. If your right hand itches, you will shake hands with a friend or take in money. Another informant tells us that if the palm of your right hand itches you will be "kissed, or cussed, or shake hands with a fool," whereas if the palm of your left hand itches it is a sign that you are going to have money.[10] Contrariwise, other informants tell us that if the left hand itches you will pay out money. If your ears burn, someone is talking about you.[11] If your right eye itches it is a sign of joy; your left eye, a sign of sadness. Itching of the nose means variously that you will see a stranger, kiss a fool, have company, or receive a letter. If your feet itch on the bottom it means that you are raring to go, hence that you will travel, some say on foreign soil. If your lips itch it means that you are going to kiss a fool. If you sneeze you should say, "God bless you," or "God bless my soul!" If you sneeze at the table the number of sneezes indicates how many more or how many less there will be present at the next meal. It is said that if you were born with a black veil over your face you will have psychic powers: "On rare occasions babies are born with a kind of black substance over their faces."

The belief is widespread that in cases of the amputation of limbs, fingers, or toes the stub will continue to be sensitive to any hurt which might be inflicted upon the amputated portion, hence particular care should be taken to either cremate or bury the amputated limb in a deep or secret place.[12] "My brother had his leg cut off and he just about went crazy. He swore up and down there was something between his toes. A fellow up here had his finger cut off, and they never thought of picking it up. He nearly went crazy, said the flies were crawling on it. He made them go back up in the mountains and find it and put coal oil on it and kill the maggots so that the finger wouldn't itch. The amputated finger was all swollen up and black, and they poured kerosene on it and burned it, and he was all right."

The body is supposed to "completely renew itself" every seven years. Tickling a person will cause him to stutter. Going barefoot will make the feet bigger. Yawn in a crowd and soon everybody will be yawning. It is bad to bathe immediately after eating. The eating of burnt crusts of bread will darken your hair. If you pull one gray hair out two others will come to take its place. Old women should make the sauerkraut; if young women make it, it will spoil. A woman should not have a tooth pulled while menstruating.

If you retire with your stomach overloaded you will have dreams or nightmares.[13] Old-time cowboys in Utah placed tobacco in their eyes to keep awake while night herding—it inflamed the eyes and caused them to burn.[14] When you "break wind" you should touch wood and whistle.[15] Eating eggs or oysters is supposed to increase passion. Place your shoes neatly side-by-side near your bed so you won't dream of being chased and not be able to escape: You can quickly get into your shoes and elude your pursuer.[16]

Determining whom you should marry has ever been a matter of concern in the lore of the folk. Probably few youngsters reared in Utah come to maturity without having plucked the petals off sunflowers, daisies, or various other flowers while saying, "He loves me, he loves me not." A modern variant of this formula is effected with a straw at a soda fountain: you go up the straw with thumb and finger, hand over hand, like a ladder, saying, "He loves me, he loves me not." The last time you are able to pinch the straw indicates the nature of the loved one's affections. A similar device consists in counting the buttons on a girl's dress while one repeats the words, "Rich man, poor man, beggar man, thief / Doctor, lawyer, merchant, chief." If there are still more buttons, begin again: the last button will be the profession of the man that you will marry.[17]

Apples are also used in love divination. The seeds are carefully removed from the core as one counts: "One I love, two I love, three I love I say; four I love with all my heart, five I cast away; six he loves, seven she loves, eight they both love, nine he comes, ten he tarries, eleven they kiss, and twelve they marry."[18] A simpler device consists in merely twisting the stem out of an apple while at each twist you say, "He loves me, he loves me not." The truth is revealed at the point where the stem breaks out of the apple.[19] Others recite the letters of the alphabet at each twist: the letter said as it breaks will be the first letter of the lover's name. The fuzz is blown off dandelions in a ritual of love divination: your hopes are supposed to come true if all of the fuzz is blown off in one breath.[20] Harking back to the Old World is the following lovely matrimonial charm encountered in Utah:

Yarrow, yarrow do I pick,
Down my bosom I do stick,
The first young man that speaks to me
My true lover he shall be.[21]

Another:

See a pin pointing clearly
It points to him who loves you dearly.

Very prevalent also seems to be the practice of hanging the wishbone over the door. The first man to walk under it is supposed to become your husband or your lover.[22] If you sleep with a piece of a wedding cake under your pillow, you will dream about the man you are going to marry,[23] or, others say, you will be either married or engaged within the year. If when shelling peas you find ten peas in a pod, you will meet the man that you are going to marry. If a couple drink together from "Matrimonial Spring" near Moab, it is believed that they will marry; drinking from the same spring will insure your return to Moab. A girl who likes pickles or lemons is in love. If a girl sits on the table, it is a sign that she wants to get married.[24] If a woman gets the front of her dress wet while washing clothes she will marry a drunkard. If a girl forgets to salt the food when cooking it, it means she will lose her beau. "Where cobwebs grow a beau will never go." Or: "Where cobwebs hang low, beaus never go." It also used to be a custom to tell a girl who was kneading bread if she left any dough in the pan she would never get married. If you take the last piece of anything on a plate you will be an old maid.[25]

A number of beliefs and sayings have been encountered concerning weddings and marriage. The widespread "Something old, something new, something borrowed, something blue," is amplified in the following:

Married in gray, you'll move far away,
Married in red, you'll wish you were dead,
Married in blue, your love will prove true,
Married in green, you're ashamed to be seen,
Married in white, you have chosen all right.

The belief is also prevalent that if you wear blue and gray to a wedding you will move far away. This rhyme asserts the importance of choosing a sunny day for the wedding:

Happy is the bride that the sun shines on,
And blessed is the dead that the rain falls on.[26]

Also: "Marry in haste, repent at leisure."[27] And, in a more somber vein:

Needles and pins, needles and pins,
When a man marries his trouble begins.

Many people will tell you that it is a bad omen for a girl to marry a man whose last name begins with the same letter as her own, and the following rhyme is quoted:

Change the name and not the letter,
Change for worse and not for better.

As elsewhere, the bride should be carried across the threshold for good luck.[28] Scissors should not be given as a wedding gift—they will cause bad luck, as will the gift of any other sharp instrument.[29] The bride's bouquet is usually thrown into the crowd; the young woman who catches it will be the next one to wed.

Not a few taboos, beliefs, and customs pertain to pregnancy and birth. A pregnant woman should not reach high above her head: the navel cord might get tied around the baby's neck. It is dangerous for a pregnant woman to work with warm meat, for touching it may cause a miscarriage. To reduce the stress of morning sickness, a chocolate candy bar or a cracker should be eaten before getting out of bed.

Mormon women as a general rule are not interested in contraceptive devices; their upbringing as Mormons has taught them that the rearing of children is woman's noblest mission. There are, nevertheless, a few folk beliefs concerning contraception. Capsules of baking soda have been employed. One informant advised us that out on the desert there is a plant that has little yellowish flowers growing along the stem: a tea made of it was said to be effective in causing abortions. Turpentine taken internally has also been used.[30] Inquiries about contraception are more likely than anything else to call forth facetious remarks, as: "Stay single, or use twin beds, and you'll keep from having a baby. Just use gunpowder in a gun to prevent conception. Take saltpeter—eat the salt and leave the peter alone." The folk have long sustained their own concepts about the use of "rhythm" in preventing conception. It is said that the two weeks before menstruation one can become pregnant, and that the two weeks after one cannot. Another informant said that a woman is supposed to be able to get pregnant only two hours during any one month. The belief is prevalent that a menstruating woman should neither have a "permanent" nor preserve fruit.[31]

To predict the sex of a child prior to birth has ever been a concern of the folk. Very common is the notion that the sex can be told by the manner in which the fetus is carried in the womb, although there is variability as to the interpretation: a baby carried high is generally, but not always, supposed to be a girl; one that's carried low, a boy. In a slightly different form, it is reported that if the mother puts weight on just in front it is a girl, that if she gets big all over it is a boy. It is also stated that the baby which kicks the hardest as a fetus is a boy. If the young child's first learned word is "mama" the next child will be a girl, whereas if its first learned word is "daddy" the next one will be a boy. It is a common belief that in wartime more male children are born than female children.[32] We have also heard that the last person who puts a stitch in a quilt at a quilting-bee will be the one to have the next baby. If following coitus the mother turns upon her right side the child will be a boy, but if she turns upon the left side it will be a girl. More babies are born when there is a full moon; this time of the month is called "a full house," or a "blitz." A mother who has heartburn before a baby is born will bear a baby with lots of hair.

The modern notions concerning the candor with which children should be told where babies come from have not always been in vogue and are still looked upon with some skepticism among rural people of Mormonia. The stork brings them, or the doctor brings them in his bag.[33] The crow may fly over and drop a baby, or it may simply be found under a cabbage leaf. "I was eighteen years old and I was alone with my mother. She hadn't said a word about the fact that she was going to have a baby although it had been evident to me for some time. When the time came I said to her, 'I'll go send for Aunt Sarah.' She was the midwife who always came. And Mother said, 'What do you suppose I want Aunt Sarah for?' And I said, 'I don't want to be here alone when the baby comes.' And she snapped, 'Who said anything about a baby being born?' "

Before World War I in all but Utah's larger cities probably a majority of the babies were delivered by midwives. When one experienced midwife was asked what she needed to perform a delivery, she replied that the only essential thing was a bitch light (a very unsatisfactory light formed by dipping a piece of string in fat). The belief is reported that a rusty axe placed in the bed will reduce the pains that accompany childbirth. Lobelia was administered at the time of delivery.

A curious process was sometimes used to cauterize the naval of a newborn child. A fresh grape was turned inside out and fastened over it with a scorched piece of tape. This was supposed to prevent infection. In another instance it was reported that a dried Malaga grape raisin was boiled, opened, and its fleshy portion bound over the navel. More frequently a scorched cloth alone sufficed.[34] It is reported that to make a delivery easier the mother should stay on her feet as long as possible.[35] Walking is good to bring on labor. In support of this it was cited that in biblical times women were tied to sticks and bounced around, which made the delivery all the more painful. We have had it reported that the organs of the delivered mother spring back into place on the ninth day.[36] When asked if this were true, a practical-minded midwife exclaimed: "Good heavens, what do you suppose they have been doing for the preceding eight days?" With reference to the troubles of childbirth in pioneer days, the testimony of a convert of Dutch-Canadian extraction is notable: "My mother never had a doctor for any of her babies; the midwife brought all of us except the very last one. Mother always had a little baby, and a lot of her twelve children came as close as thirteen months apart. I can remember that mother said she had always had a hard time bearing her children. The midwife whom we affectionately called Grandma Johnson put her over the back of a chair to help force the baby down. I don't know how she did it, and I don't know how mother stayed alive. She used to have Father wash her hands and spread clean towels over the bed and then she would mix bread while she was still confined with the baby."

We note the following rhyme about the significance of the day on which one is born:

Born on Sunday, full of God's grace.
. . . .
Born on Saturday, work hard for your living,
A child born on Sunday is loving and giving.[37]

And, a reflection on the care of a baby: "A baby rides easier in the belly than on the hip."[38]

In our interviews with Mormon folk we have been amazed at the extent to which credence is given to the "marking of babies." This consists in a belief that a baby while it is being carried in the womb may be marked with some physical or personality trait as a result of an emotional crisis which befalls the mother while she is carrying the child. To quote one of our informants: "If she craves anything, when the baby is born whatever she craves will be marked on the baby. Or if anything frightened her when she was carrying the baby, why it will be marked by whatever frightened her." We note cases where the marking was accomplished not by a craving but by its opposite. The mother in question had eaten so much fresh fish that she had developed an abhorrence of it.

On the basis of this belief, the pregnant woman is supposed to exercise very careful self-discipline: not crave anything, avoid situations which might upset her or terrify her. Moreover, if she has the slightest desire for a particular food, those about her are to do their utmost to satisfy her before the craving reaches an emotional intensity which is likely to mark the child.[39]

Occasionally direct physical contact with the object in question is said to be sufficient to mark the child, as in the case of a woman whose leg was hit by a cherry which dropped out of a tree. Her baby was born with the mark of a cherry on his leg. A pregnant woman fell down in a strawberry patch and the baby had a birthmark resembling a strawberry.

We have heard testimonials, many of them in the first person, concerning the marking of babies with various kinds of fruit; with bacon, fish, cheese, and raw meat; with a band like a snake around the forehead; with a chicken; and with crooked feet. Moreover, no less common are cases in which the child is marked not physically, but in his personality. A child with an irrepressible tendency to steal candy had been carried in the womb when his mother had had an irresistible craving for sweets. The child of a woman who was indignant that she could not continue wearing corsets during pregnancy was marked with an excessive vanity concerning her wearing apparel. A mother who was irrationally desirous that her child should be a boy gave birth to a daughter who turned out to be a complete tomboy and remained so throughout her life.

Having summarized the main tendencies in this belief concerning the marking of babies, it seems desirable to give some first-hand testimonials:

> I've got a piece of bacon somewhere on my neck because my mother wanted bacon.

> They say you can't mark a child but I know better. Because my mother . . . got so sick of fish she said she thought she couldn't stand it when she was pregnant, and I have a fish this long [measuring on her index finger and hand for about four or five inches] on my leg. She just had a horror of fish.

> I have a niece who marked her baby with a strawberry just as natural as could be. When strawberries get ripe it gets red and has dots on it.

> There is a spot on my forehead. Dad had been in town and had been hit on his head and it was all bloody, and he came in and Mama looked up and seen this, and when I was born I had this red mark on my head. It shows up most of all when I am not well.

> You can see my foot, how crooked it is. I can remember when my mother used to take my foot and straighten it up. She would set me on her lap and hold my foot straight and then let me down and she'd make me promise I'd walk on it straight. Well, later when my younger brother was born he had a crooked foot just like mine, and had to wear a brace on it. Well, she told me that fooling with my foot every day, trying to straighten it out, was what marked Will.

> —— told me that her brother was marked with a roast chicken, just as plain a roast chicken as you ever saw. Right on his thigh here. She said her mother, before he was born, went to the neighbor's house just as they were opening the oven and pulled out this chicken to baste it, and she looked at it and thought how good it was, and went home and thought about eating that chicken all day long. When Steve was born he had that chicken on him and she said the legs stuck up just like a chicken's will.

> My brother-in-law's brother was the sheriff—this is a fact—in Price. They had a jail break and the fellows got out, got an old shotgun and they shot his hand clear off, and the shot marks were on his shoulder. It killed him. They came and told his sister about it and she was expecting a baby. When the baby was born—I've seen it a thousand times—it didn't have no hand, and it had shot marks on its arm just as plain as day.

> There's a very prominent man here in town. He's just insanely jealous of his wife and there's no reason in the world for him to be—absolutely no reason. His mother told me that she marked him that way because when she carried him his father was just stepping out with everybody and anybody. They had a girl working for them and he would sit with this girl on his lap right in front of her to torment her, and any time that

he was gone she just watched at the windows for him and walked the floor. And she said, "I know I marked this boy."

Oh, well, I claim that a woman can get a craving for some particular kind of food and can mark the baby. . . . Of course they claim nowadays that you can't do that, but I claim that they used to, anyway. . . . When first I discovered that I was in the family way with my boy, I thought I could smell cheese in the middle of the night. I waked up, and oh, I wanted some cheese. I didn't have any, and I went up to my neighbor's that I knew had some, and I never tasted such good cheese in my life as that was. I ate what I wanted, and that craving was all gone, that's all there was to it. When the child was born, he always did like cheese, but [laughing] I really marked him with fresh meat. My husband was on the mountain, riding for cattle, and I was in the valley, and he came down, and he brought some fresh beef. And I said, "Well, I'd better go and start supper." And he said, "I'll cut some of that meat." And he cut some of that fresh meat, and I made up my mind that I knew just how I wanted it cooked, so I put the skillet on the stove, and put quite a bit of grease in it and got it good and smoky hot, and took that meat, the slices on my hand, and laid it in that grease, and it just all quivered, and the blood came to the top and oh, it smelled good. And I went on and put all the meat in there, and the water was in my mouth, the saliva, and I stood there looking at it, and I turned around and scratched my buttocks. And they say, "Wherever you touch yourself, there's where the mark will be." And when that child was born he had the prettiest bite of raw meat on him you ever saw. It lasted there all his life. . . . It wasn't raw. It was smooth, just as smooth, but it was just the color of red, and it had the dark red veins like it was in the meat all across that bite.

A number of taboos and beliefs relate to the care of the newborn child. For the first year it should not be permitted to look in a mirror, lest it die before it is a year old. Its nails should not be cut: they should either be bitten off or simply permitted to grow.[40] Cats should be kept away from a newborn baby; they will suck the breath out and smother it. The baby's first curls should be made by wrapping them around a finger which is carefully moistened with saliva. It is not normal for a baby to lie with its arms straight down by its sides; this is an indication that something is wrong with the child; the normal position is with the arms flexed across the chest. The belief is encountered that the child should be put upon the breast immediately after birth, that the breast prior to lactation contains a substance which acts as a kind of stimulant for the child which will cause it to have an appetite and to suckle better. Sugar teats have been used: sugared bread or simply plain lump sugar.[41] If you want a baby to go to sleep, yawn in its presence. The first tooth is supposed to bring money from the good fairy. Later on when a child is losing his baby teeth he is told that if he puts his tooth underneath his pillow the fairies will come and exchange it for money—parents carefully perform the act ascribed to the fairies. When a baby tooth is pulled, a child is told that if he refrains from putting his tongue in the hole fairies will leave money under his pillow.[42]

Wetting the bed is the subject of some folk practices. It is said that playing with fire will cause a child to wet the bed. To break a child of the habit he should be set in ice water or fed raisins.[43] A rather fearful device has been resorted to: the bed is connected up with a dry-cell battery so that upon wetting the child receives a shock which causes him to break his habit. A child should be through bed-wetting at the age of three. If a child continues to mess in his pants his nose should be rubbed in it. It should be noted that this device is resorted to very commonly in housebreaking pets. To encourage children to keep clean they are told that angels won't come to visit them if their faces are dirty.[44] They are threatened with such expressions as: "I'll throw you to the bears"; "I'm going to cut your ears off"; "The bugger man will get you"; "I'll give you to the Injins."

Tongue-twisters form a technique for folk entertainment among certain groups. In addition to the nearly universal "Peter Piper," "How much wood would a woodchuck chuck," and "The skunk sat on a stump," we have collected the following:

Baby's rubber buggy bumper.

I thought I thought,
But the thought I thought
Was not the thought I thought I thought.

Betty Botter bought some butter,
But, said she, "This butter's bitter.
If I put it in my batter
It will make my batter bitter.
But a bit of better butter
Would make my bit of batter better."
So Betty Botter bought some better butter,
Put it in her bit of batter,
Made her bit of batter better.

Theothilus Thistle, the successful thistle sifter,
While sifting a sieve full of unsifted thistles,
Thrust three thousand thistles through the thick of his thumb.
Now if Theothilus Thistle, the successful thistle sifter,
While sifting a sieve full of unsifted thistles,
Thrust three thousand thistles through the thick of his thumb,
See that thou, while sifting a sieve full of unsifted thistles,
Thrust not three thousand thistles through the thick of thy thumb.

Occasionally tongue-twisters are designed to produce a vulgar result should the inevitable mistake be made, as:

> I slit a sheet,
> A sheet I slit,
> Upon the slitted sheet I sit.

> I'm not a fig plucker nor a fig plucker's son,
> But I'll pluck figs till the fig plucker comes.

Riddling is probably less common today than it was before the inroads made upon folk entertainment by modern communications media. However, it is not difficult to encounter them still.

> Pages upon pages without any stitches,
> Guess this riddle and I'll give you my britches.
>> —Lettuce, cabbage.

> As round as an apple,
> As busy as a bee,
> Prettiest little thing you ever did see.
>> —A watch.

> As I was going across London bridge
> I found myself a piece of steel.
> I made me a coat, my daddy a coat,
> And I have the same piece of steel left.
>> —A needle.

> As round as an apple,
> As deep as a cup,
> And all the king's horses
> Can't pull it up.
>> —A well.

> A house full,
> A hole full,
> And can't catch a bowl full.
>> —Smoke.

> Little Nancy Etticoat
> In a white petticoat,
> The longer she stands
> The shorter she grows.
>> —A candle.

> What is something that is black and white and red (read) all over?
>> —A newspaper; an embarrassed zebra.

> There is a big green house, inside that is a white house, and inside that is a red house, and inside that is a lot of little black nigger babies. What is it?
>> —A watermelon.

Some riddles contain what we used to call "a nigger in the woodpile":

Railroad crossing, look out for the cars,
Can you spell that without any r's?
    —T-H-A-T.[45]

A man rode up a hill but yet he walked.
    —Had a dog named "Yettie."[46]

There were twelve knights passing by,
And twelve pears hanging high,
Each man took a pear,
And left eleven hanging there.
    —One man's name was "Eachman."[47]

If it takes a hen and a half a day and a half to lay an egg and a half, how long will it take a rooster sitting on a doorknob to hatch a hardware store? Do you give up?
    —So did the rooster.[48]

Riddles appear which are not in rhyme but which involve a direct question and answer, as:

If you are in a holy church without any windows and without any doors how do you get out?
    —Crawl out through the holes.

You are asked: "Why does the cow slobber?" The answer, "Because it can't spit." You are asked if you know how to make a match burn twice. You answer no, and your informant demonstrates by striking a match, letting it burn an instant, blowing it out, then, while it is still hot, pushing it against your hand so that it burns you.

The number of children's rhymes, finger play rhymes, and similar materials which we have encountered is extensive. While rocking a baby lying across your arms back and forth, you say, "Up with the heels, down with the head / This is the way to make cockletee bread."

"This is the way to make a house," passing your hand down the face of the baby; "And this is the way to break it up!" The hand moves up the face, brushing the nose.

Knock on the door (knuckles on the forehead)
Peek in (look in the eye)
Lift up the latch (nose is pulled)
Walk in (finger in mouth).

You lived here (touch the baby's forehead)
And I lived here (chin)
And I came to see you (strike nose with fingers as hand moves
    from chin to forehead).[49]

Here's the rooster (forehead)
And here's the hen (chin)
And here's the pullet (pull nose).[50]

A hen lived here (forehead)
A rooster lived here (chin)
Sometimes they went this way to visit each other ("walk" around
    the cheek with the first and second fingers),
Or sometimes they went the short way (straight up over the nose,
    rubbing it on the way).[51]

This is grandma's house (touch one cheek)
This is mama's house (touch other cheek)
And the mail goes over to grandma's house by ex*press*
    (press on nose).

"The beehive" (use the doubled fist):
    Here is a beehive; and where are the bees?
    Hiding away where nobody sees,
    Soon they'll come buzzing out of their hives
    1,2,3,4,5,zzzzzzzzzzzzzzz—Sting you!
    (Make two beehives and count to ten.)[52]

"The squirrels" (use the four fingers and thumb, beginning with it:)
    Five little squirrels sitting on a tree,
    The first little squirrel said, "What do I see?"
    The second little squirrel said, "I smell a gun." (sniff)
    The third little squirrel said, "Oh, let's run."
    The fourth little squirrel said, "Let's hide in the shade."
    The fifth little squirrel said, "I'm not afraid!"
    Bang! went the gun (clap hands), and away they all run![53]

"Hot Mud Pies" (song with appropriate actions):
    Tell me little housewife playing in the sun
    How many minutes till the pie is done.
    Johnny tends the oven, Katie rolls the crust,
    Annie brings the flour, all the golden dust.
        Refrain: Roll it so, and pat it thinner
                    How the morning flies,
                    Ring the bell, it's time for dinner.
                    Hot Mud Pies![54]

Pretty Master Squirrel, sitting on a rail,
Shakes his head and listens,
Curls his bushy tail.
Wish we had a shower
Think we need it so
It would make the wayside such a heap of dough.[55]

These rhymes are done with appropriate manipulations of the fingers to represent each image:

> Here's the church
> Here's the steeple
> Open the door and see no people.

Also:

> Here's the church
> Here's the steeple
> Open the door and see all the people.

Similar is:

> This is mama's knives and forks
> And this is mama's table,
> This is mama's looking glass
> And this is baby's cradle.

"Jack and Jill" is played with a piece of paper tied around the forefinger of one hand:

> This is Jack and this is Jill (show alternately the finger with
>   the paper and the one without),
> Fly away Jack, fly away Jill (hands are placed behind the back,
>   the paper is slipped from one finger to the other),
> Come back Jack, come back Jill (the child is amazed to see the
>   paper come back on the finger where he was not expecting it).[56]

The little pig that went to market has at least three notable variants in Utah:

> This little pig went to market,
> This little pig stayed home,
> This little pig had nice roast beef,
> This little pig had none,
> This little pig went "wee, wee, wee!" all the way home.[57]

> This little pig said, "I want some corn,"
> This little pig said, "Where you going to get it?"
> This little pig said, "Over in Grandpa's barn,"
> This little pig said, "Yeah, and I'll tell,"
> This little pig said, "Wee, wee, I can't get over the barn door sill."

> This little piggie says, "Me go 'teal wheat,"
> This little piggie says, "Where from?"
> This little piggie says, "Out of the wheat bin,"
> This little piggie says, "Me go tell,"
> This little piggie says, "Wheat, wheat, wheat."

Another informant counted her baby's toes to the following:

Little pee, penaloot,
Mary whistle, Mary hootle,
Big old gobble, gobble.

A baby's feet are patted to the following rhyme:

Shoe the old horse,
Shoe the old mare,
But let the little colt go bare, bare, bare.

Or:

Pit a pat polt,
Shoe the wild colt,
Drive a nail here,
Drive a nail there.[58]

We have encountered the following counting-out rhymes:

Eenie, meanie, minie, moe,
Catch a nigger by the toe,
If he hollers let him go,
Eenie, meanie, minie, moe.[59]

A Moab variant of this gives the last two lines:

If he hollers make him pay
Fifty dollars every day.

Onerie, orie, ickry, ann,
Phyllisy, fallacy, Nicholas, John,
Queever, quaver, English knaver,
Stinklum, stanklum, you be buck.[60]

One for the money,
Two for the show,
Three to get ready
And four to go.[61]

One, two, three, four, five, six, seven,
All good children go to heaven,
Some are good, some are bad,
One, two, three, four, five, six, seven.[62]

Not a few children's rhymes and sayings involve a practical joke:

Adam and Eve and Pinch-Me went down to the river to bathe,
Adam and Eve got drownded and who do you think got saved?
—The child answers "Pinch-Me," and gets pinched.[63]

Salt, pepper, and punch-me were sitting on a bench,
Salt and pepper fell off, and who do you think was left?[64]

If you had one sock and two shoes, what would you want?
   —Another sock.[65]

My father and your father had a fiddle.
My father broke your father's fiddle in the middle.
   —The listener is struck inside the elbow as his arm is
   outstretched.[66]

My mother and your mother were hanging out clothes,
My mother gave your mother a punch in the nose.
Did it hurt?[67]

Down the road I saw a big slimy snail. I one it. [The listener
   is supposed to say "I two it."—"I three it."—etc., to
   "I eight (ate) it." The supposed victim occasionally gets
   his revenge: instead of saying "I eight it," he says, "I
   jumped over it and you ate it."] [68]

One child says, "I can do such and such." If inadvertently his
   listener says, "So can I," (sock in eye) he must instantaneously
   shout, "Bull's eye," lest he be socked in the eye by the other
   child.[69]

NOTES

1. Most of the content of this article was gathered from oral sources in Moab, Utah, in
   1953, from the following informants: Inez Burr (FMC I 868, 880, 910); Ann Chamber-
   lain (FMC I 867, 882); Doris B. Ellis (FMC I 842); Mrs. Mart Fish (FMC I 896, 912);
   Eloise Hawks (FMC I 904); Opel Howell (FMC I 867, 882); Ima Irish (FMC I 871,
   913); Pearl M. Knight (FMC I 881); Mary M. Pogue (FMC I 866); LaRae Shoop
   (FMC I 874); Mrs. Spry (FMC I 895); Phyllis Stocks (FMC I 878); Mrs. Waddell
   (FMC I 911); Evelyn Ward (FMC I 878). When the informant was other than one of
   these, the note indicates the source. FMC is the abbreviation for the Fife Mormon Collection: Series I, oral sources; Series II, manuscript sources.
2. FMC I 875: Clara W. Stevens, Woods Cross, Utah, 1953; also from Moab.
3. FMC I 601: Juanita Brooks, St. George, Utah, 1954.
4. FMC I 875: Clara W. Stevens, Woods Cross, Utah, 1953.
5. FMC II 38: Clyde Fescher, WPA Writers Project, Utah, 1937; FMC I 875: Clara W.
   Stevens, Woods Cross, Utah, 1953.
6. FMC II 38: Clyde Fescher, WPA Writers Project, Utah, 1937.
7. FMC I 875: Clara W. Stevens, Woods Cross, Utah, 1953.
8. FMC I 962: Alta Fife, Woods Cross, Utah, 1954.
9. FMC II 38: Clyde Fescher, WPA Writers Project, Utah, 1937.
10. FMC I 875: Clara W. Stevens, Woods Cross, Utah, 1953; also from Moab.
11. FMC I 962: Alta Fife, Woods Cross, Utah, 1954.

12. Austin Fife, Idaho Falls, 1920's.

13. Ibid.

14. FMC II 156: Manuscript history of Zeke Johnson.

15. Austin Fife, Idaho Falls, 1920's.

16. FMC II 601: Juanita Brooks, St. George, Utah, 1954.

17. FMC I 875: Clara W. Stevens, Woods Cross, Utah, 1953; also from Moab.

18. Ibid.

19. Ibid; also from Moab.

20. Ibid.

21. Ibid.

22. FMC I 870: Clara W. Stevens, Woods Cross, Utah, 1953.

23. Ibid.

24. FMC I 962: Alta S. Fife, Woods Cross, Utah, 1954.

25. Ibid.

26. FMC I 870: Clara W. Stevens, Woods Cross, Utah, 1953.

27. Ibid.

28. FMC I 875: Clara W. Stevens, Woods Cross, Utah, 1953.

29. Ibid.

30. Austin Fife, Idaho Falls, Idaho, 1920's.

31. FMC I 257: Effie Villet, Lewiston, Utah, 1946.

32. FMC I 875: Clara W. Stevens, Woods Cross, Utah, 1953.

33. Ibid.

34. FMC II 222: Clyde Fescher, WPA Writers Project, Utah, 1937.

35. FMC II 222: Dr. Julian Stewart, Salt Lake City, Utah, 1937.

36. FMC II 277: Mrs. Luella Hardt, St. David, Arizona, 1947.

37. FMC I 875: Clara W. Stevens, Woods Cross, Utah, 1953.

38. Austin Fife, Idaho Falls, Idaho, 1920's.

39. FMC II 277: Mrs. Luella Hardt, St. David, Arizona, 1947.

40. FMC I 875: Clara W. Stevens, Woods Cross, Utah, 1953; also from Moab.

41. Austin Fife, Idaho Falls, Idaho, 1920's.

42. Ibid.

43. FMC I 875: Clara W. Stevens, Woods Cross, Utah, 1953; also from Moab.

44. FMC II 38: Clyde Fescher, WPA Writers Project, Utah, 1937.

45. FMC II 277: Mrs. Luella Hardt, St. David, Arizona, 1947.

46. Ibid.

47. Ibid.

48. Ibid.

49. FMC I 875: Clara W. Stevens, Woods Cross, Utah, 1953.

50. FMC II 277: Mrs. Luella Hardt, St. David, Arizona, 1947; also from Moab.

51. Ibid.

52. Ibid.

53. Ibid.

54. Ibid.

55. Ibid.

56. Ibid.

57. FMC I 876: Clara W. Stevens, Woods Cross, Utah, 1953.

58. FMC II 277: Mrs. Luella Hardt, St. David, Arizona, 1947.

59. Austin Fife, Idaho Falls, Idaho, early 1920's.

60. FMC II 277: Mrs. Luella Hardt, St. David, Arizona, 1947.

61. Austin Fife, Idaho Falls, Idaho, prior to 1920.

62. FMC II 277: Mrs. Luella Hardt, St. David, Arizona, 1947.

63. Austin Fife, Idaho Falls, Idaho, prior to 1920.

64. FMC II 277: Mrs. Luella Hardt, St. David, Arizona, 1947.

65. Ibid.

66. Ibid.

67. Austin Fife, Idaho Falls, Idaho, prior to 1920.

68. Ibid.; also from Moab.

69. FMC II 277: Mrs. Luella Hardt, St. David, Arizona, 1947; also from Austin Fife, Idaho Falls, Idaho, c. 1920.

Wayland D. Hand

The Common Cold in Utah Folk Medicine

The common cold, still as baffling to modern medical men as it was to their confrères of an earlier generation, claims more attention in Utah folk medical practice than any other single malady. What was once largely the concern of granny women and other folk medical practitioners in the diagnosis and arrest of the disease has lived on in families and in individuals in the form of individual folk notions and curative practices. Taken as a whole, these beliefs and customs concerning colds, and folk medical lore generally, constitute a body of traditional lore from early times that is only now being slowly discarded with the advance of medical science. It is one of the ironies of this scientific advance, and of cultural history generally, that some of the practices now falling into desuetude themselves derived from the medical learning of an earlier day.

Folk medical beliefs presented in this paper constitute only a sampling of Utah material, but they accord in a general way with folk medical lore found elsewhere in America.[1] In making no apology for a limited survey of only one small subject field of folk medicine, the author can only hope that this article will stimulate further study in a broader field of inquiry that is only beginning. Much folk medical material can still be collected in oral tradition, especially from older people, but to give historical perspective whole treasures must be unearthed from old diaries and daybooks, books of recipes, and special treatises on the part played by early-day practitioners of folk medicine, if such records can still be found.[2]

There are very few beliefs about colds and sore throats in Utah that involve ominal or causative magic. In fact, there is very little lore that deals with catching a cold. Perhaps the common ways of catching a cold are too well known for informants to have enumerated them. However, in Vernal one person at least in a family is said to come down with a cold if a cat sneezes or coughs (ominal). An informant from Salt Lake claims that the wearing of overshoes in the house brings on a cold (causative), a belief deriving from his English forebears.

Preventive measures against colds fall into magical as well as regular prophylactic treatments. We shall consider the items of pure folklore first. In 1961 a ninth-grader in a Salt Lake school reported that if you catch a falling autumn leaf you will not have a cold all winter. The wearing of necklaces, strings, and even hosiery and socks around the neck, as elsewhere, has been noted for Utah.[3] A necklace of amber beads is noted in two items from Salt Lake, both recent.[4] The keeping of a black silk cord as a protection against a cold is noted from Kearns in the 1930's, while any string around the neck is prescribed for the same purpose in an unplaced entry from 1961 designated as "an old American belief." A silk-stitched chain worn around the neck to prevent sore throat is another Salt Lake item noted in 1957, but also known in Sandy. The well-known prescription of a dirty sock worn around the neck against sore throat is recorded from Delta in 1930. This same procedure, widely used in cures, is treated below.

The wearing of asafetida around the neck, either in a chunk or in the more common asafetida bags is apparently common in Utah.[5] The theory is that by its strong smell, asafetida wards off disease. Another notion is that this noisome plant substance absorbs disease and miasmas. This practice is prescribed in five items of fairly recent date from Salt Lake, one of which represents an importation from Georgia through a Negro woman, ca. 1920. That the practice was widely known and tolerably old as such material goes is seen from entries from Ogden (ca. 1900), Bountiful (ca. 1910), Richfield (1915), Heber City (1916), Roy (1920), Layton (1934). The same preventive is noted for sore throat: Magna (1920), Salt Lake (1961), but referable to Georgia, ca. 1920 (Negro).

Garlic was worn around the neck much for the same reason as asafetida, although notions of it as a general purificatory agent are widespread, particularly in Europe. Moreover, its use in magically induced ailments (witchcraft and the evil eye), places it in the category of a general apotropaic agent. Although the practice is very old, whether the garlic is worn in a bag or in cloves, attestations in the UCLA collection are relatively recent: Midvale (1950), Vernal (1951; also 1956 from an Indian), Ogden (1957).[6] Items from Salt Lake (clove) and Magna (bag), both collected in 1963, show how both practices have persisted side by side. The wearing of the garlic in a dirty sock around the neck is noted from Midvale for 1948, and from Magna in 1963.

The therapeutic uses of onion parallel those of garlic in many ways; also here in the prevention of colds. An onion hung around the neck was prescribed in Bountiful, 1958, and this belief was noted in Salt Lake the same year. The placing of an onion under the pillow to ward off colds was noted from Bountiful in 1933, but is traceable to kinfolk coming from upper New York state. The eating of onions to prevent colds, as well as the far more prevalent use of them once a cold has been contracted, is a prescription learned from a sixty-seven-year-old woman in Salt Lake in 1964.[7]

Miscellaneous preventives include the dousing of boys' heads in water after haircuts to keep them from taking cold (1957, no place mentioned; probably Salt Lake) and the wetting of one's feet daily in salt water (Salt Lake? ca. 1900). An item from Provo, dating from around 1900, and not entirely clear, states that no child ever catches cold from its own spit or its own "pea." One more matter-of-fact view, remembered in Salt Lake from the year 1913, holds that if you got a cold or the flu, it was always due to something you had done, such as becoming chilled or otherwise neglecting yourself during cold or rainy weather. Unexplained in any way is a "rose cold," represented as being a dangerous kind of cold (Salt Lake, 1961).

In the cure of colds and sore throat, magical therapeutic agents, as in the case of preventive measures, will be discussed first. Protective and heat applications, ointments, plasters, gargles, foods, and teas and decoctions will then be taken up, in that order.

From the field of magical folk medicine, then: To cure a cold you are supposed to plant a rusty nail six feet from the east side of your house, and in two or three days your cold will go away (Salt Lake, ca. 1915). A more important item, since it ties in to the folk medical concepts of "measuring," and perhaps also to "plugging," is an item from Salt Lake dating from 1950: If you tie a lock of your hair to a stick, it will cure a cold. This item is unusual in the sense that sticks are used in "measuring," generally, and hair in "plugging."[8] The hanging of nutmegs around the throat to cure colds (Salt Lake, 1958; Bountiful, 1959) and sore throat (Ogden, 1959) implies magical connections in view of the wide use of nutmeg as an amulet.[9] The binding of asafetida on a rag around the neck to cure a sore throat (Bear River City, 1957),[10] and the hanging of an onion around the throat (Salt Lake, 1964) and on a wet string for the same purpose (Salt Lake, 1963), are perhaps somewhat less magical in character. Nondescript is the following: For sore throat tie a piece of unwashed lamb's hair dunked in brandy around your neck (Salt Lake, 1932). Other items, partly magical, but perhaps better to be explained in terms of the warding off and absorption of disease and corruption, deal with crushing onions underfoot and leaving them in the room. Four items, all from Salt Lake (1955-1963) attest to this practice, one of them specifying the treading of the onions with bare feet (1954). One of these items contains a possible clue to this rather curious usage, namely, the inhalation of the odor (1963). Onions quartered and placed in each window of the house is a kindred practice, but is not further explained (Salt Lake, 1964). The placing of a cut potato under the bed, cut side up, for the purpose of drying up a cold, is a related notion (Bountiful, 1960), although absorption rather than an exuded odor or inhalant properties would seem to explain this practice.

The binding of stockings around the neck, which appears to have been applied with some intended magical efficacy in the prevention of cold and sore throat, becomes a regular therapeutic device in their treatment, namely, as applications of warmth and protection.[11] This is especially true in the case of sore throat, which will be taken up first. Of eight items collected in Salt Lake between 1900 and 1964, four recommend the wearing of a "dirty sock" around the neck and one a sock "worn that day." A stocking worn on the left foot is prescribed in two items (1957,1958), a detail which reveals lingering magical aspects of the practice.[12] A woolen sock is indicated in an entry from 1900. Elsewhere in the state the "dirty sock" treatment is reported from Randolph (1910), Murray (1935), Bingham (1944), and Bountiful (1960). Variations include a "stocking you have been wearing" (Honeyville, 1902) and "a soiled wool sock" (Bear River City, 1957, but referable to the early 1930's). Red flannel cloths, widely known elsewhere in the United States, apparently are little prescribed for sore throat.[13] The UCLA files contain only one entry, an item from Salt Lake (1957). Important also for its magical connections is the following item from Salt Lake (1928): When you wrap a wet rag around your neck when you have a sore throat, the evil spirits are chased away. Magical rather than therapeutic also, apparently, is the application of a rubber band around the arm (N.B.!).

The binding of a dirty sock around the neck to cure colds is reported in eight texts from Salt Lake, and from Salt Lake County (Hunter), but the time span is very recent (1958 to date). Whether "a clean silk stocking" is prescribed (three entries), "a worn stocking," or "a dirty woolen sock," the practice is all to the same end. Two entries specify that the sock should be kept around the neck overnight. A related cure recommended in Hooper about 1890 is clearly magical rather than curative: If a person has a summer cold, tie a string around his neck and the cold will go away.

Applications of heat for the cure of colds, over and above the protection and warmth afforded by the proverbial "dirty sock," involve the placing of a heated brick to the neck. This may be done by putting the brick in a sack and placing it on the neck as one reclines (Salt Lake, 1962, but referable to 1920). An ice pack on one's head and a hot brick in a sack on one's neck is a variation involving the contrast of heat and cold therapy (Salt Lake, 1955). The application of bricks to the head, with no mention of heat in connection with the bricks (Salt Lake, 1955), must be regarded as exceptional. So far as the author knows, bricks are used magically only in love divinations.

The use of salves, whether those of a single ingredient or compounds, is still tolerably widespread, as is the application of plasters, a practice that will be taken up later. Rubbing oneself with goose grease (presumably the neck?) is a cure dating from the 1890's or before (Salt Lake?).[14] Even though goose grease is not as easily available as it once was, this cure is noted from the same area as recently as 1945. The greasing of the neck and chest with hot skunk oil is noted from Provo in 1945 and from Salt Lake somewhat before that. A third Utah entry, stemming from the Ozarks, was collected in Salt Lake in 1964, but goes back twenty years. Goat tallow applied to the neck and chest (1945; no place), camphor and lard (1945; no place),[15] and plain grease rubbed on the soles of the feet (Salt Lake, 1964), are other ointments involving animal fat. Raw sliced onions in kerosene, made into an ointment, was used in the informant's (Salt Lake, 1963) family "for generations."

Plasters of various kinds, widely used in an earlier day, still linger on in the curing of colds, sore throats, and kindred maladies. Plasters were made by covering brown paper, or pieces of cloth, with various curative agents. Sometimes brown paper alone was used, especially for cold in the lungs (Salt Lake, 1890's; 1944). Plasters made of animal fat include a bacon rind hung around the neck (Salt Lake, 1957),[16] a strip of fresh bacon held in place around the throat by a dirty sock (Lehi, 1957), black pepper on a strip of bacon, with the pepper next to the neck (Tooele, 1957). All three plasters are prescribed for a sore throat, the last one for sore throat in a child. Other sore throat plasters made of pork involve a slice of pork fat under a flannel cloth (1943; no place),[17] a strip of salt pork bacon with drops of turpentine applied to the neck with a woolen sock (Salt Lake, 1906), and a piece of "salted pork on your throat" (Ogden, 1919). A scatological poultice of chicken droppings placed in a cloth and tied around the neck (Salt Lake, 1915), must be regarded as a curiosity, even though the use of animal excrements, particularly sheep droppings, has lingered on into our own time in American folk medicine. Among the varieties of plasters made of vegetable products, one can note only the use of mustard plasters on the chest and back for colds (and also pneumonia) (Salt Lake, 1930, but traceable to 1888 within the informant's family)[18] and an onion plaster on the chest, also for a cold (1945; no place); and likewise on the neck (Salt Lake, 1945). Carrots in a cloth around the neck are said to relieve sore throat (Salt Lake, 1940).

Gargles prescribed include the following: Gargle with salt water every two hours—the water being as hot as you can take—to cure sore throat (Salt Lake, 1961), salt and vinegar for colds (Salt Lake, ca. 1910; 1945, no place), and gunpowder and glycerin mixed (Salt Lake, 1941; 1944, no place). Boil the inner bark from an oak tree until you obtain a dark brown fluid; cool and gargle with it three times a day for sore throat (Vernal, ca. 1910).[19]

Eating a large amount of food is a good cure for a cold (Salt Lake, 1963).[20] This theory is expressed in an old proverb, "Feed (stuff) a cold and starve a fever," which appears to be fairly well known in Utah even on the basis of a limited sampling (Salt Lake, 1961, 1963).[21] The variant reading, "Starve a fever and feed a cold," is likewise known (Payson, 1900; Salt Lake, 1928).[22] Laxatives for colds "to clean out the system," as everyone knows, are widely prescribed, but the files contain only one entry (Woods Cross, 1891).

The eating of special foods, as well as the drinking of teas and the taking of tonics, should be noted. Onions are taken in a variety of ways: Onions cure a cold (Salt Lake, 1960); eat a whole onion, go straight to bed, and keep covered up (Salt Lake, 1961); onion juice, made by putting sugar on sliced onions and putting them in a warm oven so the sugar would draw the juice out (Bear River City, 1957);[23] cooked onions (Salt Lake, 1964);[24] fried onions (Salt Lake, 1910, 1942; Provo, 1943). Raisins likewise are prescribed for sore throat (Salt Lake, ca. 1880, 1910, 1943; 1942, no place). Other foods, or combinations of foods, include yeast sprinkled on food (Hunter, 1950), and molasses and soy beans mixed together (Salt Lake, 1950), both items being prescribed for colds. Ginger is said to cure a sore throat (1930's, no place), but no details are given (See ginger tea in the next paragraph). Cinnamon and sugar mixed well, but apparently taken dry, were swabbed around the tonsils to cure sore throat (Salt Lake, 1932).

A variety of teas and other decoctions were also used in combating colds. Among the teas were hot ginger tea (Salt Lake, 1910),[25] horehound tea (1942, 1945, places not mentioned),[26] a tea made of sage and catnip (Salt Lake, 1910;

1943, no place).[27] Brigham tea goes back to an earlier period.[28] Vinegar and honey (Salt Lake, 1963), lemon juice and honey (Salt Lake, 1920), and a syrup made of vinegar, butter, and molasses (Salt Lake, 1942) were taken more in the manner of medicines than of teas. Tabasco sauce was taken as a medicine as colds were coming on (Salt Lake, 1954). A drink made of three parts mustard and two parts cornstarch water was administered for colds (Salt Lake, 1950 [Irish]). Two or three drops of kerosene in a teaspoonful of sugar was known in Provo around 1900. Kerosene on a feather heals sore throat (Salt Lake, ca. 1915), but the entry lacks details as to how the treatment was carried out.

The favorite American nostrum for colds, whiskey, did not lack adherents in Utah.[29] Taken straight—often hot (Helper, 1930)—qualified by rock candy (Salt Lake, ca. 1910; 1945 [two items]; 1950), or taken with aspirin (Salt Lake, ca. 1920), whiskey was a specific against the common cold in the homes of any save the most devout Mormons.

There is very little on the duration of colds or on their recurrence. The following two items may serve as an aid to collectors in bringing in further items in a subject field that must have endless variety: If a person catches a cold on an even day of the month, he will get over it soon, but if he gets one on an odd day, he shall have "phenomena" soon (Salt Lake, 1957). If you take a bath while you have a cold in winter time, you'll surely not recover (Salt Lake, 1964; heard originally in Mexico).

After the foregoing, it will perhaps come as no surprise that even dried rats' tails will cure a cold (Murray, 1963), but the reader must forego specific information on this engaging entry. In normal folk medical practices, as we have seen, treatment for colds is undertaken in two main ways, internal dosing or external applications. Take your pick.

NOTES

1. There has been very little published on folk medicine in Utah. Austin E. Fife's fine article, "Pioneer Mormon Remedies," *Western Folklore* 16 (1957): 153-62 (hereafter cited as Fife), is about the only general survey to which the reader may be referred. The present study rests on the author's field collecting in Utah in 1957 and before, and on material collected from Utahns and former Utahns in his folklore classes over the years at UCLA. Mainly, however, the article rests on the extensive folklore collectanea of Anthon S. Cannon at the University of Utah during the past several years. Entries are naturally weighted heavily in favor of Salt Lake and environs, but material stemming from elsewhere in the state shows that there was once a representative body of folk medicine known throughout the Utah territory. If nothing more, this study bears out the strong need to launch folklore collecting projects at several strategic spots throughout the Beehive State.

2. These rare personal documents may still occasionally be encountered in private hands, but many kinds of useful information of this sort are on deposit in public archives such as those of the Utah State Historical Society and the Daughters of the Utah Pioneers.

3. Readings from North Carolina, with comparative notes from elsewhere in the country, are to be found in my edition of *Popular Beliefs and Superstitions from North Carolina* (*Frank C. Brown Collection of North Carolina Folklore*, vol. 6 [Durham, North Carolina: 1961]: 76-357, hereafter cited as Brown); cf. nos. 1141, 1144, 2208, *passim*.

4. Brown, no. 2218.

5. Brown, no. 1099; Fife, p. 161.

6. General items in the field of popular beliefs and superstitions, published and unpublished, are being collected from all over America at the Center for the Study of Comparative Folklore and Mythology, University of California at Los Angeles. The Utah material, including a special monograph on the human body, folk medicine, and the life cycle, will be edited by Wayland D. Hand and A. S. Cannon within the next five years.

7. Brown, no. 1112.

8. Brown, nos. 828 (notes), 829 for "measuring" and 1923f for "plugging."

9. Brown, no. 2106. For a more general application see no. 757.

10. Cf. Brown, no. 1099.

11. Brown, nos. 2209ff.

12. Brown, no. 2211.

13. Brown, nos. 1140, 2208.

14. Cf. Brown, nos. 1127, 2192.

15. Brown, no. 1129.

16. Brown, no. 2188; Fife, p. 156.

17. Cf. Brown, no. 2190.

18. Brown, no. 1132; Fife, p. 161.

19. Cf. Brown, no. 2200.

20. Brown, no. 1100.

21. Brown, no. 1102, where reference is given to Stuart A. Gallacher's treatment of this old medical proverb, "Stuff a Cold and Starve a Fever," *Bulletin of the History of Medicine* 11 (1942): 576-81.

22. Brown, no. 1410.

23. Brown, no. 1113.

24. Cf. Brown, no. 1112; Fife, p. 161.

25. Brown, no. 1107.

26. Brown, no. 1110; Fife, p. 161.

27. Brown, no. 1106, 1120.

28. Fife, p. 154.

29. Cf. Brown, no. 1117; Fife, p. 154.

J. H. Adamson

Tales of the Supernatural

It hardly takes a Platonist to see how closely many of the stories of the supernatural in Utah participate in the universal types of the genre: a Utah sailor sees a phantom ship,[1] a group of boys walking through a small-town churchyard see a woman dressed in white who vanishes before their eyes,[2] a dog, by his eerie behavior, apprises a family of a death just minutes before the fateful telegram arrives,[3] a fabulous monster somewhat monotonously appears and vanishes in the fathomless waters of Bear Lake.[4] In Bear River City, Utah, old people can still remember a "teacher's trial" of a witch that took place in their childhood. One woman recalls that children were careful about witches after that; in particular, they were suspicious of a woman who was called Silk Mary Ann because she had so many silk dresses. One day this woman approached a group of children who were playing near her home and gave each of them a glistening red apple. These girls, unlike their prototype Snow White, acted prudently.

> When she had gone, one of the girls said, "We mustn't eat them. She is a witch. We must throw them away." And we all threw our apples in the ditch. (WHC. Collector: Gayle Holmgren. Informant: Mrs. Lucinda P. Jensen, Bear River City, Utah.)

Mrs. Sarah Jane Butterfield of Riverton, Utah, believed that gypsies were able to "cast spells." She was once visited by a wily and persistent gypsy woman who wished to see some money or to peer into the cupboards. Angered by Mrs. Butterfield's stout refusals, the gypsy punched her fist into a batch of dough which was ready to be kneaded into loaves. Long after the woman had gone, the imprint of her fist still disfigured the dough. Mrs. Butterfield observed and pondered. Finally she baked the dubious dough but fed the bread to the pigs. "There is no sense taking chances," she remarked. (WHC. Collector: Alice Butterfield. Informant: Mrs. Mary Jane Crump Butterfield, age 83, born in Herriman, Utah.)

Another kind of story involving the supernatural, and one that turns up quite frequently in Utah lore, is that of a dream which serves as portent, consolation, prophecy, or vision.

> The son of Alma Turner went deer hunting in the South Willow area with the son of Sam Miles, and the Turner man failed to return. Searchers who looked for him until the winter weather made search impossible were unable to find any clue to his whereabouts, and he was assumed dead. The following spring Mrs. Sam Miles had a dream in which she saw the exact location of the body sitting against a tree. As soon as the weather would permit, she took three men on horseback directly to the spot in the mountains that she had seen in the dream. There they found the body exactly as she had described it. He had, it was assumed, been struck with a stray bullet while resting. (WHC. Collector: J. Lynn Mortensen. Informants: his parents, William and Zelia Mortensen.)

A dream of consolation is recorded in the journal of Joseph Harker. After Joseph and his wife Susannah joined the Mormons, they sailed from Liverpool to New Orleans where they took passage on a river boat for Nauvoo, Illinois. During the journey up the Mississippi, their little boy John, playing with other children on the boat, caught at a string that was falling overboard, lost his balance, and plunged into the river. The horrified parents saw the little boy, brightly dressed in a kilt, sucked under the tremendous, churning paddle. After that he was never seen again. Susannah could not shake off her grief and depression. She was haunted by terrifying thoughts of her baby's body being devoured by a wild animal or a fish. But one night, she tells us, while lying in bed awake, she actually saw his body buried in the quiet sands of the mighty river. At the same time peace and comfort came to her and she bore her sorrow, from that time, with tranquillity.[5]

> Mrs. Warburton of Tooele, Utah, also received comfort from a dream. She "nearly went wild" worrying about her son in France during World War I, until she had a dream in which a great storm blew down the family barn. Her son, Van, came walking out of the debris unharmed. From that day on she never worried again. (WHC. Collector: Joyce Warburton. Informant: Miss Warburton's mother; the dreamer was Miss Warburton's grandmother.)

Utah lore of the supernatural is replete with "peepstone" stories. Such stories are found among many peoples, and they are at least as old as the account of an attempt to divine by means of stones recorded in chapter 28 of

I Samuel. It has been conjectured that Samuel may have used divinatory stones to find the lost asses of Saul. The biblical record, however, is not explicit on this point. In Utah, in any case, peepstone ladies frequently found straying animals. In the early 1900's, for example, two Dunyan sisters of Tooele, Utah, found two peepstones on Little Mountain. The one sister could see nothing in her stone except the city cemetery and the people buried there; the other, however, had a wider field of vision. On one occasion she was able to see in the stone a valuable black horse which her brother had lost. She said that the horse was standing by a stream of water near a pine pole fence. Recognizing the place from her description, the brothers went to the mouth of Settlement Canyon and found the horse standing just as Miss Dunyan had described. (WHC. Collector: J. Lynn Mortensen. Informant: his mother, Mrs. Zelia Mortensen.)

Leona D. Kennard (Fife Mormon Collection, hereafter referred to as FMC) reports three similar incidents involving the "Peepstone Lady of Logan" (so known locally). She found a cow for Joseph H. Schvaneveldt of Logan, a team of horses for a Mr. Adams from Glendale, Idaho, and a herd of cows for Cal Cressall.

The peepstone lady of Tooele, Miss Dunyan, once found a lost child, Dan Perry's small son, who had wandered away from home on a winter night, clad only in a nightshirt. Neighbors and townspeople joined in an intensive search, but could not find the boy.

> Miss Dunyan consulted the peepstone and reported that the boy was lying on the ground near two large round structures which she could not identify. After a few minutes' discussion, the townspeople deduced that the structures must be the two igloo-like coal kilns three miles northeast of Tooele in the town of Pine Canyon. They went to the kilns and found the boy lying as Miss Dunyan had described. He was revived and survived the ordeal. (WHC. Collector: J. Lynn Mortensen. Informant: his mother, Mrs. Zelia Mortensen.)

The Peepstone Lady of Logan was apparently famous for finding the bodies of people who had been drowned in Bear Lake. Miss Kennard has collected three accounts of searchers being led to the "exact spot" of a drowned body by following the directions of the seeress. In at least one instance, however, the peepstone lady's vision was something less than occult.

> One winter in the early 80's, a Mr. Hanks left his home with a horse and buggy. When he did not return at the time he was expected, his wife became anxious and a searching party was organized. The horse and buggy were found near the river. After a thorough but futile search of the surrounding area, the Peepstone Lady was consulted. She told them that Mr. Hanks's body was lying face down on the bottom of the river.

> She described the exact spot. The townspeople summoned the help of Cal Cressall and another young man of Logan who were expert swimmers. A large hole was chopped in the ice and the two took turns diving into the icy water to find the body. Cal Cressall almost lost his life because he had difficulty finding his way back to the hole. The body was never found. Twenty years later Mr. Hanks was located living in San Francisco. (FMC. Collector: Leona D. Kennard. Informant: Mrs. W. B. Jenkins, San Diego, California, aged about 70, formerly a resident of Logan, Utah.)

Still another type of supernatural story found in Utah is the ghost story. One finds many accounts of haunted places. One of these was a mountainside spring which Indians had been avoiding long before white men came to Utah. The later experience of white men confirmed the Indian belief that evil spirits consorted in the area.[6] In another instance, a place was discovered to be demonic, not because of ghostly inhabitants, but rather because a vein of ore possessed the strange property of drawing all the strength out of the bodies of those who approached it, leaving them weak, helpless, and unable to stand.[7]

Joyce Warburton has collected two instances in which a dead man's spirit appeared to members of his family. One story concerns her grandfather, Jim, who had been on such bad terms with his father that the two would pass on the street without speaking. One night, when Jim was staying in a sheep camp outside of Grantsville, Utah, his father came and said, "Jim, I'm sorry about the trouble between us. I'm leaving and I want to make it up with you before I go." They sat down and talked in a friendly fashion for a few minutes; then Jim's father left. Later Jim heard that at the time when he had thought his father was visiting him at the sheep camp the older man had actually died at home. (WHC. Informant: Miss Warburton's mother.)

A similar incident is also related by the same informant.

> Many years later when I was in Salt Lake City by the bedside of my first husband, who was dying, I had left my two little daughters in Grantsville with my parents. The night he died my mother, father, and two younger brothers were at home with the girls. They swear to this day that Jack (my husband) came to the house, entered, and spent some time tenderly watching his children before he quietly left.

The various types of stories we have dealt with thus far are common to the lore of most peoples. Utah, however, does produce a few types of supernatural stories which arise from her own folkways. The first of these types, to which belongs a remarkably large body of lore, is centered around the Three Nephites.[8] These three supernatural beings are first mentioned in the Book of Mormon, according to which Christ, after his crucifixion in the Old World, visited the New World and founded a church among a group of fair-skinned Hebrews. These Hebrews, it is said, had found their way across the ocean hundreds of years earlier. Three of their number requested from Christ the same gift that, traditionally, John the Beloved had requested in the Old World, i.e., that they should be allowed to tarry until the Master should return. Jesus granted their wish, at the same time promising them that they should never taste of death, feel pain, or know sorrow, "save it be for the sins of the world."[9]

The Nephite stories have a number of interesting characteristics and relationships. To begin with, the legend of the Nephites is quite similar to the legend of the Wandering Jew. Another characteristic, although not an invariable one, is that these aged wanderers, like the gods of Greek legend, knock on doors of mortals and ask for food. The act of healing or the giving of advice, invariably associated with their appearance, is often a reward for hospitality extended. Sometimes they promise, after the manner of the prophet Elijah (I Kings, 17:14), that hospitable people shall never again lack food.

One motif appearing in all the stories is the vanishing of the Nephite immediately after he performs his errand of mercy. On at least one occasion, the horse a Nephite was riding vanished also. The deathless ones are almost invariably described as old men with white beards. They have, so far as is known, never appeared to anyone except Mormons, although they have appeared to Mormons in many lands and climes.[10] The following stories illustrate significant aspects of the lore.

I

This incident occurred in Tooele, Utah, around 1860. The McLaws' family home was situated on the west side of Tooele, somewhat apart from the other homes. One day a man appeared at their door and asked for food. He was told that the supply was meager, but that he was welcome to share what they had. After he had eaten, he thanked Mrs. McLaws and told her that she and her family would never want for food. Then he asked the way to Grantsville. The house was located in such a way that Grantsville could be seen across the valley, and Mrs. McLaws asked her young son Robert to step outside and show the stranger the way. Robert went outside but could not see the man anywhere. Around the house for many blocks in every direction stretched the open fields. The stranger had disappeared. (WHC. Collector: J. Lynn Mortensen. Informant: Mrs. Ruther Hector, daughter of Robert McLaws.)

II

A young girl had severely burned her hand and the doctors had little hope that she would ever have full use of it again. One afternoon an old bearded gentleman came to the door and asked for something to eat; he was admitted by the girl's aunt who fixed him something to eat in the kitchen. As he ate, he looked at the girl and said, "What's the matter with the young lady?" When told of her accident, he said, "Do you mind if

I give her a blessing?" The mother agreed and the old man blessed the girl, promising her that she would regain the full use of her hand. The old man returned to the kitchen and the aunt followed him a moment later. He was not there. The aunt went outside, as did the girl's mother, and looked all around the house and into the street. The man was nowhere to be seen. The house was situated in a wide, flat field. It was possible to see a mile in each direction without obstruction. (WHC. Collector: Robert P. Sherwood. Informant: Mrs. Rex Winder; born in Rock Port, Summit County, Utah, in 1880's. Informant was the little girl in the story.)

III

When a boy, my father, Ferdinand F. Hintze, was sent out into Neff's Canyon to find the cattle in the fall. He became lost in the mountains. As night had come on, he figured he would just have to die because he was so lost. To his great surprise, a stranger came by, a very old man on a white horse. The man called him by name and asked what he was doing away over here. Ferdinand told him that he was lost. The stranger told him to climb on his horse and he would take him home. When they arrived near home, the old man let the boy down. The boy walked a few steps, turned around to thank the old man, but he had disappeared. (WHC. Collector: Penny Florence. Informant: Mrs. H. S. Florence, who was told the story around 1919 by her father, Ferdinand F. Hintze.)

I was able to follow up a recently reported appearance of one of the Three Nephites. When visiting in Carey, Idaho, in 1952, I was told that a young man from that town, serving on a mission for the Latter-day Saints in the vicinity of Boston, Massachusetts, had seen one of the wanderers. The details were meager and vague. Many people knew of the incident, but no one apparently had heard a specific account. In 1954, on a visit to Boston, I made inquiries and was able to establish the following facts. Three young Mormon elders were speaking in the open air on the Boston Common. They were in some difficulty from hecklers in the crowd when an old man with a beard appeared and asked for the privilege of the rostrum. He took questions from the crowd, answered with dignity and acuity, and, when no more questions were asked, descended from the portable pulpit and disappeared. The young missionaries, not only impressed but actually shaken by the experience, immediately began to speculate rather boldly as to the nature of their champion. They were disillusioned, however, when they saw the old man on two subsequent occasions. Ultimately they discovered that he was an aged member of the "Josephite" sect who was willing to help some of his "Brighamite" kin. (Informant: Professor Rulon Y. Robison, formerly of Boston University, now living in Darien, Connecticut.)

The lore of the Three Nephites is undoubtedly Utah's most interesting contribution to American folklore. It is a rich and varied material in which these wanderers, who transcend both time and space, appear sometimes at crucial moments to relieve suffering or to save a life and sometimes on simpler errands such as the giving of a suit of clothes to a missionary in a strange land or a word of hope to some despondent Saint. They have even been known to help bring in a threatened crop for a man who had delayed his own harvest to help sick or elderly neighbors.[11] Such stories still circulate, though less often, through the Mormon country; but they have left in the lean river valleys an aura of mystery, of awe, of compassion for suffering. Jesus in faded jeans asking a handout might characterize them best. One should remember, too, that the stories recorded here were gathered by college students from people who were children, at most, when the appearances are supposed to have occurred. As a result, the accounts lack the fervor, the intimacy of detail, and the frequent flavor of illiteracy that marked the original stories. For the authentic flavor of an earlier era one should consult Hector Lee's fine monograph (see note 8).

Less widely known than the Nephite stories, but a distinct genre also, are the stories of those who were rewarded or punished through a supernatural agency for their loyalty or opposition to the Church, its practices, or its duly constituted authorities.

I

The Reverend Lamb, who was a Methodist minister, was bitter toward the Mormons. He fought them verbally and finally wrote a book against the Book of Mormon, calling it "The Golden Bible." When he published it, he went totally blind. His wife came to Mrs. Riggs, my mother, and said, "I suppose, Mrs. Riggs, that you would call this retribution." My mother retorted, "Why, I certainly do, Mrs. Lamb." (WHC. Collector: Mrs. Emma Rae Ashton. Informant: Mrs. Emma Rae Riggs McKay.)

II

When the pioneers first came to Morgan Valley, they had little food and had to eat the roots of plants and wild herbs to survive. It has been said that some of the Saints were eating water hemlock (which is very poisonous) without ill effect. Then, as the story goes, the people were told not to eat the root of the water hemlock or they would die. Everyone had eaten it up to this point without ill effect; one man decided that he could continue. He died shortly afterward. (WHC. Collector: Robert P. Sherwood. Informant: an old farmer, unnamed, whose father had come with the first settlers to Morgan Valley and had told it to him.)

III

In the Mormon Church, young boys 14 to 16 years old administer [offer the prayer and then pass to all members] the sacrament of the Lord's Supper. On one occasion one of these young priests, before performing the ritual, concealed a package of cigarettes in his coat pocket. This was a sacrilegious act inasmuch as tobacco is forbidden to the Saints. In the middle of the prayer, the boy's voice faltered, he was unable to continue and had to leave the meeting. (Collector: J. H. Adamson. Place: Carey, Idaho. Time: ca. 1918—a common word-of-mouth story.)

Another feature of Mormon life which produces tales involving the cooperation of the supernatural is belief in continued revelation. Although it is official Church doctrine that only the president of the Church may receive revelation binding on Church membership, nevertheless a surprisingly large number of unofficial prophecies continue to circulate and Mormon folk life is still often lived, if not in the hush of great expectations, at least in the hope of something evermore about to be. For example, in Wayne County, Utah, the Saints once attempted to settle south of the Capitol Reef Monument. But the Fremont River flooded them out; it was promptly renamed the Dirty Devil. At that time a prophecy began to circulate that some day a "stake of Zion" would flourish south of the Reef. In 1952, in the company of Adrian W. Cannon of Salt Lake City, I talked with half a dozen farmers in the vicinity of Torrey and Teasdale, Wayne County, all of whom knew of the prophecy although none knew who had made it. All felt that it was likely that the recent uranium strike in that locale was the beginning of the fulfillment of the prophecy.

I

Aunt Susa Young Gates, a daughter of Brigham Young, was staying here at our home. One day she pointed to a small mound near the present high school and said, "Some day a temple of the Lord will stand right there." She also said that terrible disasters would strike the eastern part of the United States, and we would see houses and tents closely packed in all the open country around the town. (Collector: J. H. Adamson. Informant: W. L. Adamson, born 1882, Heber City, Utah. The incident took place in Carey, Idaho, around 1915.)

II

A curious circumstance occurred on Sunday at meeting in the old Brush Bowery. The people were all very much depressed by their situation: no civilization nearer than St. Louis, clothing and supplies almost used up or worn out. President Heber C. Kimball, a jolly old gentleman but a true prophet, got up and spoke a little about the conditions of things existing. To cheer the people he said, "I will now prophesy that next summer in the streets of Salt Lake City you will be able to buy goods cheaper than you could in New York." A listener pulled him by the coattails and said, "Brother Kimball, I don't believe that." "Neither do I," said the old gentleman, and sat down. Nevertheless it came true. In the summer of 1850 the gold diggers came rushing through on their way to California. They had started from the East well fitted out with wagons and goods, but the gold fever began to strike them so hard that they seemed to go wild: They sold their teams, wagons, and goods for almost nothing, and bought old mules or horses, packed a little grub on them and away they went. (WHC. Collector: Joyce Warburton. Informant: Richard Warburton, her great-grandfather.)

There remain several motifs of supernatural lore in Utah not mentioned in this paper: the faith healing of cattle and horses, appearances of Satan, possession by evil spirits (called the legion), visions of gold mines or other hidden wealth. Even so, the collector of folklore in Utah today finds that the designs of Providence and the agents for their fulfillment are not as numerous and companionable as they once were when a friendlier heaven was a conduit, not a curtain, when the sky was, as Wallace Stevens says, "a part of labor and a part of pain, . . . not this dividing and indifferent blue."

Austin E. and Alta S. Fife

Unsung Craftsmen

The Pace Ranch in Castle Valley (Grand County, Utah) is located at the base of the magnificent La Sal Mountains in a setting that is, in our estimation, not equaled elsewhere in North America. But beyond its scenic beauty the ranch is notable because in its buildings one can trace the evolution of the types of personal dwelling houses which have been built and used in the Rocky Mountains from the time of the arrival of the very first Anglo-American settlers.[1]

In a low hill are noted four dugouts—the first dwellings built by the rancher. By means of an excavation into the hillside the back and two sides to the building are formed. Although the natural dirt and rock of the hill sometimes sufficed for the walls and floor, they may be, as in this case, lined with natural stone. A wall of this same material forms the front. The total space consists of one room, about ten by fourteen feet, with a single door and a small window at the front. A roof was constructed over this with poles covered over with brush and dirt. In 1953 the four dugouts of the Pace Ranch still served as coops for barnyard fowl, a saddle house, and a storage bin. On flat ground, or in areas where timber was abundant, this one-room dugout may have been replaced by a conventional log cabin of the type built widely on the fringe of the American frontier wherever pioneers were moving west.

After a few successful crops or the sale of the surplus from cautiously husbanded herds of cattle had made it possible, a more commodious dwelling was erected: a two-room rock or log house with dimensions of about thirty by twelve feet. A sharp gable roof protected the natural stone. One room served as a bedroom, the other as a living room and kitchen. A wall directly across the middle of the building separated the two rooms, and a symmetrical façade was achieved by placing two windows and two doors in the long side of the building both at the front and at the rear. Others built this structure of adobe or even brick, but the same floor plan prevailed.

This basic two-room building pattern appears abundantly throughout Mormon country. Impressed by the large number of exterior entrances in such small dwellings, the tourist has glibly termed these houses "Mormon," equating the number of exterior doors to the number of wives in the polygamous household. However, on more careful inspection it is noted that the number of outside doors served a more practical function. Toilet facilities were outside. Neighbors were not close even in the villages because the size of lots was large. Hence privacy within the family—which had been so difficult for the first pioneers to preserve in their one-room houses—was achieved not via the expensive use of interior hallways but by the practical expedient of exterior doorways.

These typical two-room stone or adobe houses proved functional in another way. When additional crops permitted the enlargement of the home one could quickly achieve prestige within the community by the addition of a porch along the front of the house. This gave shade and cooled the interior rooms. In some cases these front porches have subsequently been screened or glassed in. At the same time a lean-to was frequently added at the rear, somewhat deeper than the full front porch, providing two additional rooms which served now as a bedroom and kitchen, leaving the two original rooms of the dwelling to serve as a bedroom and parlor. The roof slope of the front porch and of the rear annex was decreased by about one-half, giving the characteristic hat-and-brim-like contours of a great many old houses in the West. Later, when people were affluent enough to build houses which were initially large enough for their needs, they built four rooms and a front porch all at once, still maintaining the basic plan which we have described.

Lest there be some who are skeptical of the validity of our treating the architecture of Mormonia as a folk art, let them be reminded that up to the middle of our own century in rural areas and in small towns houses were rarely built following architectural plans. In 1954 a contractor in Moab advised us that he had never built a house from blueprints: up to 1946, the houses in that town which had been built according to professional plans could have been counted on the fingers of one hand.

It should be noted that in effect the frontier builder had created a building technique which is almost "modular"—a practical building design to which component parts could be rationally added at later dates, or the combination of which, in groups, could effectively result in the construction of larger houses. We note, for example, that the two-room house type that we have described was enlarged to four rooms by slightly increasing the exterior dimensions, by adding an upper story over the two lower rooms, and by thickening the center partition to provide for a stairway. Often a rather magnificent early house was built combining this plan in the form of a T with an upper story, giving a six-room house, six exterior entrances, and one to three full balconies. Here indeed we have the polygamous home *par excellence*!

It is significant to note that a food storage facility was built close to nearly all houses on the frontier up to the 1900's, when it tended to be replaced by a basement in which both food storage and heating facilities could be installed. This food storage facility consisted in its simplest and earliest form of a "root cellar" directly behind the house. An excavation was made about four feet below the surface of the ground with a stairway going down to it. The walls were sometimes natural dirt, more often lined with rough stone. The roof was characteristically built of logs, brush, and dirt. Later it was enlarged and improved, built of cement, adobe, or bricks, with a gabled roof. Tables, shelves, and other useful storage facilities were properly installed along the walls. This facility served an exceedingly useful purpose in the days before the advent of ice boxes and refrigerators. All of the root crops—turnips, beets, parsnips, carrots, potatoes—could be properly stored, and home-canned fruit effectively kept herein. Often at least one wall of the facility was reserved for cooling and processing milk. Sometimes a trough was placed against this wall in which water circulated. The milk was strained into pans and placed on slats over this running water. Milk products were sometimes prepared here, sometimes taken to the house where heat was available for the making of "clabber," or cottage cheese. Later, when a market developed for the sale of cream to dairy concerns, the hand-propelled cream separator was often installed in the cellar.

Not uncommonly we note that this facility was enlarged into a two-story structure. Grains, seeds, dried fruits and vegetables mold or rot quickly in the dampness of a cellar. In a two-story facility all of the utility that we have just described was still available below, and above, the colonist had a convenient dry-storage area with an outside entrance. In these more elaborate facilities a platform at the level of the upper story was built about three or four feet above the ground from which it was convenient to load and unload supplies from wagons. In certain communities, when the economic level of the people permitted, these buildings were made large enough to serve multiple uses: sometimes a stove was installed and the family laundry was done there rather than in the kitchen. Canning of fruit could be done there, and the cooking in hot weather, so that the living quarters did not have the heat from a coal or wood stove added to the hot summer sun. Sometimes one section of the building was partitioned to hold coal, wood, and other farm necessities such as axle grease, garden implements, coal oil, etc. Onions, ears of corn, and other dried foods were often suspended from the rafters.

The first settlers operated by necessity on an almost self-sufficient basis, each family striving to produce all of its living requirements by its own toil, or at most by bartering with neighbors. It should also be kept in mind that in almost any rural area of Mormonia today it is possible to find families with the most modern orientation of their economy living next to families who still live almost as did the children of the first generation. During the 1950's households still existed in small towns in which there was no running water or interior plumbing, where wood and coal stoves still served for heat, where coal oil lanterns or Coleman lamps gave the only light, where feathers gathered from one's own fowl served to stuff pillows and ticks or the straw from one's own wheat to stuff the mattresses. In the same block one might find the most modern heating, lighting, and plumbing fixtures—telephone, carpets, refrigerator, freezer, electric range—all the conveniences of the mid-twentieth century.

However, since the folklorist is at heart a bit of an antiquarian, let us retrace our steps to the economy of rural Mormonia around the close of the nineteenth century. The pattern was set by Brigham Young who repeatedly emphasized the essentially pastoral nature of the lives of the Saints and about whom one informant advised us: "I am just as sure as can be that if there had been no Gentiles come in to Salt Lake City the cows would be pasturing in the streets today."[2] Husbands were to get for their wives a heifer or two, chickens to take care of, a few pigs. The springs were supposed to be dammed up and spawn of mountain trout planted therein. Potatoes, parsnips, carrots, beets were to be grown for winter storage and the tops fed to the animals. Fowl were supposed to be good for the gardens that the women were growing, since they destroyed insects. A little patch of lucerne was to be planted near the house so that the heifer would have grazing and so that the women of the house could cut armfuls to take to the domestic animals. The ideal Mormon wife was one who could sustain herself and her family essentially without benefit of the husband, especially if he had more than one wife.

The era of the efficiency of American industry had not yet dawned. Canned or frozen foods were not available, nor the unlimited range of other domestic articles, wearing apparel, farm machinery, and equipment. Nor was the cash income of the first generation pioneer sufficiently abundant to buy these things had they been available. The food produced via the domestic animals, the garden and adjacent land was supplemented by the abundant use of wild game: deer, antelope, bear, rabbits, wild fowl, fish. We are acquainted with one farmer on the slopes of the La Sal Mountains who had killed a score of deer during 1952; venison was the staple diet for his family of nine children. Fish from the local streams—trout from the mountains, and suckers and carp from the swampy areas in the valleys—were also a vital food source. We are reminded of a story the setting of which is in the early days of Utah when food was extremely scarce. There was an unpalatable variety of fish which was available in great quantity and which was eaten until all the settlers were tired of it. The narrator at this point proceeds to explain to you an exceedingly elaborate recipe used to make the fish more or less edible. After his extensive rigamarole has been pushed almost to the point of absurdity, he explains that after all this has been done you must throw the fish to the hogs and eat the plank on which it has been prepared.[3]

The family per se was only a kind of subunit in the more cohesive unit of the community. "Bees" were organized on the slightest pretext to peel, can, or dry peaches, apples, apricots, to gather wild berries, to make preserves. Common herds of cattle and sheep were maintained to which each family contributed a given number of animals and from which it derived a corresponding proportion of the returns. These group activities were essential to the economy of the community and were creative in the manner in which they gave cohesiveness to social and economic life.

Wood was gathered in adjacent canyons for cooking and for heating. Certain varieties were "coked" and rendered suitable for the blacksmith's operations. Tallow candles were made in crude molds, or "bitch lights" were improvised when coal oil was not available by putting the end of a twisted piece of cloth in grease. Water was purified by settling it with fragments of cactus placed therein. Soap was made by every family. In the 1950's there were still households where it was maintained that commercial soaps were not satisfactory. Even the lye from which soap was produced was manufactured locally from the ashes of native woods.

The butchering of a domestic animal for meat was a significant event in the life of the household, and since meat could not be kept indefinitely it was a common practice to distribute cuts from the butchered animal in the community: one could expect reciprocation in kind when his neighbor's turn came to kill an animal. These were occasions when the poor, the widowed, the infirm also benefited by the generosity of their more fortunate neighbors. The animal fats were husbanded for the making of soap and for other household uses. Hides were preserved and tanned for subsequent use by the shoemaker and the harness maker or made into rugs, chair seats, clothing.

In the first decade following the establishment of communities grains and corn were produced in exceedingly small quantities. Gleaning was resorted to in order to reap the maximum return. White bread was relatively uncommon. One informant relates that she was at the neighbors' when they graciously offered her a beautiful biscuit made of white flour. "I couldn't eat it," she said. "I just held it in my hand. The woman asked me, 'Lucy, why don't you eat your bread?' And I said, 'I'd like to but I want to take it home to show my mother!' " [4]

If grains were available for bread, greater difficulty was encountered in the procurement of satisfactory materials to make it rise. Both salt and saleratus were used, and the yeast jar was a precious item on the shelves of a western pantry. Corn was grown in the early years almost as commonly as wheat. Informants born in the 1870's still remember the elaborate processes necessary in converting corn into hominy, a staple in their diet. Popcorn was grown and did good service in welding the family together in delightful evenings of entertainment when the corn was popped before the assembled family, salted and buttered, or sometimes molded into delicious balls with the use of cooked syrups.

Sweet foods must have been exceedingly rare until the development of the sugar beet undustry in the first two decades of our own century. Corn molasses was made in most communities. The occasional settler who had a swarm of bees felt blessed indeed, and the wild bee trees that youngsters encountered during their fishing and exploring escapades among the cottonwood trees in the river bottoms were windfalls of honey which lent a rare and delightful addition to the drab diet of the pioneer, the sure-fire occasion for a "candy pull." We note that honeydew was procured. It consisted in a kind of sweet juice or sap secreted by certain willows at infrequent intervals during the year or deposited on them by aphids. The branches were bent down and rinsed off in water, then boiled down to produce sugar.[5] Cider and vinegar were made locally. Ladies who drank tea would rinse out the last bits of sugar left in their cups and put them in the vinegar jar.

The fare produced in the garden and on the farm was supplemented by such things as watercress gathered in the stream beds, by the occasional use of bulbs of the sego lily, and almost universally by the use of "pig weed."

It is difficult to say something definitive about the folk arts and crafts of Mormonia which relate to fabrics and clothing. Change rather than continuity is the characteristic to be noted. When settlements were first undertaken wool was cautiously sheared from the sheep, even gleaned from the bushes and shrubs where the passage of the animals had left occasional strands. It was washed, carded, spun, and woven into fabric for the simple costumes of the first settlers. Hides were tanned and leather prepared for use in harnesses, shoes, chaps, saddlebags. Even shoelaces were made from the tanned skins of cats. Tanning processes were brought west with the pioneers or learned from the Indians. Jackets and trousers made of buckskin were common. The first settlers early discovered that they could make dyes in four or five essential colors from available plants: sagebrush for yellow; a mixture of blue vitriol and tag alder for brown; indigo for blue; madder for red.[6] Wives of farmers who had no sheep solved their problem by cleaning, cording, spinning and weaving on shares. Usually they were permitted to keep one-half of the finished fabric for their toil. Knitting has been a continued occupation of Mormon women, although today as elsewhere they use manufactured yarns and designs supplied by women's magazines or the yarn trade.

Once fabrics had been produced locally or, later, secured from afar, the final and consummate women's skill consisted in the blocking out, cutting, and sewing of these fabrics into the finished costumes of the family wardrobe. Even in the earliest days women did their utmost to work out their costumes after the latest available styles.

The feathers of domestic fowl played a significant role in the economy of the household as stuffing for pillows, mattresses, and cushions. Some youngsters had as a regular chore the gathering of feathers dropped by the chickens in the course of each day's pecking about the coop or yard. Wild ducks and geese were a boon not only for the meat they supplied, but also because their feathers were of better quality for pillows than those of domestic fowl. Hats were made locally either from woven wheat straw or from remnant pieces of fabric. To make a brim, several thicknesses of fabric were sewed together, then dipped in a concentration of sugar and water or some other starching agent and ironed to make them stiff. The results were satisfactory until the first rainstorm, when you could get a quick transfusion of energy by sucking the brim of your hat! The starching process, of course, had to be done all over again.[7]

In men's clothing homespun and buckskin gave way early to overalls and jumper, or, in the cattle country, to trim trousers called "Oregon City pants" and a Stetson hat. A baby's layette consisted of two or three long dresses, a couple of inner-blankets, some flannel bands, home-knit stockings, and a half-dozen or so flour-sack diapers.

At least one pioneer craft is as significant, as finely developed, and as universal as it was in the earliest days of our history. Commercial blankets may well be used on the beds of some people in the rural West, but few self-respecting women fail to display with pride their homemade quilts. Many a Mormon grandmother will explain that no descendant of hers has gone to the altar without having received as a beloved personal gift a quilt of her grandmother's workmanship. The techniques of fabrication and the designs have been passed along from generation to generation and the making of the quilts is not infrequently accompanied by some of the most agreeable social life of the adult women. Selection of the design and the careful husbanding of remnants are matters of individual initiative. This is also true of the long period during which the scraps are cut carefully to the proper shapes and dimensions and sewed into lovely designs. It is usually also an individual project to mount the quilt on the frames, to spread out the batting, and to get it ready for "quilting." At this point, however, it is common practice to invite in friends—with especial attention to choosing those with a reputation for careful workmanship—who as a group apply their agile needles to the quilt while they sip their chocolate (tea or coffee in the case of non-Mormons) and talk about things that interest them. All that remains now is the final binding before the quilt is ready for display and use. Each design has its name, its unwritten symbolism, and its appropriateness to the social situation in which the quilt will enter upon its life of intimate utility. We have noted the following most prevalent designs in the single community of Moab: star (in several variations), spider-leg, log cabin, sunshine and shadow, wedding ring, Dresden plate, nine-patch (in numerous variations), broken dish, Japanese fan, sunflower, trip-around-the-world, pinwheel, black-eyed Susan. Today these quilting enterprises may constitute regular projects by such organizations as the Relief Society and the Daughters of the Utah Pioneers, and the results of their toil are contributed to welfare projects.

We note five different types of homemade quilts, although the patchwork type previously described is by all odds the most common. Very common in earlier days was the crazy quilt, or crazy-patch. Generally these quilts were more ornamental, made of lovelier fabrics and—when successfully executed—works of art which make of them true heirlooms. Lovely bits of silk, velvet, or similar materials were husbanded for years, cut into random shapes and sizes, and then joined together with an intricacy of needlework which defies the imagination. It was a fetish that the seam along each side of a patch should bear a different embroidery stitch; scores of stitch-types may appear, hence, on the face of a single quilt.

Less often we note appliqué quilts and quilts which are either embroidered or which bear hand-painted designs, not uncommonly of floral or animal subjects (the last two especially for the beds of children).

Practical quilts were made from cheaper fabrics and with less time-consuming methods. They are usually called "camp" quilts or "boys' room" quilts. The unworn portions of used clothing of heavy weight such as men's suits or overalls were cut into square or rectangular patterns, sewed together, and then, instead of being quilted, were tied at frequent intervals over their surface to hold the batting in place. Few are the cowboys, lumbermen, hunters, fishermen, prospectors, or miners of the Rocky Mountain West who have not set out on their sundry quests with a bedroll made up of these camp quilts. They were also commonly used on boys' beds, being more adapted to the rough wear they would get there than the lovely ones which adorned their sisters' and mothers' bedrooms.

Rugs were and still are made as a kind of folk art, and almost every household had a "rag sack" which received all discarded clothing suitable for this purpose. The rugs may be either braided, woven, hooked, or crocheted, and designs are achieved which are truly decorative even where a utilitarian purpose is paramount in the mind of the craftsman. Weaving frames are kept by an occasional member of the community. The contents of the previous year's rag sack are suitably prepared and sent to her periodically. She weaves and returns a beautiful throw rug at a modest craftsman's fee and you can pick out the pants you wore to Lem Hellman's wedding every time you sit down on the bed to take off your shoes!

It is a common misconception that folk arts and crafts are a kind of monopoly of the female members of the household. Careful scrutiny reveals that the men have been equally creative. In the working of leather, buckskin, and horsehair, in the use of wood, and in the solution of practical engineering problems of the farms—in the building of fences, gates, and agricultural equipment—their ingenuity, working with the patterns that tradition has given them and with the materials at hand, has produced articles of undisputed beauty and utility.

At a campground on a Rocky Mountain fishing stream we encountered a craftsman who, with pocket knife and patience, had carved a beautiful chain out of a strip of solid wood cut from a nearby tree. At Moab we saw a magnificent collection of lamp bases made from the gnarled and twisted trunks of cedar trees that had been whipped by desert winds for decades. This artistic creativity involved hours of searching the ridges of the La Sal Mountains, the careful drying of selected trunks in the farmyard, the stripping of bark by hand, rubbing with sandpaper and pumice, delicate staining and varnishing—the end result a demonstration of folk creativity which is a delight to look upon.

If the Indians were the first to avail themselves of the hair of horses' manes and tails to make lariats, hackamores, bridles, hatbands—and we are not sure that they were—Rocky Mountain craftsmen soon learned to vie with them in skill and workmanship. Disastrous inroads are now being made on this art by the cold anonymity of industry. Yet the collector who faithfully pursues the back country can still buy specimens of horsehair braiding which in beauty and loveliness excite the mind. No rider was so proud as the one whose horse wore a hackamore consisting of thousands of individual strands of hair assembled in little bundles according to color, meticulously woven into bands, reins, and sliding knots where no single end of a hair was visible save in the tassels. With the rider's matching hatband or belt it was a symbol of the unity of mount and horseman that built the cowboy myth. Snakeskin hatbands and belts were also made.

However, the creativity of the man of the frontier usually had a more practical goal. After all, his first concern was with the economic security of his family. In years of maturity he was likely to leave off the more artistic and less practical crafts of woodcarving, horsehair braiding, carving whistles out of green wood, or making balls from twine and buckskin, to solve the problems on his farm. Fences were essential to the protection of his animals, and a visible symbol of ownership. Their design was conditioned by the absence or scarcity of commercial products such as nails, bolts, wire, hinges, and latches. For the most part the Westerner was content to use patterns which had come down through centuries and across continents, provided these designs were suited to native materials. Zigzag pole fences, the horse-and-rider fences, or the complex rip-gut fences built by the actual weaving of short straight pieces of cedar, all erected three-quarters of a century ago, still stand at many points in the Rocky Mountains and do good service as they did at their building by the first settlers.

But fences are only a half-solution to the problem. You have to be able to get animals in and out of the fields as desired, and this requires gates, the construction of which presents challenging problems. The simplest way was to slide single poles between two vertical uprights. To open the gate then required considerable time and toil, for each pole had to be dropped separately, the cattle driven through, and each pole raised to its place. It was not long before ingenious ranchers discovered that if smaller poles were used and all the poles attached to each other you could slide them out and turn them a quarter way around as a unit. Even this required the consumption of precious time which the rancher could ill afford. Besides, a good gate was one which could be opened and closed from horseback. Hence, more efficient hinges and latches were necessary. The hinge most commonly encountered involved the planting of a discarded wagon wheel in the ground. The sharpened point of the vertical post of the gate turns effectively therein. Sometimes the axle of the wagon itself was attached to the base of the gate to turn in the wheel in which it had turned for decades. Not uncommonly the concave surface of old Indian grinding stones formed satisfactory hinges: the rounded bottom of the vertical upright on the gate will turn in the concave stone effectively and so turns still in many a rancher's gate.

Throughout the Rocky Mountain area it was soon discovered that rainfall was so slight that hay could be stored outdoors the year around if it was suitably topped to shed water. As hay production increased, the problem of stacking it into high, compact butts called forth the best of folk resourcefulness, and derrick types of amazing ingenuity evolved. They show an evolution from a simple vertical pole anchored by guy wires to an intricate structure so sturdy that it still appears at innumerable points on the horizons of Utah decades after its utility has been superseded by more efficient devices. Only within the last two decades have the farm implement manufacturers succeeded in building machines to stack hay which could compete with these older, inexpensive, locally built stackers whose silhouettes, like the spirits of ancestors, still fall across the farmyards of the living.

Men of all cultures and all educational levels seem to be possessed by a kind of "collect-o-mania." We are not referring here to collecting which results in the institutionalized collections of museums, historical societies, and antiquarians, but to individual collecting which expresses the true folk mentality. Throughout Mormonia these collections appear in the homes of all classes of people. Sunday afternoon excursions to gather arrowheads were and are organized. Rock collections are common. For example, we note a woman who takes pride in displaying a collection of rocks gathered by her or by friends, or by friends of friends, one from each state in the Union. Petrified wood, bones, and fossil-bearing rocks, ores, seashells, all appear in folk collections. Indian relics are common. We have seen entire flower beds surrounded by Indian corn-grinding stones, by clam or abalone shells which have been procured on an excursion to the California coast. Antler collections are common and are sometimes used in ingenious crafts, such as the making of hatracks, coat hangers, chairs, and benches. More frequently they appear simply piled in the yard, attached above the door of the house, over the garage or barn door as a kind of memorial to man's superintendency over the denizens of the wild. They appear of course commonly to decorate public buildings such as pool halls, beer joints, bars, lodges, barber shops. A woman will display with pride her collection of salt and pepper shakers; she may even specialize in those which are replicas of dogs or some other animal. Sometimes there is a fetish connected with the procedure with which the collection is made: it must be comprised of gifts rather than purchased items, and not more than one must come from each giver. We could add collections of teacups, ornamental spoons, centennial dishes, replicas of animals of every description, firearms, knives, shaving mugs, etc.

To conclude our brief excursion in the realm of the folk arts we must visit a graveyard. Characteristically it is located on some high, rocky plot unsuitable for tilling. A few roads circulate among the graves which are arranged in orderly plots. It is seldom visited except for an actual burial, or yearly on Memorial Day. In the rural areas the graveyards may not always be irrigated and kept green, though a few ornamental cacti will survive despite lack of care, or such rugged plants as castor beans and native grasses. We note unmarked graves, graves marked only with the undertaker's temporary metal plaques which contain a paper identification, or with wooden slabs some of whose identifications have totally worn off, simple markers from native stone, a few of which seem to have been carved by hand or painted in colors that contrast with the stone. Predominant, of course, are the usual commercial brands of markers which are professionally done outside the community, shipped in and planted as an enduring memorial to the deceased and his family. The symbolic ornamentations that appear most commonly include doves, lambs (especially on the graves of children), various plant and floral ornamentations which most frequently resemble ivy, holly, lilies, roses, or clover. Gates, frequently with a star, the sun, a crown, and, rarely, a cross, are noted. A single heart may appear carved at the top of a stone. We note occasional carved replicas of the Mormon temple in Salt Lake City. Clasped hands are a common symbol. A hearth and hearth logs appear, a chain and anchor.

Textual inscriptions on the gravestones constitute a kind of folk poetry that is worthy of attention. Those which conclude this paper were noted in the

cemetery at Moab, Utah, in 1953. Most often the inscription is a simple statement of love, hope, sorrow:

> In God we trust.
>
> Those whom we never cease to love we never lose.
>
> Honest, courageous and intelligent.
>
> She was the sunshine of our home.
>
> Courage, hope, remembrance.
>
> Let our Father's will be done.
>
> Gone but not forgotten.
>
> The world is better for his having lived.
>
> Prepare to meet me in heaven.
>
> Budded on earth to bloom in heaven.
>
> Our little lamb, our little child lies sleeping here.
>
> May we meet at the gates.
>
> She was a kind and affectionate wife and a loving mother.
>
> We will meet again.
>
> My darling daughter, fairer than a rose.
>
> We can safely leave our boy, our darling, in Thy trust.
>
> One of Christ's jewels, she shines in her beauty, a gem for His crown.
>
> Sleep on in thy beauty, thou sweet angel child.
>
> We loved him in life, let us not forget him in death.

Not uncommonly the inscription constitutes a poetic couplet as:

> In the Kingdom of Grace
> Grant a little child a place.
>
> No pains, no griefs, no anxious fear
> Can reach our loved one sleeping here.
>
> Our darling one hath gone before
> To meet us on the blissful shore.

Less often the inscription is more elaborate and constitutes a four-line or even
longer verse, frequently from a known author. We note the following:

> A light from our household is gone,
> A voice we loved is stilled,
> A place is vacant in our hearts
> That never can be filled.
>
> Life is real, life is earnest
> And the grave is not the goal.

Dust thou art, to dust returneth
Was not spoken of the soul.

Sleep, noble warrior, sleep,
The tomb is now thy bed,
Cold on its bosom thou dost rest
In silence with the dead.

We loved this little tender one
And would have wished him stay,
But our Father's will be done,
He shines in endless day.

Just a thought of sweet remembrance,
Just a memory fond and true,
Just a token of affection
And a heartache still for you.

One precious to our hearts has gone,
The voice we loved is still,
The place made vacant in our home
Will never more be filled.

Our Father in His wisdom called
The boon His love had given,
And though on earth the body lies,
The soul is safe in heaven.

NOTES

1. Except for a few items it is impractical to give a bibliography for an article of this kind. It is written on the basis of interviews and observations made by the authors during fifteen years of vacation trips in Mormon country. In the few footnotes used, FMC is the abbreviation for the Fife Mormon Collection: Series I, oral sources; Series II, manuscript sources.
2. FMC I 410: Dick Barnes, Bountiful, Utah, 1946.
3. FMC I 564: L. M. Hilton, Ogden, Utah, 1946.
4. FMC I 910: Mrs. Lucy Burr, Moab, Utah, 1953.
5. FMC II 371: Winford Bunce, Moab, Utah, 1937.
6. FMC II 379: Winford Bunce, Moab, Utah, 1937.
7. FMC I 833: Otho Murphy, Moab, Utah, 1953.